D1472261

IRON
BRAVO

IRON BRAVO

HEARTS, MINDS, AND SERGEANTS IN THE U.S. ARMY

CARSTEN STROUD

BANTAM BOOKS
NEW YORK · TORONTO · LONDON · SYDNEY · AUCKLAND

IRON BRAVO

A Bantam Book / March 1995

Library of Congress Cataloging-in-Publication Data

Stroud, Carsten, 1942–
Iron bravo : hearts, minds, and sergeants in the U.S. Army / Carsten Stroud.
        p.   cm.
ISBN 0-553-09552-8
1. Persian Gulf War, 1991.   2. Crane, Dee, 1941–   .   I. Title.
DS79.724.U6S77   1995
956.704'42—dc20   94–22187
                                                              CIP

Published simultaneously in the United States and Canada

Bantam Books are published by Bantam Books, a division of Bantam
Doubleday Dell Publishing Group, Inc. Its trademark, consisting of the words
"Bantam Books" and the portrayal of a rooster, is Registered in U.S. Patent
and Trademark Office and in other countries. Marca Registrada. Bantam
Books, 1540 Broadway, New York, New York 10036.

PRINTED IN THE UNITED STATES OF AMERICA

BVG   0   9   8   7   6   5   4   3   2   1

For Linda

CONTENTS

Fighting Joe Hooker
once said
with that tart unbridled tongue of his
that made so many needless enemies
"Who ever saw a dead cavalryman"
the phrase stings
with a needle sharpness
just or not
but even he was never heard to say
"Who ever saw a dead congressman"
and yet he was a man
with a sharp tongue. . . .

—STEPHEN VINCENT BENÉT
commenting on the dead
at the First Battle of Bull Run
in the poem,
"The Congressmen"

CHAPTER ONE

CRANE

Crane lived alone.

Every night he did sets of military fifties with his feet propped up on the ladder-back chair beside his bed, his hands braced on the hardwood floor, cranking them out in fast sets of five, puffing and huffing through the count. He could feel the bones in his body like bamboo machinery within a casing of blood and flesh, feel his muscles tug and stretch, eyes fixed on the worn wooden planks, on one peg in one single board, his mind empty, watching but not seeing the wooden slats of the floor come at him and pull back and then come up again, as if someone was opening and closing a coffin lid to make sure the guy was still dead.

When Crane could do no more of these, say two hundred or some nights it was three—some nights it was only fifty—then he'd let go and he'd slam, shaking and boneless, onto the wooden floor and then he'd roll over and stare up at the ceiling of his apartment.

He'd stare at the fan going around, an old wooden-blade fan like the one that lifer assassin in *Apocalypse Now* had been staring

1

at—an inside joke for Crane—and he'd lie there for a moment, trying to keep his mind blank, which was sort of like trying to drive with your eyes closed, but sooner or later he'd realize he was starting to think about the unit and then he'd realize he was *already* thinking about the unit so it was time for crunches.

Crunches were hard the way Crane did them—hands behind the neck and lifting the shoulders with the belly muscles—chin jerking down toward his flexed knees, not a big move, but hard still, especially if you're forty-nine.

Crane did these in bursts of five, until the pain in the belly was serious pain, like a muscle was about to rip, or when the light in the room got slightly pink in color from the blood that was pounding through his head.

Crunches done, Crane would lie back again, chest heaving and his breath raw in the back of his throat, watching that fan go around, hearing the muted beating of the blades, and the sound of the wind in the trees like a river running past.

After a while his lungs would stop burning and he'd crawl up on the side of the bed, sit there for a minute, head pounding, and then he'd reach under the bed and push the .45 out of the way and tug out the easy-curl bar.

He'd rest his elbows on the tops of his knees and curl the bar with sixty pounds on it, roll it out and wind it back in, again and again, watching the machinery work—all upper-body stuff because that was where the mind was and you had to tire the mind out somehow, otherwise it would give you trouble.

Behind him the empty bed was like a huge, snow-covered field and he tried not to think about it. Carla used to ask him, Dee, why the hell don't you come to bed? And Crane would try that, stop working out, come in and lie down with her, cuddle up, try to get to sleep.

That part was very sweet, nothing about sex or trying to make something happen, but just being there in the bed with someone he loved and who was a good person too.

It was sweet, very sweet, so of course it didn't last. What would happen, not every night, but most, was Crane would have one of those—not a dream, really, because it wasn't anything in his dreams that bothered him. Crane didn't have dreams. Not ones that he could remember. But most nights, something would snap him up and, well, Carla found it hard to deal with, and she was a girl who needed her sleep.

It seemed to Crane that it wasn't ever the big things that killed his friendships with women, it was the small stuff, the day-to-day. No matter how hard he tried, there was just something about him, something rocky inside that made him hard to take. So Crane understood that Carla needed her sleep and that what was happening to him was tough on her.

Hell, Crane needed his sleep too, but he understood.

He understood completely.

But the thing was there, and after a while Carla went back to staying at her place. They still saw each other—Carla was a receptionist in a doctor's office, and she worked part-time at Harry's Uptown on Poyntz—but Carla was really too young to understand how some things had no solution, some things just had to be handled any way you could handle them, and working out late like Crane did, well, that was the way he handled it.

Crane knew a lot of guys who had handled it very, very differently, put it out of the way big-time, so this looked pretty reasonable to him.

But Carla, working for a doctor, thought that there weren't too many things that couldn't be fixed by medicine or doctors or having a positive attitude. Carla had read a couple of magazine articles about Crane's problem—his dysfunction was what she called it— and she had a theory that Crane was in something called deep denial and was suffering from hypervigilance and was not confronting effectively, and more along those lines. Carla had her doctor all primed up and was talking about something called Prozac or Pronzac or something like that. Whatever it was, there was no way Crane was going to take any of it, and no way he was going to sit around, chat with the docs about why he was having trouble or even *if* he was having trouble. Frankly, it was none of their business and it was only Carla's business in a sideways sort of way because they had been living together and had what Carla called a relationship.

The thing was, what was bugging Crane was no different than what was bugging a lot of other vets and for that matter just a lot of other people who happened to be in their forties. One way or another, every guy—every woman too—who makes it to his forties is a kind of vet, he's been through some shit or other, and life being what it is, a guy gets worn down and develops some weirdness, some hitches in his get-along. Better to leave it be, and stay away from the doctors. Especially that. His life in the machine was a day-by-day thing now—his eyes were going and he needed glasses to read so he didn't read much around the troops and it seemed that nobody was speaking very clearly anymore, he had to keep asking people to say that again, and they'd say it but afterward they'd give him a look, that sideways look—well, let it come out that Crane was seeing some civilian shrink and the battalion Personnel guys would be leaning on him to take his Early Out and disappear. Which was exactly what it would feel like. Crane had seen it happen to other lifers and it always started with some goddam doctor.

So Crane was nervous of doctors, based on his experience, but he was a reasonable guy and he understood how a person who respected doctors might see things differently and he had tried to be reasonable with Carla.

But the effort of being reasonable without actually doing what she wanted had eventually had an effect on them, and so Carla was now living out more than she was living in, and Crane was still doing easy-curl forearm work on the side of his bed at nine-thirty at night.

It was too bad and Crane wasn't happy about it, but he had done all he could to cooperate. The thing about Carla—maybe the thing about women in general—was that a man, anyway a man in his forties, had only so many ways to talk to a woman and most of them didn't involve words, they had more to do with doing things for her.

For instance, Crane had gone out in all kinds of Kansas weather to look for that hellcat of hers, and he made it a point to see to the oil and the transmission fluid in her car, and he had always helped around her dad's house, the old guy being a widower and his son not being real handy, and once he had even gone to some kind of office party, met the doctors. Man, they were a confident bunch, and very happy about themselves, lots of fast talk and jokes and flirting with the nurses and the office staff, even with Carla, and Crane just standing there watching it all, Crane wondering what they'd do if he stepped left and drifted one of them in his chops, let him know that flirting with a guy's date was something polite men didn't do. He didn't do it, but he gave it some thought.

Thing was, he liked to spend time with her, which is another way a guy tries to say what he feels, and it was a puzzle for him that this wasn't enough for her, that she seemed to need something—not something he couldn't give her, because he would have done whatever it took—but it was like, Carla was waiting for it to come to him on his own.

But he had no idea what *it* was supposed to be.

Women wanted talk and it had been Crane's experience that talk just sort of let the air out of life, especially with women, so Crane missed her, but he still hit the weights pretty hard every night.

Afterward he'd get up and lay his gear out—boots and battle dress uniform and a white tee shirt, not regulation but what the hell, the new tees looked like baby shit in a mustard sauce—and then he'd go stand under the shower for a long time feeling the hot water run over his body, breathing in the steam, looking for that feeling of stillness and fatigue to come over him.

When it did he'd step out and towel down, hang the towel to dry, get into a robe, then go into the kitchen. He had to go through the living room and tonight that was a bad idea because some of Carla's stuff was packed up in boxes waiting for her brother to come over and get them. Crane made sure not to let it get to him.

In the kitchen he'd stand at the counter and he'd pour two fingers of Laphroaig into a coffee mug with the Big Red One patch on the side and he'd sip it slowly, a kind of unconscious ceremony for him, although you would have had to watch him do it to realize that it was in the way Crane did things that he showed who he was.

The scotch was good scotch, maybe the best there was, although it had taken Crane a while to get used to it. His father used to go on and on about this scotch and that scotch, could be a little hard to take, but when the old man died Crane had for some reason started drinking it and now he enjoyed it very much.

Crane liked the way it was smoky and reminded him of woods in the fall when he had been a kid in Lake Placid, maybe leaves burning somewhere with that thin blue smoke hanging over the wet shingles.

There was a blue distance in the Adirondacks but up close with the leaves turning and everything red and rust and bright yellow under a blue sky, it was all somehow brand-new and not the end of things at all.

Crane would stand there and think about things as little as possible, just look out the window at the street down below and feel the scotch go down, feel it like a blue flame but not burning, just warming.

Tonight there was rain.

In August the rain always smelled of dust down here, the sweet-grass smell was something you got back in the spring, but the leaves were very dry and the rain pattered on them like little grains of rice falling on a tin roof.

He liked the way the yellow lights under the cottonwood trees all the way up the street were glowing in the soft rain, and the light seemed to settle down on the walks like snow drifting down, not Adirondack snow, deep and soft as cream, but Kansas snow, which was mostly light and lacy, though it could cut like broken glass, and a couple of times a year it came down on the base so deep and white the yellow stone buildings looked like ships stranded in an ice field, and the silence was as deep as the snow, voices carrying over the blank white spaces.

But now it was summer and all along the leafy street there was a nice yellow glow from the windows of the houses and even though it wasn't dark yet—it was only about nine-thirty and the twilight was just deepening—you could get that summer evening feeling from the way everything looked and smelled.

A door opened down the street and a couple of kids came along the lane and got into a blue convertible. College kids from Kansas State, not Army. You could always tell the Army kids, even in civvies, with their cue-ball heads and their bony kid faces. The college kids were better fed and better dressed.

There was the sound of an engine racing and music came through the cloth top on the convertible, something with a heavy bass beat. Crane watched them pull away with an odd feeling in his chest but he did not think about what it might have been.

He felt tired now and was ready to go into the bedroom.

It was a nice bedroom, although he had liked it better with Carla's things all around it, the bedside table covers, the extra lamps, and things that women liked to buy, things that you didn't know you wanted until they'd just go ahead and buy one of them while you were out. You'd come home and there it would be, and she'd be looking at you, hoping you'd see it right off, maybe betting herself you wouldn't, but Crane always did.

Now it was back to a wooden floor and a wooden bed with an old crazy quilt and flannel sheets, one campaign chest from his father that sat on a wooden bench, and a chest of drawers, and over the bed the bronze crucifix from his mother's coffin, and a gooseneck lamp for reading, and a stand-up mirror to check the uniforms every morning, and on the wall some pictures his brother had taken of their home in Lake Placid and the mountains around it and three framed certificates from the noncom school at Fort Leavenworth. And a black-and-white shot of Barker and Weeks and Arnie Mauldar and Crane, the four of them leaning against the bar at Inkeys in Junction City, way back in '65, all of them looking like skinned chickens, a month after the Big Red got orders to Vietnam.

That was it. Nothing else.

Other guys, they had it all up there, the ribbons and the old snapshots, the campaign stuff and the beer mugs from the Milan—218 Truong-Tan-Buu Street—coasters from the Arc-en-Ciel, the Sporting Bar on Tu Do, the Blue Bird, Annie's Bar where all the DEROSed grunts would hang out, waiting for a flight back to the world, and the faded pieces of military scrip, blood chits, copies of the *Grunt Free Press,* homemade patches, and ashtrays made out of 105 shells.

All that shit to show they'd been in-country, like being in-country was some kind of bus tour, go to see the House of a Thousand Animals or the Schultz and Dooley Museum in Utica— see the world, meet interesting people, and blow their doors off. But not Crane.

All that stuff just made him sad, made him feel like he was on the way to being one of those sleeve tuggers you saw around, guys who were aching to let you know they'd been there, been inside it all.

Inside what?

If you'd gone to a lot of trouble to crawl up a bull's butt, would you bring back souvenirs?

Now and then one of the new kids would ask him, maybe after a class or during a drill march, ask him about his war. Crane would be sitting down in the bush somewhere, picking ticks out of his socks or trying to show some boot how to clean his A2, and a couple of the green ones from Benning would be standing around, looking down at the way his hands worked, and looking at his Combat Infantry Badge.

Crane could feel it coming and a lot of the time he'd get up before the kid could ask him, walk away toward one of the squad leaders. He had to, because whenever somebody asked him he always ended up talking *around* the pencil thing, because they weren't up to that shit, not by a mile.

He had told it once, to a real crusty young boot who needed an education, and ended up in front of the colonel, who had slammed him hard for screwing with the morale of the FNGs— the fucking new guys. Still, when he was quiet like this, or sometimes when he was working, he'd look down at the pencil in his hand and see it all over again.

———

Ever since the Big Red had deployed to Vietnam, they'd been playing a cat-and-mouse game with a very hardcore VC unit, the 9th Division. They'd hunted them all over a place called the Iron Triangle territory—forty square miles of swampy jungle and rice paddies and villages in between the Saigon River and the Thi Tinh River, about thirty-five miles northwest of Saigon, pegged into the wet green marshland by the villages of Ben Cat, Ben Suc, and Phu Hoa Dong.

Ben Suc was the biggest ville, over six thousand dinks, every one of whom paid taxes and cached stores and generally helped out the VC any way they could.

The Iron Triangle was covered by marshes and rice paddies but there was a lot of dense forest around Than Dien in the north. It had been a hideout for the Viet Minh ever since the Second World War. By the time the 1st reached the place, it was infested with VC, riddled with tunnels and bunker complexes, and every yard of trail was fire zoned or booby-trapped. Intelligence was sure the area held at least six hundred tunnels and over a thousand linked bunkers, none of it visible aboveground due to the dense foliage. It was a hell of a place to send green kids from Kansas. For the Big Red One—the 1st Division—and for Crane, the Triangle was an endless maze of green jungle and tracer fire and an enemy they hardly ever saw until it was too goddam late. The Triangle taught Crane how to hate in that deep silent searing way that made you a good soldier and ruined you as a man.

In '66, they'd run Operation Attleboro, that was Edward H. de Saussure's idea, the brigadier general in command, which damn near finished the 196th Light Infantry and ultimately dragged in the 1st under William DePuy. Attleboro ran for seventy-two days. It included B-52 strikes, murderous artillery support, and endless brigade-level sweeps through the villes and jungle, making sporadic contact, running green troops into VC ambushes, taking sniper fire, losing guys every half hour, rounds coming in from nowhere, kids going down, toe poppers and pungi traps all over the place.

They had one hundred and fifty-five guys killed and eight hundred wounded. The VC lost—so they were told—over eleven hundred men, which was hard to believe because they only pulled in half that number of weapons. And somehow the VC 9th slipped back into Cambodia and they had to do it all over again the next year, in Operation Cedar Falls, and El Paso 1, and then again in Operation Junction City in March of 1967.

Now by this time, most of the guys Crane had shipped out with were either dead—Arnie Mauldar erased by a mortar, Barker zapped by a sniper during Attleboro—or sent back to the World, or were safe in some rear-echelon clerk job in Saigon—except for Webb,* who, being fugazy, totally nuts, took a door-gunner job. But Crane had somehow slipped into a state of mind where he couldn't face *leaving* Vietnam and going back to Lake Placid to argue with his brother over the war and put more flowers on his mother's grave.

Not that he hadn't tried.

Everybody in the war got two weeks' leave in the middle of his tour, usually to Guam or Tokyo or the beaches in Phuket—all things considered, it was a bad idea because when the grunt came back to the bush, he had lost his rhythm, his sense of timing, and sometimes he didn't have time to get it back before he zigged when he should have zagged and got his ticket punched for good.

Crane had been to Phuket and Bangkok—there was a city had the right name—so he talked his Six Actual into an extension and he went home to Lake Placid to see the folks.

His brother was older than Crane, and was at the time into some postgraduate sociology thing in Buffalo and he had a lot to say about the war, took the high ground, saw the whole thing in a global perspective, a problem of cold war positioning and the military-industrial complex. Listening to the man talk, Crane felt a couple of things, like, first, the guy was probably right about the war being a rat-fuck and they were all pawns or something, part of a global game. You could sense that from the officers, especially field-grade Pointers in for their six months of Real War and then back to the world and up the ladder.

The other thing he felt was, Hey, fuck you, man. I lost people over there and you're pissing on their graves.

Between listening politely to his brother talking from behind his beard and listening to his father's emphysemic breathing, and looking at the way the house was falling apart now that his mother was dead, well, somehow the world just seemed too damn complicated and his brother's droning voice made him jumpy and

*Not his real name.

once he dreamed about slicing his brother's throat with the edge
of a C-rats can, took the carotid right out of the meat like a length
of pink plastic wire.

Crane went back to Camp Alpha at Long Binh and told the
clerk he'd re-up and about three weeks later he had blown his
fifteen hundred on hootch-girls and stereo gear in Cam Ranh Bay
and he was back in war zone C, a sergeant now with his own squad
to waste, busting his butt in the Triangle again.

Only now they had a VC deserter named Gap Ky, in on the
Chieu Hoi program—"Open Arms"—a skinny, dark-skinned dink
with a slight cast in his left eye who had a little English and smiled
too much.

So it came to pass that in March of '67, during Operation Junction City, Crane was part of a patrol sweep that took them around
Katum Airfield and by this time Crane was feeling a little salty—
he'd been in the war for two years now, and most of it had been
spent chasing the goddam 9th Division all over the Iron Triangle
for no discernible gain—and he remembered walking a Ranger-
style patrol single file up a long slow valley, staying off the path,
Crane watching Gap Ky up ahead with Suarez, the point grunt.

Now, Gap Ky was a dink, Chieu Hoi or no, and none of the
guys in the platoon trusted him much. Gap Ky had a face like a
ferret and bad teeth and he was always sucking on a leather strip
dipped in *nuoc mam* sauce—the rotting fish sauce that every dink
in-country slopped all over everything they ate. In every ville you
found it, a stinking cauldron of the stuff that you could smell from
six klicks out.

Once on a perimeter check Crane had gotten in real close with
a VC sapper trying to free a satchel charge that had got hung up
on the razor wire. Crane nailed him on the hop, blew his leg off
with a three-round burst, and was onto him in a half step with his
bayonet fixed—only guy Crane had ever killed with a bayonet in
the whole stupid war. He rammed the short iron blade into the
sapper's belly and had to trigger the piece to get the blade back
out—Charlie was wrapped around the barrel like a jumbo fried
shrimp on a stick—and when the barrel blew the iron free, underneath the smell of cordite and wet cotton and mud, Crane got

a stiff blast of that goddam *nuoc mam* sauce, boiling up out of the dink's belly along with the blood and the bile, that dead fish smell.

Nuoc mam sauce carried on the wind, which meant that Charlie could smell it too, and the thing was, in the bush, smell was everything. You could always tell a green boot because he washed a lot, and the smell of soap and aftershave, that carried on the wind. Charlie could smell you coming like a basket of lavender, set up and grease a whole patrol. So nobody washed, but the *nuoc mam,* Christ, that stuff smelled like a ten-day corpse in a paddy.

Gap Ky said, and it was true, that the VC stank so of *nuoc mam* themselves that they could hardly smell someone else's *nuoc mam* at two hundred yards, but it made Crane nervous anyway, and as a consequence he hated Gap Ky for making him nervous, and he especially hated the smell of *nuoc mam* sauce, so all in all he had by this time gotten to the stage where he was walking this patrol near Katum about five yards behind Gap Ky and all he could think about was borrowing Zippo Baxter's 60 and stitching his name down Gap Ky's backbone.

Which is, of course, when the shit starts, up front at point, where Midget Suarez trips a wire and tugs a pinless grenade out of a tin can tied to a tree and the grenade goes *crump* and Midget Suarez gets divided in three pieces, and then the whole jungle opens up on them.

The guys went herringbone, taking cover left and right, getting their fire out pretty good, and Crane went forward with Zippo and the M60 to where the corpsman, Wybowski,* was lying down beside what was left of Suarez, staring at a roast-sized chunk of Suarez that was slick and pink and was twitching along the jungle floor like a huge slug. Wybowski was wide-eyed and dazed, crazy-grinning up at them, and as he turned to say something to Crane about this phenomenon, the side of his face blew off, and some of what they later figured out were Wybowski's teeth hit Crane in the face and one of Wybowski's bone bits sliced into Zippo's left eye.

After that things were pretty hazy for Crane. He remembers taking the 60 from Zippo and Zippo doing the loading, slapping

*Not his real name.

a new belt into the 60, remembers Zippo looking for the glove he carried so he could put it on and change the barrel because they'd blown out fifteen hundred rounds and cooked the first one and now it was too hot to touch.

Now all around them guys were shouting and firing and putting out rounds with the bloop gun, which went *phutt* and then *wham* as the round bit in, leaves and twigs flying everywhere, rounds snipping and zipping and shrieking in, men taking rounds going *hoof* and grunting and falling, helmets flying off and then someone was yelling—Crane knew the voice—it was his—and the fight was over and Charley was gone.

And so was Gap Ky.

They searched the whole perimeter with shaking knees, their throats dry and their eyes burning with cordite. Gap Ky was gone.

Now that was the end of it for then. They medevacked out with six dead and two so bad that Crane and Murphy* thought real hard about shooting them before the slicks got there. Especially Wybowski, the corpsman whose brains were all over the front of his shirt but who was somehow terribly alive. Crane looked at him over the sights of his Colt while the rest of the guys did a grudge sweep looking for Gap Ky and capped off the only wounded dinks they could find. Then it was back to the Tactical Operations Center and they got Murphy to go for a little Intox and Intercourse.

But after two days at China Beach and another week of easy duty Crane and Murphy ran into an ARVN sergeant who told them that they had taken four VC alive three days back, in a sweep south of Katum, and one of them was a Chieu Hoi deserter named Gap Ky. And since everybody knew that Crane's platoon had been cut up bad in an ambush set up by Gap Ky, the ARVN Intelligence guys had kept Gap Ky alive and were prepared to sell him to Crane and Murphy for five hundred dollars.

That same night, Crane and Murphy got in a Jeep and drove over to the ARVN camp at Shin Loi mansion, where the ARVN sergeant grinned big and took them to a tin hootch where they found Gap Ky and three other VC in the ARVN G2 cells.

*Not his real name.

Gap Ky was in bad shape but he was in good enough shape to recognize Crane and Murphy. It took two ARVN soldiers to hold his head and a third to keep the rag in the dink's mouth while Crane and Murphy took turns hammering two olive-drab pencils into Gap Ky's ears while Crane looked right into Gap Ky's eyes and watched the impression the whole thing was having on him, smelling Gap Ky's *nuoc mam* breath, seeing the way his eyes were changing, knowing that Crane's face in the half-light was the last thing Gap Ky was ever going to see.

Murphy ponied up the five hundred out of Suarez's scrip cache and they left the hootch and drove back into their base in silence as a big red sun went down into a steaming green jungle and the road ahead of them twisted right and left like an open vein in the slanting red light.

The next day the ARVN troops took Gap Ky and the other three VC out into the bush and hung them upside down from a banyan, gutted them, cut their genitals off and hung them from the pencils that had been hammered into their brains through their ears. The pencils had gold letters embossed on the side that read, in Vietnamese, *"duma,"* which means "fuck your mothers." It was an ARVN thing, PsyOps or some shit, but for Crane the main effect was that he could never look at pencils quite the same way after that, and when the boots asked him about the war the first thing that came to mind was usually the thing about pencils.

So, no, he didn't have a lot of souvenirs on the wall in his apartment.

Crane set his clothes down in the hamper in the closet. He looked over the uniforms there, each one in an olive green suit bag. His Class As and his dress blues, six sets of BDUs pressed and starched by Monte's First Call Cleaners in Ogden, six pairs of boots shined and buffed like black stone.

Still feeling that stillness and the tiredness, he got into bed and lay on his back and stared awhile at the ceiling fan, listening to it whisper and thrum.

One blade was slightly off-balance so it had a kind of syncopation to it that lulled him. He reached out and turned off the gooseneck and the room was filled with soft evening light, blue and velvety, fading into darkness.

In a while it was very dark in the room. Outside the rain came down through the parched oak leaves with a soft hissing sound. From somewhere down the block music was drifting through the mist. . . . Crane's breathing slowed . . . he was doing pretty well. His mind was . . . he was doing okay. . . .

Crane slept.

Thirty-six minutes later he was sitting upright in the bed with his heart slamming away on the inside of his chest and his throat clamped shut. He was staring straight ahead at the black rectangle of the open door that led into the hallway. In his bones and belly he was listening as hard as he could listen to the silence in the hallway, knowing that something he heard, something wrong, had wakened him, and now he was just sitting there trying to get his breathing under control, trying to hear over the machinery of his body.

Moving as slowly as he could manage, he leaned over to the side of the bed and dragged the Colt out from under it. He felt the hammer with his right thumb and flicked the safety off. The safety was oiled and silent but it made a faint metallic thunk that seemed to bounce around the empty room.

He sat there with the piece on his lap for maybe three minutes, straining to see into the blackness, struggling to hear over the roaring in his ears and the hammering in his chest.

Which is why Crane lived alone.

———

Crane's apartment was in a combination wood-and-brick house in the western end of the town of Manhattan, Kansas. The people like to call it the Little Apple of Kansas; it's a pretty little Great Plains town with solid yellow-limestone and wooden buildings and big wide avenues shaded with cottonwoods and alders and oaks.

Manhattan is a complicated community, home to Kansas State University as well as the huge Army base known as Fort Riley, a few miles to the west of the town. Generally, the two camps live comfortably together, although the caste system is clearly defined and most of the military families attached to the 1st Infantry Di-

vision stay close together, mistrusting, with some reason, the dif-
fering sensibilities of the college families. A lot of the older
soldiers still carry hard feelings against college kids, developed
during the Vietnam years.

The fact that Crane lived off the main post wasn't unusual. Most
senior noncoms and many of the married rankers lived somewhere off post, in trailer parks or walk-up apartments in Junction
City or Ogden or, less often, in Manhattan. The main post housing
at Fort Riley is reserved for senior officers—from majors on up—
and the troop housing up on Custer Hill is spartan.

At the southern end of Crane's street you run into Fort Riley
Boulevard, which extends west about fifteen miles, turning into
Highway 18 and passing through the little scrub-town strip called
Ogden and on into the east gate of Fort Riley.

The gate is made of rough fieldstone and sits in a small valley
between two shallow bluffs that rise up north and south of the
two-lane blacktop road. Go another three miles along this road
and you see on your left a fifty-foot stone cairn, half-hidden in a
stand of cottonwoods, reached by a short gravel turnoff that leads
down to a clearing by a stretch of old railroad track.

This cairn is a monument to those men of the 1st Infantry Division who trained near here, at Camp Funston, and who were
shipped overseas from Fort Riley and other posts just a few years
after the turn of the century, shipped out to become a part of the
American Expeditionary Force sent to help the British and the
French in their struggle with the German Army. The year of their
departure was 1917, and it was in that year that the long self-
regarding innocence of the United States would come to an end
in the blood and ruin of the First World War.

There are no names on the cairn, but the records show that
one of the men who trained here was a sergeant, perhaps a little
like Crane, and like Crane he was in charge of a small unit of men
who went off to war in the spring of that year, 1917.

It was also in that year that the 1st Infantry Division received
both a name and a terrible distinction, and the twentieth century
began to develop and refine its murderous character. In 1917, the
1st Infantry Division saw the true face of war.

CHAPTER TWO

THE WINE COUNTRY

JULY 1918

Regarding the commencement of that brutal war, little needs to be said here, except to echo Robert E. Lee's observation that it is well that war is so terrible, else we should love it too much. Most of the war love had bled out of the conflict by July of 1918, when a unit of the 1st Infantry Division was slogging down a parched and dusty cartway in the Champagne country of France, toward a low line of trees at the edge of the great sweep of grain fields between the Aisne and the Marne rivers, between Soissons and Reims in the southeast. There the Allies had the Germans in a bulging pocket—all that remained of the Ludendorff offensive— and the French, being tired and decimated, had called upon General Pershing for help.

The men of the 1st Infantry had marched for a day and a night in showers and then in heat, through a great litter of guns and tanks and a heaving sea of plunging horses, gun limbers, muddy shouting men, Legionnaires and blue-black Senegalese, Moroccans in bright blue and scarlet, through platoons of the U.S. Marines who had made names for themselves in Belleau Wood the month just passed, through all of this confusion toward a low line of trees in the east, the beginning of the forest at the edge of the town of Villers-Cotterêts, in France, where the long placid dream of the nineteenth century was grinding to an end in a vast mill-work of steel and iron, blood and machines, stupidity and nobility.

It was high summer, the twilight not coming until after ten that evening, and since there was no moon, the forest had darkened into an impenetrable blackness by the time Private James Rose and the men of his unit reached their position in a forest that had, in its time, sheltered a great evil by the name of Gilles de Rais.

They were at that time known as the 1st Division—named at Lafayette's tomb in Paris the year before, and now part of Pershing's promise to French field marshal Foch to support his counteroffensive against the German breakthrough back in March.

Many of the men were late of the National Guard, and had ridden with Blackjack Pershing on his punitive mission down into Mexico, chasing Villa and the Army of the North. Some were cavalry troopers who had been pulled in from the west, and there were men from Albany and Lake Placid as well as soldiers from Ohio, Maine, and the Midwest, all sucked into the great vortex of the war, caught up in the cheers and the girls and the lying percussive pulse-beat of the military drums and the military bands.

They had been on the march for close to twenty-four hours, and they had had neither food nor water nor rest on the road. As they marched, grunting under their packs, one man's eyes fixed on the trenching tool of the man in front, all around them the glory of the last century was sinking into the earth.

Lancers in shining cuirasses, plumes sodden in the rain, and horse guards with their sabers rusted and their mounts blown and heaving, all the chivalric majesty of nineteenth-century warfare, it was all being fed into a churning mechanical hopper, and the gateway to all of that was just beyond this forest. Rose and his platoonmates collapsed into the blackness under the trees just as the night sky cracked open and a shimmering downpour filtered through the leaves and spattered on their helmets.

They slept badly that night, listening to the shouts and the curses of officers looking for lost platoons, catching fleeting glimpses of one another in a sudden crack of lightning, hearing the jingle and stamp of horses, and the coughing and spitting and moaning of thousands of men in the dark, and the monotonous droning rain.

All through the night Rose and his friends smoked and talked and worried in the silences about what might happen in the morning. The word was out that Harbord was forming them up for a big assault, Marines and infantry, in the service of the French general Mangin, along with these Foreign Legionnaires, and the Moroccans and the poilus and the Senegalese. They were going to begin a barrage around dawn, and then they'd go up in waves and head for the Germans, thousands of whom were dug in beyond the forest, in the fields and hills to the east, with the Marne River at their backs and General Ludendorff watching them like a fat old vulture.

It was said that the Germans were not expecting the assault, that they were demoralized and ready to run, that they would be so cowed by the shelling that not a single man would raise a weapon. It would be a walk for the 1st Infantry, so they all said.

After a while, they slept.

At 4:35 on the morning of July 18, 1918, a 75-mm cannon opened up with a short, sharp crack, and in a minute all sixteen hundred guns were firing on the German lines. The sound was massive, shattering. Rose felt himself literally bounced off the ground by the concussion, and the shells made a sound like fabric ripping as they arced overhead. When they hit, the explosion was short, sharp, deep, gone in the flick of an eye. Trees and earth and bits that looked like men would fly up into the air, into a little whirlwind of earth and dirt, and other rounds would slam in, again and again, until the whole field was like a tossing sea of brown and green waves and flying grasses all the way across the grain fields to the town of Berzy-le-Sec.

And it was true. They had surprised the Germans. Rose and his platoon, up now and deployed along the treeline and in the field north of the forest, could see German soldiers who had been trapped in the grainfields, harvesting wheat for bread. Now they lay like bundles of torn clothing or they ran toward their lines across the field. They all felt a great exultation, a sudden rush of power and awe, as they watched the shells come in and saw the enemy scattering.

All along the front, the Germans were falling back, and then the barrage stopped and there was a shout from the sergeant— Manning was his name—and now they were up and running, screaming, Rose's throat was raw, and under his hands his tommy gun felt hot and heavy, his boots heavy in the churned earth, the helmet bouncing on his skull, and all his friends were around him, running and shouting under a bright new morning, across a wheat field in France, for reasons none of them could name.

Now the line was four miles wide, and all along it Rose could see the men advancing. Just beside them were those Moroccans, cheering and jubilant, and beyond them, away to the south, the Marines, also screaming and cheering. Now they were coming up on a ditch, they had to leap it, and the French were waving them on, and Rose thought how fine it all looked, and then a shell slammed into the earth a few yards to his left, in the middle of a running mass of men, maybe a dozen of them.

A man to Rose's left was in that instant transformed, it seemed to Rose, into a wet cloud of flesh and scraps of cloth. His forward leg, it went on another step, and then the rear leg, now attached to nothing, an obscene joke, it came tumbling up and then Rose felt warm blood and something hit his battle-dress jacket, a clump of something. Other men were reeling—in a complete silence now—although their mouths were open and from the way their veins were thickened and their eyes so widened, they must have been screaming—red faces full of blood and eyes wild—but Rose ran on out of that, carrying his tommy gun, ruined now by a piece of shrapnel, so he gave his ammunition to another man running beside him, and now he and his sergeant, Manning, were running through the wheat field and there was no one around them.

Everyone else was dead or down with wounds. They looked back and saw nothing in the tall grain. They ran on now, Rose weaponless, Manning with his rifle, in silence as all around them the guns were pounding and men were falling—they were being watched at this point by the writer Pierre Teilhard de Chardin, who was a stretcher-bearer and a priest, and he wrote later about ". . . the vast upland of the Soissons country dotted with groups of men advancing in single file. . . . On all sides great bursts of smoke. . . . Over all this there rose the sound of a continuous light crackling, and it was a shock to see among the ripening crops little blotches that lay still. . . . Here and there a tank made its way through the tall corn . . . like a ship sailing the seas. . . ."

Rose and Manning, just the two of them, walking forward now, out of wind, came across the ruined body of a German soldier, who screamed at them in German, asking to be shot, but they looked at him for a time and then walked on toward the town of Berzy-le-Sec and after a while it was clear that there had been a great victory, for there were lines of German prisoners filing past them toward the forest and as they went by some of them were cheering at Rose and Manning and what they were saying was Yes, go on, finish it, finish this goddamned war.

Rose and Manning found other men of their company and went forward as far as a ravine that opened up near the village of Vierzy, south of Berzy-le-Sec. It was a sharp sudden gash in the fields and the Germans had set up machine guns nearby, so that there had to be a halt while some tanks could be brought up.

But Rose and his friends were surprised when a squadron of French cavalry—heavy dragoons in their steel cuirasses, lancers with pennons flying, a full mounted troop—came wheeling out of a little wooded copse on their right. The cavalry drew sabers and formed for a charge, Rose thinking how magnificent they looked.

They shaped up and steadied, the tips of the lances came down, the sabers shimmered along the line of horses like a flutter of white wings along a far shore, and they kicked into a slow trot—cavalry by the book—and then into a canter—don't blow the mounts, they'll founder—dress the line there, stay abreast—skirmishers out, sabers coming forward—and then put the spurs to them, a headlong charge toward the gorge in front of Vierzy. They looked quite unstoppable to Rose, but Manning, who had been with Pershing in Mexico and knew something about cavalry and machine guns, had a grim face and nothing to say.

Now the machine guns were still crackling and chattering, and there was some sporadic fire from their lines, but mainly the Germans in the field and up in the gorges were quiet, so that Rose could hear the sound of the cavalry, and hear faintly across the grainfields the sound of the dragoons, who had been taught since Napoleon to come forward with the low, moaning, growling cry that had terrified infantry for centuries, a sonorous droning like a hive of bees.

Now the earth was drumming with their hoofbeats and the jingle of harness and they could hear the horses huffing and snorting with the effort, see the deep brown shining skin of the animals.

The first German shell landed at the left of their line. The squadron rode into it and some went down, and then the shells came down like hammers, like fists on a tabletop, and the little horse figures jumped and tumbled like cups and saucers as the shells slammed into the earth all around them.

In a minute it was over and there was nothing but butchery and shredded meat in the wheat field, and Manning shrugged and looked even grimmer. Then they got the word and they all got up and went out across the field to take the Germans on foot, which they did.

So that was the beginning of battle for the 1st Infantry Division, and that evening they bivouacked a half mile from the village—they'd take it from the Germans tomorrow—and there was food and some hot coffee, so the ones who were still alive agreed that this battle thing was okay and not as bad as they had thought it might be.

And they were easy in their minds because they had been to the gate of the thing and looked inside and not been afraid. They were soldiers now and had done their country proud. Manning, the sergeant, saw to it that everybody was in shape and fed.

Sometime during that night they changed in an important way—at least at the time it seemed so—and in the morning when the sergeant woke them up they felt for the first time that they were part of something big, something they could be proud of, they were 1st Infantry, and all of this seemed to settle in around the sergeant, who looked as though he had grown an inch during the night, and was full of jokes and rough talk and made them all feel strong.

Hell, this war was going to be over soon, and he was part of a good crowd, they were all good men, all soldiers together.

While the soldiers were sleeping, General Pétain went to Mangin, the general who was in charge of this battle, and he told Mangin that, while a great breakthrough had been achieved, Mangin would have to stop it there. Mangin, who had built a huge wooden tower in the middle of the forest of Retz so he could see all the way across to Berzy-le-Sec and the gorge at Vierzy, was extremely upset and asked Pétain why the hell he would have to do this. And Pétain said, Because you are extended now and cannot be reinforced and I have no more men to feed to you. And Mangin, who knew that across the way the German generals, Ludendorff and Hindenburg, were talking, making plans, and using the time to halt the collapse and to get ready for the next day, looked at Pétain very hard. Pétain held his ground and said it again. Mangin must stop here because there were no reserves to bring up, and these troops, the Americans and the Moroccans, were blown and should not be extended, or the Germans would cut them up. Then he left, angry.

Mangin watched him go—arrogant bastard—and he realized after a while that Pétain had said he would send no more men, since he had none. But he had not said for Mangin to remain, it was not a direct *order*, and Mangin said to himself—and then to his Chief of Staff—Well, if we cannot have more men, we will continue this assault tomorrow with what we have. And he gave that order. There would be a new assault in the morning, which should reach all the way to the Marne and drive the Germans away from Reims, which they were threatening.

But the next day they did not have the surprise and the Germans were waiting for them a little before Berzy-le-Sec as the 1st Infantry Division—ten thousand men under arms—came out of their positions and started to cross the rest of that long sweeping valley before Soissons, at the edge of the great forest of Retz, where Gilles de Rais once lived.

It was Champagne country, we know the names from labels—Château-Thierry and Epernay and Pérignon and all the little vineyards—and a lot of good red wine also comes from there, deep and rich and red, with a tannic acid taste and a long farewell.

This was the country that lay in front of Rose and Sergeant Manning as they saw to their weapons and listened to their officers on the morning of July 19, 1918. They crouched in trenches and heard their officers tell them about the objective, and then it was five-thirty and a Very flare went off, and the first wave stood and got ready to climb up and go forward at the Germans.

Which they did, in their thousands, all down the long line, Marines and the rest, the Senegalese and the Foreign Legion, and the 1st Division, Rose and his platoon behind Sergeant Manning, who was yelling to them, telling them who they were.

There was a sweep of land ahead, and then they had to run up a little crest, and it was as if that little crest of land was the lee shore. They ran up it in a crowd of men, helmets bobbling, hunched forward as if into a strong wind, and they could hear the ratcheting chatter of machine guns up ahead. Their boots slipped on the trampled grain and the mud beneath it so that by the time they reached the top of the little hill, they were almost at a walk.

The major was an old soldier and had been with Pershing for a long time but when he cleared the rise Rose saw him at the top, staggering, coming to pieces, shredded by a sheet of fire from the massed machine guns on the far edge of the field.

Seconds later all the officers were dead and Manning ran forward, turning back to say something to Rose—looking right at him—and then he was coming apart as well. Rose ran to him, crouching down in the face of the endless stream of rounds coming at them, and Manning was choking on his own blood. He said something to Rose and Rose let him down easily and stood up, the men looking at him.

He waved at them, said something, what it was he couldn't remember, and then he ran down the slope and out across the field, firing as he ran, with his friends all streaming down the slope behind him, firing and shouting, heads down, leaning forward, shoulders hunched as if they were walking into a strong wind. All men do this when they have to walk into fire—they did it at Antietam and the Second Bull Run and even at LZ Bitch—not that it does any good, but it is the same sometimes with people who have been shot; you see wounds in their hands—clean through—that they got when they saw the gun come up and tried to stop the round with their hands. Soldiers have their habits. This hunching of the shoulders and the lowered head, they're understandable.

Now try to imagine this. . . .

You are on the fire step of a trench, up to your puttees in mud, wet through and through, in a mumbling press of men, all staring up at the ragged lip of the trench. Far to the east there's a pale pink light and the sky is turning the color of a dirty cotton bandage. You have a long Springfield bolt-action rifle, at its muzzle a seventeen-inch bayonet. On your head a tin pot strapped so tight under your chin you can't swallow. In your belly you have three cups of tea fortified with very strong rum, so that even your toes are warm right now. You have not eaten because you have been told that a belly wound will be even worse if you have food in your stomach. So the rum has gotten into your head and calmed you a little, although your left knee is shaking a bit and you can't seem to stop it.

Now all through the night you have tried to sleep, although the dead from the last assault are still out there—men you knew, a kid from Brooklyn who traded you chocolate for socks on the march, another boy who was going to be a printer when he got back; his father, who had been killed in a fall from a building, was a bricklayer and had left him the money *if* he would take care of his mother, who had TB. And there was a man from Ohio, his face was extremely freckled and his hair a carrot red and his eyes were almost sky blue, so that when he smiled through the mud on his face, he looked like all the colors of the flag. The boy talked about his farm, he was worried about the farm because the cows were sick and needed medicine.

The day before they had all been alive, as alive as you, standing on the fire step just like you are now, and waiting for the major to blow his whistle, waiting for the .75s to open up. And then they were dead, shot through the left eye, or blown up by a shell, or opened up from the crotch to the breastbone by machine-gun fire. You watched a man stumble forward—it was the printer—his feet tangled up in his own entrails, and another man, you had to jump over him, running, breathless, that damned useless tin-pot helmet wobbling around on your head, your gear jingling and shaking, your boots sucking in the mud, your legs on fire, while he lay in the mud on his back, naked from the waist down, his clothes blown away, leaving him white and naked and very bloody and his pubic hair was very red and his white skin mottled with freckles and his eyes—that vivid blue—staring up into the rising smoke . . . they all died.

So now it's the next day, and you are going to do this again. Even though you can see very clearly that it's a bad idea, that your leaders simply do not know what they're doing, that they're using nineteenth-century battle tactics, massed infantry and frontal assaults, against a twentieth-century creation, the machine gun. The level of stupidity has reached the criminal, but you are still here, still on the fire step, waiting to go, instead of doing the sensible thing, turning around, shooting the major, shoving that whistle up his dead ass, and going back home to Cincinnati.

Now what you have come to know is this:

At the beginning—which may have been the day before yesterday—you figured, Hell, some of us will die, but not me. You're young, you're quick, you're just simply and irreducibly *you.* You've lived behind those eyes and in that skull for twenty years, for God's sake! You've looked down at these hands, shaved this face, washed those toes. You've danced to the music and hungered for the ladies and read the books, filled your mind up with memories and connections. You have *plans,* for God's sake. You don't have *time* to be dead! You are the pulsing *center* of every vibrating moment, it all swirls around *you,* and *you* are not like these dead ones here, who were unlucky, or made a mistake, or simply ran out of time.

But not you.

That's what you thought yesterday, anyway. And then you went for that slow jolting jog across the wheat field and there was that white rippling fire all along the treeline, that sound like popping corn—such a small sound, not *huge* like the shell bursts that started to hunt you, that came cracking up out of the dirt on your left, as sudden as a bone breaking—and then there were *bits* of men on your jacket, and little wasp sounds of shrapnel humming past your head, and now more of that little popping-corn sound and the scattering, pattering rickety-ticketing of the machine-gun rounds slicing through the tall corn . . . and after a long hallucinatory time, you were back in the trench with your lungs on fire, and all those boys who started out with you—well, you looked around at the other faces and for the men who weren't there and suddenly you reached the *second* stage of knowing.

Okay, it *can* happen to you, even though you are the center of everything and if you die it will all be snuffed out. So what you have to do is be *smarter* than the dead ones. Take more care. Shoot straighter. Run faster. Dodge. Dive. Kill better. Kill quicker. You can learn all this. You can keep yourself alive. And out there in the wheat field you can see some wonderful sights, learn other things, for instance blood will glow in the dark if you leave it for long enough. And rats can live through anything. And rats will eat anything.

But sometime during the early hours—maybe not then, maybe later, but soon—you'll get to the third level of knowing about war. It's not just that you *can* die out here, if you're not quick and lucky and smart. It's that you *will* die out here, if you stay here long enough.

There are only three ways this thing can go.

One, you'll get killed outright about ten minutes from now.

Two, you'll catch a massive wound and spend the rest of your life in a basket by the side of the park, pissing into a diaper and living on liquids while all your friends talk across the top of your head.

Or the war will end and you can go home.

That's it. There are no other possibilities.

You lean your forehead against the stock of your Springfield—

or your M16 or your M1 or your pike or your scabbard, it doesn't matter, because this is the heart of the whole thing and always has been—and you try to figure out a way around it, and there isn't one way. Not one.

You are now facing your own extinction. You are about to die. Or worse, but whatever it is, it is *now,* not later, not next year in Jerusalem, not after a long and happy life, toppling into the roast at a Sunday dinner decades in the future, no happy toddlers calling you Pop, no more slow, sweet hours of a summer night with a scented wind stirring the curtains and the old bedboards creaking. No more cold beers, no victory parades, no drums, no bugles. Just a white moment while your limbs turn to water—there was a man who caught a round in another war and when it hit him, he stood up and asked his friend to *walk* him, to keep him walking, one leg in front of the other, as if this wound that was killing him could be walked off, shaken off, as if death was like sleep; they even slapped his face.

This is a very concentrating moment, a soul compression that no one who has not been there can truly understand, and because no one who has not been there knows what it is, we go on having wars.

So the major blows his whistle and you, having no choice, go up over the edge and out into the wheat field again with only two things to help you. One, if you don't go, maybe the major will shoot you, because that's why the officers have pistols, to shoot the cowards. And two, if you *do* go, then someday the war will end and somebody has to live and it *might* be you. And that's why men lean into oncoming fire as if it were rain, and walk across wheat fields that are blowing up all around them, and it's also why they don't talk about this sort of thing afterward.

As for Private Rose, by the time he had reached the Soissons road that went to Paris, he had gone through these changes, and now there was only Rose and one other man. They fell down at the ditch on the west side of the road and looked across at the treeline. Fires flickered across the line, German machine guns, traversing mechanically, sweeping down anything standing. To their right the 6th Marines were coming out of the trees and into that fire, seeming to melt and run away into the ground like water, whole platoons of men falling in line.

The man with Rose had gone as far as he would, but Rose stood up and started across the road. He fell, chipped a tooth, and a fan of machine-gun fire swept by above his head. He rolled over on his back and looked behind him across the field. He had come five hundred yards from the little ridge where Sergeant Manning had died and there was no one left but him. He put his head back on the road and in the terrible silence that descended he could hear, above the pounding of his heart and the whistle of breath in his throat, the cries of wounded men. The sky was very blue and he lay there for a while and looked up at it in silence.

Later the field was taken by the 6th Marines and what was left of the 1st Infantry Division. By the time Rose and another man— all that was left of his unit—reached the village of Berzy-le-Sec, Ludendorff had withdrawn his men behind the Marne.

It had been a great victory, and although many of the men who had come up two days before were now dead or shattered by shell-fire or ruined by terrible wounds, the commanders agreed that the 1st Infantry had fought very well—"played up" was how Field Marshal Sir Douglas Haig put it later, "played up well"—and after that they looked kindly on Pershing, who had once seemed un-willing to commit his Americans to the Great Alliance.

And Rose?

He fought well, as he recalls, although with somewhat dimin-ished fervor, until the second phase of the battle for the Argonne Forest in October, when, late in the afternoon, a round from a German machine gun hit him in the foot and he was sent to the rear and his war was over.

The French word for the injury was *un petit blesse,* which trans-lates as "a little wound" but the Americans called it "the little blessing," which it was.

Around Berzy-le-Sec and Soissons, between July 17 and July 22, the 1st Infantry Division lost seven thousand men. By the Armi-stice, they had suffered almost one hundred and fifty percent ca-sualties, close to twenty-three thousand men, as veterans fell and replacements were fed into the machine.

So this is why you can come along that westbound highway from Manhattan, Kansas, run through Ogden and into the east gate, and find that stone obelisk commemorating some of the men who trained at Camp Funston and Fort Riley, and then shipped out for France in 1917, and caught a shell or took a round or were simply vaporized.

A little creek runs by this monument, and in the late summer the cicadas buzz in the cottonwoods and a dry Great Plains wind rustles in the dusty leaves.

And now we know Manning the way Crane knows him, as a sergeant of the Regular Army, who rode with Blackjack Pershing against Villa in Mexico, and who, for reasons that remain unclear to us but might resonate with Crane, drowned in his blood a few hundred yards beyond the old forest of Retz, in the Champagne country of France, near Berzy-le-Sec, where they say the wine is very fine, and everyone agrees that it must be something in the soil.

CHAPTER THREE

CIVILIANS

AUGUST 1990

As Crane remembers it, he had been pacing his apartment and getting more and more jagged, which happens to everyone, but single people feel it more, the same way one cat will always sit at the window looking down into the street, but two cats will keep each other busy, find something to ruin.

So ten minutes later he was dressed in his civvies—Dockers and a polo shirt actually, part of the new clothes Carla had taken him out to get, Carla feeling that all Crane needed was a new attitude—and was out in the Caprice heading east on Fort Riley Boulevard as the wipers ticked and clicked and made greasy arcs on the window and the streetlights smeared themselves across the glass.

At Eighth he made a left and drove slowly past the library, and then he turned right onto Poyntz. The wide street was slick and shiny with the rain, empty except for a cluster of cars halfway down the block. He cruised along it at twenty until he reached Harry's Uptown, where he found a slot between a metallic green BMW and a racy-looking Seville. The Army-tan Caprice looked a little sorry there and Crane smiled as he locked it up.

He could hear music coming from Harry's, maybe Billie Holiday. Harry's Uptown Bar was on the ground floor of the old Wareham Hotel, right in the middle of the six long, wide blocks that people thought of as downtown Manhattan. The limestone face of the Wareham Hotel was wet with the rain and the deep-set windows were black and empty, but the ground floor was lit up and people were milling around in the bar.

Crane shoved the door open and the music broke over him, the voices and the press of people smelling of Boss and Chanel, tobacco and beer, everyone in suits or sports jackets, crisp white shirts and silk ties and all the women flushed and smiling and bright with talk, teeth wet and lips red.

Crane found a space by the service slot and waited for the bartender to notice him. Harry's clientele was mixed, lawyers and clerical staff from the Riley County Courthouse down the street, some doctors and staffers from Memorial Hospital, some college kids and instructors from Kansas State.

Not a bad crowd but maybe a little too pleased with how things were going for themselves. Crane didn't mind them as long as they gave him some space and didn't expect shop talk from him. He didn't come here too much. It was Carla's territory anyway, and Crane was edgy around people like this, people he thought of as The Young and The Ruthless. People like that usually looked down on the grunts from Fort Riley, although it was hard to believe any of them would have jobs if it weren't for all the shit going on up on Custer Hill. It wasn't Kansas State University that kept this town going.

There was no doubt he was Regular Army, even in civvies. The haircut alone was enough to give him away, but his thin and angular frame and his bat-eared face like an elbow, full of seams and cracked around the eyes, and the way he held himself—something he couldn't have changed by now even if he thought of it— marked him off and set him outside, that is, if people bothered to focus on him at all.

Right now this crowd was all wrapped up in their own wonderfulness so Crane felt pretty safe, could just snag a cold beer and settle down, listen to whoever was on now, something jazzy with a lot of horns—Duke Ellington doing "Willow Weep for Me."

Carla wasn't behind the bar. Crane had not expected her to be there, although he wouldn't have been unhappy to see her. The new kid was in something agricultural at the university, Crane tried to remember his name—Tory, right?—and he called to the kid over the loud talk and the music.

Tory brought him a Miller Genuine Draft but no glass so Crane reached over the side of the bar top and got himself one. That was another thing with these people, always doing whatever they saw in a commercial, the cool guys don't drink out of glasses, so now, go into a bar anywhere in the free world, you don't get a glass for your beer anymore.

Right beside him he had a couple of guys, Levi's and pricy cowboy boots, polo shirts, heads together talking about how the health system in America was on the edge of falling apart. Taking it very seriously too, from the sound of the talk.

There was a TV on behind the bar, something for Tory, Crane figured, Tory being a youngster and not able to go too far from a television set. Tory had it tuned to CNN and he was keeping an eye on it as he mixed and dipped and popped for the crowd along the bar. Crane looked away from the television set and concentrated on his Miller, only half listening to the two guys next to him who were convinced the country's health system was a corpse that wouldn't lie down.

Tomorrow was going to be a hard day. The G4 officer had let all the senior noncoms know that there was going to be a "surprise" CMMI sometime during the morning—Command Material Maintenance Inspection—although the noncoms always called it Coneheads Manifesting Minimal Intelligence: bean counters and bumboys from the Command Support Services section, clipboards at Lock and Load, inventory control printouts hanging from every orifice. Everyone from the noncoms on down would be climbing all over the Bradleys and the motor pool depot and the company arms compound with at least two CMMI pogues on his ass, looking to see if every bolt and oilcan was precisely where it was supposed to be and tagged in precisely the correct way.

All of this military energy and ambition ended up with Captain Wolochek, a lean yuppie-looking West Pointer. Wolochek knew the name and status of every one of Baker's two hundred and four troopers, so whenever the pogues from CMMI dropped in and screwed up the training routines for the whole battalion, Wolochek would get all raspy with DerHorst, a lifer sergeant in his late thirties with ambitions for rank, and DerHorst would get jumpy and bad tempered with Crane. The thing was, if it wasn't a good CMMI then it would affect Wolochek's OER—his Officers Evaluation Report—which went straight to the Department of the Army in Washington.

This kind of situation was generally referred to in army jargon as FUBAR, which meant Fucked Up Beyond All Recognition. So Crane sighed and stared into his glass, which was now empty, and tried to enjoy the music, which Tory was just now in the middle of shutting off.

Crane had his mouth open, ready to say something to Tory, but Tory had his back turned and was looking at the television set. On the screen there was a large map of Iraq and Kuwait, with arrows pointing into Kuwait from the Iraq border. Crane's heart blipped and skipped. One of the guys next to him called out to Tory to turn up the sound.

And now the whole bar got real quiet as the CNN announcer introduced a Washington bureau reporter, and the picture then cut away to a brief clip of President George Bush.

In a steady voice but with a kind of angry vibrato underneath it, Bush announced that he had just been advised that several tank divisions of the Iraqi Army had just overrun the Kuwaiti defense forces and had taken over the entire country. The Iraqis had made their move at dawn, and estimates of the size of the invasion force varied but the figure one hundred thousand troops had "not been denied," which meant it was probably three times that. There were unconfirmed reports of Iraqi atrocities coming out of Kuwait but that contact had been broken off abruptly. War had come to the emir's palace itself. The emir's brother had been killed.

War.

Crane felt a weird kind of dropping-away sensation, as if he had just lost a great deal of weight or the gravity in the bar had been turned off. He could feel the cold from the Miller bottle in the bones of his left hand. He had a kind of warming sensation running up the back of his neck.

They did it. They actually did it.

Bush had been snarling at Hussein off and on for the last year, and to an Army man the signs were all there. Bush was getting ready to do something, make a point, fight the "wimp factor," get out there and nail some raghead balls to a door, and it looked to Crane as though this would do the trick, and besides there was all that oil.

War.

War in the desert.

They'd all had the doctrine brief back at the REFORGER war games exercise in Germany last year; oil supplies had been one of the probable ignition points for sending in the U.S. Army. And Kuwait had, what, ten percent of the world's oil, so it was a high-risk scenario and they'd all played it out last year at the National Training Center in the Mojave. The 1st was mechanized infantry. That meant infantry trained to fight in tanker wars. Infantry that rode alongside tankers in armored personnel carriers. Infantry that fought mounted or dismounted but infantry that was designed for exactly this kind of war. Infantry that had been war-gaming Soviet battle tactics in the Mojave, going up against the permanent OpFor units stationed there, units that used Soviet T-72 main battle tanks and Soviet engagement strategies. And the Iraqis had been Soviet trained and Soviet equipped and the Iraqis used precisely the battle tactics that the 1st had been drilled in at the Fort Irwin NTC. And the 1st was part of the VII Corps, and the VII Corps was "tasked" for exactly this kind of operation. If the U.S. decided to do something about the Iraqi invasion of Kuwait, it was a dead-solid certainty that the U.S. would do it with the VII Corps.

Christ.

Crane stared at the screen and thought these thoughts while

the bar started to react to the news, people slamming the bar top, voices all rising together, and somebody was tapping him on the left forearm, and Tory was in front of him, also watching Crane's face. Crane looked to his left and saw a flushed, bearded face, one of the young doctors beside him.

"You Army? Excuse me, but Tory says you're Army?"

Crane nodded and lifted his empty Miller up in front of Tory, raising his left eyebrow.

"Yes, sir."

"What are you, an officer?"

"No, sir. I'm a sergeant."

"I'm sorry, I don't mean to—what do you think they'll do?"

"Who?"

"Who? Us. What'll we do?"

"You in the reserves, sir?"

"Me? No, not personally."

"So you mean what'll Bush do?"

"Yeah . . . I mean, I guess they brief you guys about all of this stuff way ahead. You don't have to say anything you don't . . . it's just, how's this look to you?"

Tory came back with his beer. Crane looked down the bar, at all the people chattering and moving around, and back to the television where some guy was standing in front of the White House with a mike in his hand. He had the exact same look on his face as everybody along the bar, a look that was half nausea and half thrill, the look of the guy with a guaranteed note from his doctor, he's not gonna go.

But damn is he interested in the look on your face.

"Well, sir, it looks pretty early."

The man looked disappointed, checked his friend to see if he was behind him, came back into Crane's face.

"We're not gonna let this—I mean, Hussein's—he'll get all the oil and, well, we're gonna—somebody's gonna have to get in there, stop that, because there's no way—"

"I understand that, sir. It's just that, from a military perspective, it's very hard to go in and root someone out, especially if the guy has time to dig in and get ready. From a tactical point of view, it's better to defend than to assault, like a three-to-one advantage, so the problem here is, Hussein's *in* and the best way to handle a situation like that is not to let it happen in the first place because whoever has to go get him *out* is going to have a very bad time."

There was something going on in the guy's face. Crane couldn't make it out, but when the guy spoke it all fell into place.

"So you don't want to go in there?"

"No soldier wants to go anywhere near a war." Crane looked the guy over, thinking about how far into this he should go, was the guy worth the trouble? Well, he was a citizen, wasn't he? Like an employer, in a sense. And sometimes you never knew, sometimes it was a good idea to get the civilians to try to see things better.

"Look, I don't mean we don't want to fight, sir. Fighting is what we train for. I'm just saying that, from a tactical consideration—it's like in medicine?"

The man's face brightened up. He was back in home country now.

"Say a guy comes in, he has lung cancer. The sooner you get to him, the more you can do, right?"

"Absolutely, but I can see where you're—"

"Yes, sir, I know you can. But you see, that's what it is. It's better for the guy that he never started smoking in the first place. What we have here, we have a government—no offense to them—but they see things in a political way, use Hussein to back off the Ayatollah, that sort of thing. But then, things change, and suddenly we're not friends with Hussein anymore, and now we got to get in there, take the guns and stuff we gave him last year away from him this year. That sort of thing, it gets on your nerves, because it didn't have to happen that way. You see what I mean, sir?"

"Yeah . . . of course, and I guess, it's been a long time since we went to a real war, right? I mean, no offense, but Panama and Grenada, they were more your police actions, right? Not like Vietnam—were you in Vietnam, Sergeant?"

Crane was going to say no he wasn't but Tory spoke up, said that Crane was a Silver Star and had a couple of bongs and bolo badges, so that took care of that.

"Yes, sir, I spent some time there."

There was a look on the man's face but Crane couldn't make it out.

"My dad was there, a place called Why Drag, something like that?"

His *dad*? Jesus, how old was this guy?

"You mean the Ia Drang?" Crane was starting to regret this conversation.

"I guess so. I never asked him. Was that a bad place?"

Was the Ia Drang valley a bad place? How the hell did a guy answer a question like that? Just *asking* a question like that meant the guy had no right to a polite answer. Crane let out a slow breath and pulled at his Miller.

"Was your dad in the Air Cav?"

The guy's face went blank for a moment, then brightened.

"I don't know. He was in the Seventh Cavalry. Used to get razzed about it, like he was with Custer at the Bighorn. Is that Air Cav?"

"Yes. The Seventh Cavalry was a part of the First Air Cavalry Division."

"I thought they'd be separate units. You know, First Cav and Seventh Cav? Were they the same?"

Jesus.

"Sir, a division is made up of several different brigades, and a brigade is usually made up of battalions, and a battalion is made of three or four companies with about two hundred men in a company ..." The guy was looking around for Tory and holding up his glass. Crane felt a sudden chill flood of embarrassment and shut his mouth while Tory filled the guy's glass again. The Ia Drang valley. Christ.

Yes. It was a bad place, a very bad place for Company C of the 7th Cavalry. The Cav was new to the Nam, and the whole Airmobile thing was still being worked out. They dumped six choppers packed with cherry grunts into a landing zone made of mud and elephant grass. The 33rd North Vietnamese Regiment had the zone all sited in, just waiting for the slicks. LZ Bitch was the name they gave it later. The 7th had lost ninety percent of that company. The Air Cav had learned to fight in the Ia Drang, but not before it lost a hell of a lot of FNGs. LZ Bitch was studied at the noncom war-fighting school in Leavenworth. It was the classic case of a screwed-up Airmobile assault. What got to Crane was that this kid—was he maybe thirty?—that this man hadn't bothered to find out what the "Why Drag" was all about. The guy was talking again.

"I'm sorry, you were saying—about companies?"

"Never mind. And yeah, the Ia Drang valley was a bad fight. Your dad never told you about it?"

"Well, yeah, but, you know . . . war stories, right?"

Crane's jaw tightened and he looked down into his glass. The man was still talking, speaking for all of them, it seemed to Crane.

"But this time, this one, maybe we ought to get in there, do the thing right this time?"

"Yes, sir, maybe we should. It's just that . . ."

"Hey." The guy's face was smiling but somehow Crane didn't feel the smile was supposed to include him. "Look, I'm sorry. I've been pushy. I mean, what the fuck, hey? Who needs it, right? We have enough problems right here in town. We don't want another Vietnam, right, Sergeant?"

"Yes, sir. That would be right, sir."

The man smiled again, thanked him, and turned back to his buddy, and they spoke in lower tones, so that Crane knew his part in their evening was over, and that one way or another he had confirmed something about the Army that they always suspected, which was that the U.S. Army couldn't fight. It was too bad, but there it was.

Crane looked at the back of the guy's head for a while, thinking about saying something to it.

But what? Even more to the point, why? Times like this, Crane felt the difference between himself and the civilians the strongest. This guy's dad was a grunt in the Cav, probably a blue-collar guy, but *he's* a doctor, pulls down sixty, maybe seventy thousand a year. Worked his butt off all the way through med school, long hours and no pay. Now he's out in the world, got it all sewn up, and to a guy like that, Crane is just some poor scratch farmer, family plays the banjo, has nine kids each with one eye bigger than the other, sleep all together in a bed with a rope mattress, run corn liquor across the state lines, just another cracker soldier boy who couldn't make it in the real world. Why else would a grown man still be in the Army, unless he couldn't take the heat in the outside world?

Crane wanted to say something strong, something that would shake the guy out of his attitude, but all he could think of to say was one word.

Kasserine.

And that wouldn't have meant much to the guy, but the last time the 1st was sent to the Middle East—Africa, really, but it was desert all the same, exactly like the desert in Kuwait—they had gone to Tunisia.

And on February 19, 1943, Rommel's Afrika Korps Panzers had come on them, out of the sandstorm, come straight into them and they had lost a hell of a lot of guys, blown into meat, blown away in their boots, hand-to-hand in places, and the name of the place where this happened was the Kasserine Pass.

It was on the colors, one of the ribbons, and one of the 16th guys was a Medal of Honor winner, Bob Henry, but everybody knew, including General George S. Patton, who took over the 1st after Kasserine, that anybody who had been there would always find the room go quiet as soon as he came in.

The Kasserine Pass was one of those battles where you either court-martial the commander or you call him a hero.

That was the Kasserine Pass, and it was in Africa, which was, as far as Crane cared, just the same as Kuwait, a land where no American ought to go just to get killed in a tank battle.

But how could you get this guy to see that?

You couldn't.

Because everybody knew the U.S. Army couldn't fight.

Goddam Vietnam.

Vietnam was like this weird old uncle the Army had, something they had to keep in an attic and not bring up in polite conversation. It was hard being the first American army to lose a war, take all that condescending bullshit from some yuppie doctor who would have been the first one wearing a bra to the induction center if he'd gotten a call.

They all believed that the U.S. Army had gotten its ass kicked in Southeast Asia—even though they had never lost a single full-scale fight with the VC or the NVA and had, in fact, pounded the North Vietnamese into jelly by the end of 1969. But there was a story, one of the generals had pointed all that out to Giap or some other dink honcho at the Paris peace talks and the guy had thought it over, looked back across the table, and said, Yes, that was true, but it was also irrelevant.

And since then the Army had handed the American people nothing but excuses.

Excuses for the Son Tay raid, a real hot Special Forces op that had worked like silk except for the fact that no POWs were actually *in* the Son Tay camp when the Special Forces guys got there.

And then there was that enormous fuck-up in the Iranian desert, when a chopper had flown right up into a C-130 plane and the next day we still had all those hostages in the U.S. embassy in Tehran but now we also had Iranian newsreels of dead U.S. airmen and smoldering U.S. aircraft in some raghead wadi east of nowhere.

And Grenada, where the press made sure that everybody found out about the Ranger drop on the airfield where a bunch of Cuban truck drivers shot the shit out of them as they hung up there in their parachutes.

And Panama. And the poor bloody jarheads in Beirut, blown out of their bunks by one raghead with a ton of C-4 plastic explosive in the back of his truck, and, let's see, William Buckley, the CIA station chief tortured to death by the Syrians in 1985, and the Marine colonel, Higgins, hung like a gutted pig and videotaped twisting in the wind, and what does George do in the name of the American people?

He throws a barbecue on the White House lawn.

Crane had lived through all of that, and he knew what the guy was thinking. And what was there to tell him?

That it wasn't true? That it wasn't as simple as that?

Tell it to the Israelis, who once handled the problem of a KGB assassin squad working out of Lebanon by kidnapping the brother of one of the KGB men, cutting his balls off, and sending them to the man himself.

Maybe the guy was right.

Maybe America wasn't up to it anymore.

Crane downed the rest of his Miller and dropped a ten on the bar top and went back outside. The rain was softer now, and the clouds were ripping apart overhead, the moonlight showing around the edges.

Crane started up the Caprice and headed back west on Riley, thinking he might go on out to Junction City and look for some of the guys in Baker. As one of the senior noncoms he ought to be around where the troops were, because the war talk would be burning them up and the kids would be full of questions, full of crazy war panic, half-mad, half-glad, and desperately in need of a simple, straightforward answer. And in Crane's heart he knew what that answer would be.

He rolled westward along Fort Riley Boulevard and cleared the last lights of Manhattan. The road rose up into a saddle pass and curved left again and down through a lowland valley, and in the far west there was still the faintest tinting of red fire on the underside of the cloud drift. He held the wheel tight and felt his heart in his chest and the tightness in his throat. Later, when he had a chance to think it over, he realized that he was afraid, but that what he was afraid of wasn't the idea of a war in the desert.

He was afraid of being left behind.

CHAPTER FOUR

LAST POST

NOVEMBER 1990

William Least Heat Moon has observed that if you could stake a wire into downtown Seattle, Washington, and run it all the way southeast to Key West, Florida, and then stake another wire in the middle of the walkway at Battery Park in New York City and stretch that wire three thousand miles to the intersection of Hollywood and Vine in Los Angeles, your two wires would intersect—almost—in the middle of the cavalry parade square at Fort Riley, Kansas, the geographical and military heart of the United States.

The land around Fort Riley is rolling and graceful, although there are passages where the yellow bones beneath the thin skin of red Kansas earth burst up in jagged eruptions of sawtooth limestone cliffs. The fort is huge, covering nearly one hundred square miles if you include the tank ranges and marshes to the north, and it is sheltered from the hard winds that come up out of Oklahoma by a long yellow limestone bluff that runs along the southern border of the fort, about a mile from the Kansas River. In this broad river valley the Kansas wanders in long shallow loops and arcs in between banks of ocher earth, bordered throughout its length by cottonwoods and oaks planted by the first settlers in the state. A bridge crosses the Kansas beside Marshall Field, and the road runs up a winding tree-lined circuit that leads you into the groves and shaded lawns of the main post of Fort Riley.

As you roll up the curving two-lane blacktop past the first out-buildings, the fort looks more like the grounds of an old university. Classical buildings constructed of yellow limestone dream solid Republican dreams under massive oaks with dusty green leaves and thick black gnarled branches. Separated by broad reaches of parks and grassy slopes, the fort is composed of grace-fully situated nineteenth-century stone halls, low wooden outbuild-ings painted a soft ocher yellow accentuated with green-painted wooden trim and balconies, in a web of winding streets lined with trees, shaded and sheltered from the brutal Kansas sun and the bitter Kansas winters, heavy and rooted, weighed down with the passage of years and worn by the passage of men.

On a low rise of green grassy hills, in orderly and tree-shaded rows, the senior officers' homes are made of yellow square-cut stone two feet thick, with wraparound green wooden verandas and open porches full of bright wicker couches and easy chairs, and each house sits in a little shaded park of green grass marked off by white picket fences. Trikes and bikes and skateboards lean up against the walls. Swing sets and drying laundry flutter in a soft Great Plains wind, cicadas drone in the heavy heat, and the leaves rustle and whisper. A great silence seems to lie over the main post, muting every step and rising with the sweet-grass smell out of the ground.

In the middle of the officer's enclave a little rough-cut yellow-stone church sits in the middle of a broad park, under a massive black oak, beside a later and more graceful church. This is St. Mary's Chapel, built by the 6th Infantry troopers, who had arrived here in 1853. St. Mary's lies a few hundred feet from the site where General Custer's house used to stand, and it is the church where Custer and his wife, Libby, went to service every Sunday during his posting here in 1866. It was in front of this little chapel that

Custer was first introduced to the officers of the 7th Cavalry, which Custer was to lead to glory and ruin over the next ten years.

Across the gentle reach of grass, beyond the bronze statue of a cavalryman, three small cannons sit under the oaks and alders. They are Battery Rogers. They are painted dark green and in gold letters on their barrels these words are painted:

DUTY

HONOR

COUNTRY

The plaque beside them reads:

NAMED FOR THE WARRIOR
RECON COMMAND SERGEANT MAJOR
WHOSE HIGH PROFESSIONALISM AND COMMITMENT
TO THE ARMY, ITS SOLDIERS AND THEIR FAMILIES,
EPITOMIZE THOSE VIRTUES WE CHERISH SO GREATLY
IN THE ARMY'S CORPS
OF NONCOMMISSIONED OFFICERS

Past this memorial, a walkway leads to the cavalry museum and beyond that to Patton Hall, named for General Patton, who was stationed here before the war and who led armored divisions from Fort Riley across Sicily and deep into Germany. And on every street sign and carved into the stones are the names of famous military men who once walked these parks and halls: Sheridan, Pershing, Pickett, Mosby, Jackson, Meade, Burnside, Longstreet, Lee, Grant, Terry, Custer.

When the first companies of the 6th Infantry arrived here in 1853, the site had been named Camp Center because it was very near the geographical center of the land that would eventually become the United States. The name was changed to honor Brevet Major General Bennet Riley, who had just died in Buffalo on June 9th.

In 1853 there was nothing on the site but a few rough tents. All around the fort the vast Kansas Territory swept away, an eternity of rolling grassland and soft hills where the Kiowa and the Cheyenne and the Arapaho hunted and rode as they pleased, chasing herds of buffalo so immense they took three days to pass a landmark and where the only roads were the great rivers, the Kansas and the Missouri, the Republican and the Platte.

For the troopers of the 6th, the future consisted of stone cutting and building, of endless Kansas winters and sudden firefights with raiding Kiowas and Cheyennes and Comanches, of hardpan summers and beans for dinner and beans for breakfast, a time of great silences under a boundless arc of blue, of the soft rustle of wind in the limitless grasslands, of swift storms and sixty-mile-an-hour winds, of funnel clouds and whiteout blizzards so sudden and complete that a man could freeze to death in a drift fifteen feet from the camp circle.

The voices now lost were mostly Irish, but there were Germans and Scots, Frenchmen and Italians, and Canadians who'd come down for adventure, small men in the main, as you can see from the boots and jackets they left behind, few of them taller than five four or five five, weighing in at an average of one hundred and thirty pounds, most nearly illiterate, but many well-read and educated, remittance men and second sons, or bankrupts from back East, or cashiered runaways serving under another name. They were usually twenty-one or twenty-two, and the noncoms—Civil War veterans for the most part—were in their thirties and forties. Although their accents and backgrounds ranged from Silesia to the Bowery, over half of them were native-born Americans, second-generation men in a country not yet a century old, men for whom the echoes of the Revolution could still be heard, for whom the fight at Valley Forge was a story told by the men who fought it. It's hard to realize how new the nation was in those days, and how completely the myth of the New World had possessed and driven even the worst of them, how the possibility of a new life, of an eternity of second chances lying just beyond the treeline or just across the river had made them crazy and noble and ruined and redeemed, living six lives in thirty years, made weightless by the frontier, drifting on the ceaseless Great Plains wind like thistle-down or dried leaves. It took a Civil War to hammer down the meaning of the country they were riding over and dying on.

In 1865, after five years of brutal war, the nation felt itself at the brink of a brave new definition, and many thoughtful citizens were aware of the poignancy and ambiguity of a victory bought at the price of nearly a million dead men. Somehow they sensed that a ritual of recognition might be healing, a completing and enveloping act that would close the circle once again and free them to take the country forward.

So many men had been killed in the conflict that thousands of women spent the rest of the century in a kind of undeclared intimacy with other women, sharing homes and lives in what came to be known as Boston marriages. At Arlington and Gettysburg and a thousand other cemeteries around the nation, white marble stones or white-painted crosses sprouted up out of the farmland like a new and terrible crop. At Antietam it had been possible to walk a mile over the battlefield and not once step on the earth, but make the whole passage on the bodies of dead men. The evening of the day that the Second Battle of Bull Run had been fought, the sound of men crying out for water or release, the sound of thousands of men gasping for life or choking in blood was like the noise of a crowd at a game, and when you stepped over a rise and looked out across the patchwork farmland under the night sky the sound would swell up as it does when you walk out of the halls and down into the stadium itself. In the fighting around the cornfield men had fallen before Confederate volleys in company formation, going down a hundred men at a time, and they were found there the next day, dead in their ranks, with all their wounds in the fore. It would take fifty years for America to raise enough young men to die in such numbers, and with such a selfless courage, in the mud and barbed-wire entanglements of the First World War. Surely something powerful and noble and eternal must follow from the decimation of an entire generation.

So, in 1865, they came in their thousands to Washington, and by the evening of the twenty-second of May, there wasn't a room to be had in the city and people were sleeping in the parks and along the marshes by the monuments and the Capitol Building. And everywhere you looked there were soldiers, some gaunt and wolfish looking and bearded from long campaigns, others shattered and borne on litters, some skinny and ill with faces oddly out of time with their age, as if old men were staring out from young men's eyes, and many of them walking in phalanxes of faded blue, with shiny medals on their rough woolen tunics.

And each one of them wore a kind of ashen solemnity on his seamed and weather-burned face, and all their hands were scarred and raw looking, wrists sticking out of ill-fitting jacket sleeves, boots bound up with burlap or stitched and torn, burned in the fore by campfires of last winter's bivouac.

But they were soldiers, all of them, and no one who was not a soldier could look at them and not feel a certain diminishment as he watched them go by, a transitory smallness and a sense of being at the edge of something great, of having missed it all and let it go by.

The night of the twenty-second of May passed with the sounds of rough music in the beer halls and canteens, and the city wives stayed indoors while their men went to listen to the songs and hear the stories on the front steps and along the curbs and the shaded parks, and all through the night there was something in the air, something heady and intoxicating.

At nine in the morning, the Army of the Potomac led off the march down Capitol Hill and along Pennsylvania Avenue to the White House, where President Andrew Johnson and the notables waited on a pine-board bleacher covered in bunting and flags. And all along the way it was roses and songs, the tumult of the crowds, and military bands honking and blatting, a flourish of brass and the leathery thump and boom of the drums.

They played the "Battle Hymn of the Republic" and "Marching through Georgia," the "Battle Cry of Freedom," "Hail Columbia," and "When Johnny Comes Marching Home." Women and old men cried and the soldiers passed steadily, endlessly, a river of faded blue and blurred pale faces, passed by the old President and down toward the mall and across the river and out of the sight of the crowds, passed away to their discharges and their pay

books and the rest of their lives, and in the distance behind them
they heard the bands strike up again, thinly, a breathy rattle carried over the wind from the town. Another army, and more songs.

In two days more than two hundred thousand men passed in
review on their way toward their honorable discharges, their pen-
sions, and their farms if they had one, or toward the factories and
mills and shops of Baltimore and Cincinnati, the steel towns of
Pittsburgh, or the teeming streets of New York City.

The war was over, the nation—though scarred and deeply divided—was whole again, at least on the maps on the walls of the
Washington bureaucrats.

Now that their attention was not pulled south to Virginia and
the shattered Confederacy, they began to look west again, to the
Mississippi and to the Missouri and beyond, and what they saw was
the reason for the war, the bright promise of the New World, a
wilderness of dreams and possibilities that the nation had paid for
in blood and war—that Lincoln, like Moses, had seen from a
mountaintop—and when they went to the banks of the Mississippi
and the Missouri, they looked westward into the dying light, and
thought about an army, and what would be needed to take the
territories.

Because, while the men of the Army of the Potomac and the
Army of the Shenandoah—each man a volunteer as are most of
the men who fight the cataclysmic wars—were passing in review,
and the terrible war was ending, and a huge civilian and conscript
army that at times had numbered three million men was now dispersing and fading away, the Regular Army soldiers—the lifers and
professionals—were still at war out in the Far West and the Colorado Territory, where they had been fighting since 1803.

They were fighting in places like Minnesota, where the Santee
Sioux had been raiding farms and settlements since 1862, and in
New Mexico, where Kit Carson was fighting Mescalero Apaches
with a column of volunteer cavalry, bringing them to battle at
Canyon de Chelly, Arizona, in the midwinter of 1864, and, there
was fighting in a hundred other places along the Platte, the Yel-
lowstone, the Snake and the Tongue, the Picketwire and the Rio
Grande.

By 1867, two years after the end of the Civil War, the Regular Army was engaged in brush-fire wars and trail-guarding operations from Fort Peck and Fort Buford in the northern Dakota Territory, all the way south to Fort Hays and Fort Riley in Kansas, to Fort Union in New Mexico and Camp Supply in Oklahoma.

Crazy Horse and Red Cloud of the Lakota Sioux killed Lieutenant Fetterman and a hundred men under his command two hills away from Fort Phil Kearny in northeastern Wyoming in 1866. The fort was abandoned and burned the next year, and the Bozeman Trail closed. Even today you can see the twin rutted tracks of the old Bozeman Trail as it comes down a grassy bluff and runs by the site of Fort Phil Kearny. Two hills east of the fort, Interstate 90 comes looping up out of the Dakotas, running in the shadow of the Bighorn Mountains, still following the route of settlers and miners coming up from the Oregon Trail to work the copper mines of western Montana.

Southern Cheyennes put half of western Kansas and most of eastern Colorado to the knife all through 1867 and well into 1868. A Regular Army colonel named Forsyth engaged the Cheyenne on the Arikaree Fork of the Republican River in western Kansas in September of that year, and George Armstrong Custer, leading 7th Cavalry troops from Fort Riley, attacked a Southern Cheyenne band on the Washita River in northwestern Oklahoma in the early winter of the same year.

All along the frontier, the little wars burned bright and the smell of grass fires and buildings blazing sometimes reached all the way back to Kansas City. The fighting got worse in the early 1870s, and the size of the Regular Army had reached twenty-five thousand men—its legal limit—by the time Custer and his command was wiped out by the Northern Sioux on June 25, 1876, northeast of the Bighorn Mountains, at a place called Greasy Grass.

By the end of the 1870s, Fort Riley was a major military reserve, a solid encampment of infantry and cavalry and Artillery that looked in those days pretty much as it does now, part of a massive network of forts and cantonments that stretched all the way to Washington and Oregon. It was out of major forts like Riley and

Leavenworth in eastern Kansas that new recruits and replacements
from the depots at Jefferson Barracks in Missouri or David's Island
in New York were dispersed to line forts all over the nation, part
of the Regular Army's Indian War. Regulars fought Blackfeet in
Montana, Nez Percés in Idaho, fought Snake Indians and Ban-
nocks in northern Utah and Wyoming, Utes in Colorado, Modocs
in northern California and Oregon, Apaches in New Mexico and
Arizona, Kiowas and Comanches in Texas, Oklahoma, and Kansas.

The Indian Wars swirled around Fort Riley for nearly thirty
years, until December of 1890, when, in the space of two weeks,
Sitting Bull was assassinated by Dakota policemen and Big Foot's
ragged band of Lakota Sioux and Cheyenne were wiped out by
the 7th Cavalry at Wounded Knee, near the Pine Ridge Reserva-
tion. And after the Indian Wars, there was Villa and his Army of
the North, and after Villa was chased back into Mexico by Pershing, there was a little war in Puerto Rico, and outlaws to hunt
down, and hundreds of little skirmishes, while across the ocean
much larger plans were being made in Prussia and Moscow.

The promise made at Appomattox was kept, the frontier
brought into the Union, and whether the reality was as noble and
as fine as the citizens who came to Washington for the Grand
Review hoped, there was no one alive at the time who did not
understand that the nation had been bought and paid for by soldiers.

———

The life led by infantry and cavalrymen at Fort Riley in those days
was a hard, bleak eternity, some sense of which you can get from
a look at the *General Orders of the Post* and the *Regimental Book of
the 7th Cavalry,* on display at the Fort Riley Cavalry Museum:

5:45 A.M.   TRUMPETERS ASSEMBLE.
6:00   REVEILLE AND ROLL CALL.
6:30   MESS.
7:30   FATIGUE CALL—VARIOUS POST DUTIES.
8:00   SICK CALL.
8:55   TRUMPETERS ASSEMBLE.

9:00	GUARD DETAIL ASSEMBLE.
9:45	RECALL FROM FATIGUE DETAILS.
9:50	BOOTS AND SADDLES.
10:00	DRILL.
11:00	RECALL FROM DRILL FOR INFANTRY AND ARTILLERY.
11:30	CAVALRY RECALL FROM DRILL.
11:45	FIRST SERGEANTS CALL—MORNING REPORTS.
12:00	RECALL FROM FATIGUES OR DRILL—NOON MESS.
1:00 P.M.	DRILL FOR TARGET PRACTICE.
2:00	FATIGUE DUTY.
4:15	RECALL FROM FATIGUE DUTY.
4:30	STABLE CALL—HORSE CARE AND GROOMING.
SUNDOWN	ASSEMBLY OF TRUMPETERS AND ENTIRE GARRISON— FULL DRESS. SOUND RETREAT—ROLL CALL.
8:55	ASSEMBLY OF TRUMPETERS.
9:00	TATTOO—DRUMS—ROLL CALL OF COMPANIES IN FRONT OF QUARTERS. FORMATIONS.
9:30	LIGHTS OUT. TAPS.

Breakfast was usually beef hash and dry bread served with black coffee. Dinner was beef again, and dry bread, and black coffee. Supper was frequently beans and hardtack and more black coffee. At Riley each trooper got a trace of quinine in an ounce of rye whiskey every morning, and now and then there would be prunes, if the quartermaster was dedicated. The Army encouraged each company to create and tend a vegetable garden, and the company mess fare could be improved if the first sergeant who ran the company funds made good arrangements with the fort's sutler or—if there were any—the local citizens and farmers. For that matter, it was up to the first sergeants to run practically every aspect of the soldier's life, and few rankers had any kind of direct contact with an officer beyond a salute and a courtesy, which is how most soldiers like it even in modern times. A ranker's day was run by sergeants and it was by the sergeants that the Regular Army lived, worked, fought, and died.

At Fort Riley, almost every noncommissioned officer was a vet-

eran of the Civil War. The outside world might have forgotten
their names, or even the location of their bones, but they had—
and still have—a kind of immortality at Riley; many young noncoms today can tell you stories about this sergeant or that corporal, his passion for radishes, or what he did for a ranker who was
having an affair with an officer's wife, or who knew Gustav Korn,
Comanche's keeper, who was killed at Wounded Knee, after which
the horse faded away and was buried somewhere on the grounds
of Fort Riley. Sergeants and noncoms were in those days, and in
these times still are, the essential memory line of the Army. An
army lives through its sergeants, and it is through the sergeants
that an army remembers what it has learned about war and military life.

Even in the last century, it was up to the sergeants to enforce
discipline—usually by toe-to-toe combat if it came to that, and it
often did. Sergeants were the point of collision between the officer
caste and the enlisted men, and it was at that connection that the
Regular Army of the Indian Wars forged its strongest bonds. It
was also up to the sergeants to be a father to their men, to protect
them from unreasonable or incompetent officers, to see that they
were well fed and well led and well buried if they were killed, and
all of this for less than a cowhand could make in a fortnight.

At Riley in the 1870s, a sergeant major earned twenty-three dollars a month, a saddler sergeant made twenty-two dollars, as did a
first sergeant, a corporal made seventeen dollars, and a private
soldier earned thirteen dollars a month. Out of this a man was
expected to pay for much of his gear, to have his uniforms tailored
and patched, and if he wanted better fare than he could find at
the mess, he could get it from the commissary at outrageous mark-
ups. It was common for butter to go for two dollars a pound,
potatoes for ten dollars a bushel, and coffee essence, an early form
of instant coffee, was a dollar a box. Milk, eggs, and fresh meats
were hard to come by and usually purchased by a company fund
managed, again, by the first sergeant. Sowbelly bacon was generally loathed and most of it was traded to local "tame Indians" for
venison or pemmican or buffalo jerky. And out of their cash the
soldiers had to pay for shoemakers to rebuild the issue boots,

made by surly inmates at Fort Leavenworth Military Prison. They
were a black-leather-and-brass-screw abomination so ill fitted that
it didn't matter which boot you put your foot into. Men would
pay five dollars for a good fit, and many of them deliberately
walked the boots through creeks and marched until they dried,
just to get the soles to soften and shape to their feet. Old-timers
bought boots and used uniforms from discharged men, and no
experienced campaigner wore his best uniform on a march, because whatever was ruined had to be replaced out of his monthly
uniform allowance, and the uniform allowance, if not used, was
paid to the man as earned savings when he left the service, and
was often the only real pension the soldier could look for. Only
thirty-year lifers got a full Army pension, and most men served for
less than five years.

And when they got paid, it was, until 1879 at least, in Army
scrip—just like in Vietnam—and, as in Vietnam, scrip was generally discounted by fifty percent at every grog shop and whorehouse
within a day's ride, so money was even scarcer than it looked.
Whatever a man managed to save from the sutler and the com-
missariat and the quartermaster sergeant was usually eaten up by
credit purchases—tobacco, whiskey, chocolates or prunes or
canned goods—and deducted at the point of payment by the civilians running those stores.

If a soldier needed extra money, there was always a man in the
unit who would lend him some—at fifty percent interest, payable
at payday, and gamblers often got the rest.

When the money was gone, the diversions were few and simple.
Entertainment after taps was usually a song and poker, and there
was always someone in the unit who could play a guitar, or a fiddle,
or who had a fine tenor voice. The rare man who could read well
and who had books would sometimes give a reading to the unit,
sitting on a rail-back chair with his feet on the barrack-room stove
guard, a pipe in his mouth, giving his best to something by Walter
Scott or Hawthorne or merely reading the latest newspaper—
about six months old—from Wichita or Kansas City. Often as
the evening pickets went by they'd hear the singing coming over
the lawns and parade grounds of Fort Riley, see men sitting by the

red glow of the stove fire or under the yellow light of the kerosene lantern, their faces bright with heat from the stove, pipe smoke drifting in the still air, and in a way and for a brief moment get a glimmering of what there is about Army life that makes some men miss it more than home and family. Even in modern times, that feeling can still come over anyone with Army in his background, but the feeling is usually brief, as brief as it was for those long-dead men.

Still, you can walk along Sheridan Avenue today, under the dusty oaks, with the Cavalry Parade Field on your left and Custer House on your right, and it's possible to hear the ghost voices singing soldier songs in company formation on the lawns in front of the old stone houses, the officers and their wives standing on the green painted verandas, the light slipping away and the first hard bright Kansas stars showing in the gathering night.

Maybe that was the best of it, and perhaps it was made even sweeter by the brevity, because when you listen to the old songs, such as "Annie Laurie," "Shenandoah," "The Good-Bye at the Door," "Little Footsteps," "Dreary Black Hills," or, the cruelest sweet song ever sung, "Danny Boy," you hear the sadness of loss and the hope of glory, and see the blue columns as Libby Custer last saw the 7th Cavalry, a battalion of ghost soldiers passing over the green earth and slipping away into the light. They were death obsessed and maudlin and unbelievably tough, even the worst of them, and if a sad song gave them a moment's peace, they had sure as hell earned it.

Out of Riley, they campaigned in winter, because it was easier to find the hostiles in the winter, and winter campaigning in the Kansas Territory was murderously cold and dangerous work. Few veteran troopers of the era escaped their service without losing skin or worse to frostbite, and even the heavy buffalo coats issued at Riley weren't much help against sudden temperature drops to fifty below zero and wind gusts up to thirty miles an hour. In situations like that, troopers holed up in Sibley tents sleeping two or three to a blanket—the origin of the Army term "bunky"— and waited it out while the horses died in the drifts outside.

And summer campaigning had its own brutality, long marches

across a burning anvil of prairie hardpan under a sulphurous sun, twenty or thirty, sometimes forty, miles a day with the scouts out and the skirmishers on the flanks, and perhaps a bad death at the end of it if you were lucky enough to actually find a hostile.

The fights were rare and brief, a sudden ambush from the tree line, a party of charging warriors on fleet little ponies while you circled the supply wagons with the horses and mules inside and you, on foot, worked the Springfield or the Sharps outside the lager, trying to hit a warrior at fifty yards on the fly while the bullets spattered into the dust all around you or blew splinters off the wagon boards and the sergeants bellowed and bullied the feckless and the fearful.

Wounds were worse than death. If you caught a round, it meant being dragged fifty miles in a travois with a minié ball in your liver, or suffering a wagon-bed amputation without benefit of anesthetic, much less antibiotic. Arrows were in a way worse than rifle rounds, because the heads were made of soft iron and were bound onto the slender wooden shaft with animal glue and sinew thongs. When the head hit bone, the tip bent and spread out, and the blood in the wound softened the animal glue so the head usually stayed in the wound even if the shaft was drawn out. Few men could stay still enough to let the camp surgeon root around inside the wound trying to retrieve the head, so many men decided to just leave the thing in and hope for the best. They either died badly a few hours later, or they lived through it and carried the arrowhead to their graves years later.

An Indian fight was short, sharp, brutal; few were sustained battles, although there were terrible exceptions, at Greasy Grass or the Lava Beds fight against Modocs in northern California. It was usually a kind of guerrilla war, an insurgency war of hit-and-run and maddening pursuits over a rolling ocean of prairie grass and dry washes, and any man taken alive by a Kiowa or a Dakota faced a very ugly death.

In a fight that took place in west Kansas in the 1870s, two infantrymen from Riley were separated from their company, surrounded by Kiowas, and brought to ground. In full view of their fellow infantrymen lagered a hundred yards away, the Kiowa war party stripped the two men, scalped them, cut their throats, sliced off their genitals, tore out their hearts and disemboweled them, and all of it was done in less than two minutes. It was assumed that at some point in the proceedings, the two men managed to die. That kind of death was a commonplace in the Kansas Territory, and not always confined to soldiers. There wasn't a trooper at Fort Riley who hadn't seen the *kakeshya* torture of women, even children, all along the Platte and the Republican during the Cheyenne wars of the late 1860s: arrows thrust up anuses and vaginas, dreadful butchery and dismemberments, sinews pulled from limbs like threads out of a garment, hearts cut out and burned, skulls crushed and opened, and slower endings beyond description.

It was a hard era and the men who fought in it had a kind of toughness that may not exist on the planet today, but the traditions and the myths and the memories established at Fort Riley and throughout the Great Plains from 1865 to 1890 have a strange kind of half-life at Fort Riley today. You don't see that toughness in the young men and women who serve there now, and no reasonable person would expect to. These are different times, and they are different people. But it is there, and when you find it, it's often in the voice or the stillness or the manner of one of the noncommissioned officers, doing what noncoms have done for armies for five thousand years.

The grounds of Fort Riley are out of time, perhaps even out of the main line of American life. On this slow November afternoon in 1990 the silence is thick as dust on all the walks and parks. The Kansas runs slowly in her banks and a soft wind stirs the dry leaves and raises yellow dust along the banks. And far overhead a thin contrail cuts a feathery white line across the high and endless blue like a diamond cutting through a blue glass bowl, heading into the east. From the officers' homes by St. Mary's Chapel soft music is coming, and children play in the yards. But up on Custer Hill where the enlisted men have their quarters, in low red brick flats and concrete blocks, there is only stillness and a sense of time suspended.

All the men are gone. Their bunks are stripped and their rooms are locked. In the alleys and the motor pools yellow dust shifts and settles on the cleared desks and the tool benches and the parade squares. Down the long hallways filled with amber light from the setting sun, the eternal barracks smell drifts in the dead air: floor wax and boot polish, gun oil, sweat, dry cotton and old clothes, hardwood, brick, and bone white walls. From across the flat parade squares comes the faint far-off sound of a cadence, the man's voice as harsh and dry as a crow's call, and the answering shuffle and thump of a lone platoon, and music from an open window a half mile down the line, something from the forties, maybe an old lifer dreaming of the Good War in his bachelor's bed, dreaming of the past as it rolls away from him down a long corridor of years, hearing the distant sound of the march and the music and the voices of men coming up from under the ground, coming through the hardwood planks and the yellow stone walls, rising up out of the hard Kansas clay, the slow silent resurrection, a legion of dust and dreams.

All around the fort the yellow grasslands and the soft timeworn hills and the silver veins of the river and the streams recede into a blue haze. In the east the sky deepens into sapphire and midnight blue. On the interstate the heavy trucks grind their way up the long grade toward Junction City and Denver and the coast. At Harry's Bar the talk is going around, all the young doctors and the lawyers are saying witty things and leaning in close to each other and the room is full of music and on the stand behind the bar the television is tuned to CNN, and if there had been a pause, a momentary catch of breath, they might have heard the sound of all the silence at the fort, and seen the empty places on the street where soldiers used to be.

But they didn't hear the silence and they didn't see the missing soldiers, and perhaps they never will.

CHAPTER FIVE

SWEET GRASS

In the pale light of a Kansas dawn, Crane was standing with the rest of the Baker Company sergeants at the edge of the hardpan under the wing of a massive dark green Hercules from Military Airlift Command. They were watching the loadmaster try to get her point across to Captain Wolochek.

The humvees were too wide—six inches too wide—to load them in a Hercules in pairs. They had to go in single file.

Wolochek was not very happy to hear about this, although like any competent officer, he was up to date on PUSH logistics and the movement of hardware. Somebody somewhere should have ordered up a Starlifter or made other arrangements for the humvees. But they hadn't, and it was on Wolochek's head now. Wolochek was a good officer as officers went, but he did not look like he was enjoying his nose-to-nose with a female loadmaster from the Military Airlift Command who was explaining to him at the top of her lungs that it was not her goddamned fault that the military buyers hadn't bothered to ask *her* how wide a Hercules

59

actually was, and that these goddam humvees wouldn't load double-wide in *any* Airlift transport, not even a C-5A Galaxy. In her opinion, of course. Sir.

The reason why they were all mustered here today was that Saddam Hussein had made it clear he had no intention of giving up what he had taken, and President Bush had dropped a Rapid Deployment Force into Saudi Arabia in the hope that Saddam would think twice about barreling on into that country too and turning it upside down.

Anyone with any tactical sense understood that it would be the job of this small trip-wire force to die in as spectacular and globally symbolic a way as possible if Hussein came down into Saudi, because there was precious little else they could do. In the meantime, the entire U.S. Defense Department was scrambling to get some serious iron down on the ground in Saudi Arabia, in case the White House and the United Nations wanted them to actually *do* something about the Iraqis.

For Crane, the scramble had begun in earnest the morning after they had all watched the news of the Iraqi invasion in August, and it had continued at a brutal pace until this November day, which found them mustered at Forbes Field, waiting to board a fleet of C-130s from Military Airlift Command, and watching Wolochek confront the reality of the too-wide humvees.

Crane found this early sign of a military FUBAR oddly comforting, and he tried to convey this stoical acceptance of things military to his subordinate sergeants on the flight line.

Brett Huckaby, the 3rd Platoon sergeant, shifted his webbing and grinned at Crane from under his Kevlar helmet, his small blue eyes shaded against the rising sun. He had nicked his chin shaving and there was dried blood on his helmet chin strap.

"Good thing the Abrams are going by sea, huh, Top?"

"Don't call me Top. DerHorst's Top," said Crane.

Dave Fanand, thinner than ever and even more worried looking than usual, said something that was lost in the blast of a C-130 engine revving up.

"What'd you say, Dave?"

Fanand leaned into Crane's ear. He smelled of Scope and Brut.

"I said, the kids are pretty uptight."

Gil Noshaug, the 1st Platoon sergeant, snorted.

"Of course they are. Hell, they're going to a goddam war! If they're not nervous, they don't understand the situation."

Fanand shifted his footing. "The thing is, don't you think the captain ought to, you know, say something. . . ."

Shabazz, Baker's official homeboy, a hard-nosed black man from the 'hood, kicked his ALICE pack and tightened his chin strap.

"Like what, man? Some fucking *speech*? 'Yo, troops, we going to Saudi to kill for Exxon. Everybody gets a free gallon of gas and a dead otter if they come back alive.' "

Huckaby and Noshaug disapproved of Shabazz's blunt language but since Shabazz had done better than they had at the NTC, they had both relaxed a little around him.

"You really think that, man?" asked Noshaug in his Connecticut Yankee cadence.

Shabazz leered at Noshaug, who was shorter but heavier.

"Why *else*, Gil?"

Crane looked at him hard.

"You telling your squad that, kid?"

Shabazz lost his smile.

"No, Sergeant—but it's true all the same, no offense."

Dave Fanand spoke up again.

"That's what I meant. Most of the kids, they think like Shabazz, they think the whole thing's all about oil. That's why I think Wolochek ought to say something to them."

"Dave, if it ain't about *oil*, what's it about? Man, word up!"

Fanand found Shabazz's homey slang more than a little grating but he respected him as a good judge of his men and their morale. Thomas G. Rhame, the major general in command of the 1st, had issued a mission statement to be read aloud to every company and corps by their commanders. In it, Rhame had talked about their duty to confront aggression wherever they found it, and their duty to obey the Commander in Chief, but he'd stayed away from the issue of oil supplies, leaving it up to platoon-level leadership to deal with troop motivation. Even today, on the morning of their deployment, the issue was a hot one down at the squad and fire-team level.

Crane had his own feelings about the purpose of the war, but he also remembered very clearly that the U.S. had fought damn hard and lost a lot of men—thirteen thousand KIAs—fighting to protect South Korea from an aggressor, and South Korea had no oil at all, and, in Crane's view, had been protected for no other reason than to defend a democracy. Still, Fanand was on target. The squad leaders had better find something uplifting to tell their troops. Crane picked up his ALICE gear and his rifle and looked around at the squad sergeants.

"Dave's right. These kids are looking at their first war. So are all of you. I personally don't give a dingo's pecker whether you guys love this war or think it's a rat-fuck from the get-go. This isn't Disneyland, it's real life, and most of real life is a rat-fuck. If you don't believe me, go find out what they really put in Mickey Dee's special sauce. You guys weren't hired as political analysts. You're eleven bravo, Combat Infantry. You guys get in there, make them feel like they're doing something that counts. You don't, they're gonna drop you all in the shit when you can least afford it. Okay?"

They all nodded, stunned, faces set and solemn. Crane left them and walked away, looking for DerHorst.

All around him hundreds of troopers and support battalion personnel were lying around on the cold tarmac in full combat gear, with ALICE packs and field radios, their weapons stacked and stowed, everybody in the new "chocolate chips" desert camou-flage BDUs, the Kevlar "Fritz" helmets that Crane couldn't get used to. Noncoms raced around with clipboards, half an eye on the gathering storm front coming in from the southeast, officers clustered around the HQ posts, and down the line at runway nine, eleven massive dark green and black C-130s with subdued mark-ings sat in the pale light, misted in a light fog, engines coughing and whining. Around them the Kansas prairie rolled away like a pale green ocean.

After fifteen weeks of intense preparation, Crane and DerHorst, the four platoon sergeants, Huckaby, Fanand, Shabazz, and Noshaug, and the squad leaders had Baker Company ready for transport to Saudi.

Baker had four infantry platoons of roughly forty men each, along with a headquarters company and an antiarmor company equipped with TOW antitank vehicles and an M113, a vehicle with one machine gun. Each platoon had three rifle squads, a command section, operating with four Bradleys each. Although each platoon was led by a lieutenant, Junior Grade, the effective operations of the platoon were in the hands of the platoon master sergeant, the various squad sergeants, and the fire-team leaders. Civilians sometimes wonder why there are so many sergeants and squad leaders in an infantry unit, but the soldiers know why: in a firefight, the leaders thin out fast. The more sergeants you have, the more leaders you can afford to lose.

Crane had the job of overseeing the squad sergeants and making sure that their troops were properly trained, properly briefed, and in good mental and physical condition. In other words, Crane was Baker Company's whip.

The last fifteen weeks had been filled with reports and training lectures and slide shows. Now and then, when he had the time, Crane would take a breath and think about how much *stuff* the modern U.S. Army grunt had to remember. Back in the days of the Indochina War, you had to remember seven or eight things, mainly:

Never put your foot where no one else has put his.

Dead brush at the top of the trail means an ambush.

So does *live* brush.

Their tracers are green. Ours are red. The difference is important.

M16s without a *C* under the barrel will sooner or later jam up and kill you right when you can least afford it.

Never be the first to wade through a murky stream. That's what prisoners are for.

Never stand up in a firefight.

In these times of what Crane thought of as Nintendo combat, the technical elements of even the simplest infantry operation were infinite and maddening. Crane and the other sergeants ran endless cyclical lectures drilling the troops on just about everything the Army could think of to kill somebody with:

This is an A-6 Intruder warplane. This is an Iraqi Fishbed.

Cheer for the first one. Blow the second one out of his shorts.

This is a Tomcat fighter. It can track twenty-four targets at the same time and hit six of them at once. This is a Hornet long-range fighter-bomber. It can deliver seventeen thousand pounds of gravity and laser bombs and it can drop all of them down your grandmother's cookie jar from halfway around the world. This is a Harrier, a Marine airframe, and they love this plane because it can do everything the Tomcat and the Hornet can do and it can do it backward.

This is an A-10 Thunderbolt. It kills tanks. Make sure you are always where you are supposed to be because someday one of these will be looking down its gunsights at you and asking someone sixty miles away if it can kill you now. This is a B-52. We had them in the Nam too. If we had our way, we'd get some of these guys to drop a few tactical nukes on Iraq so you could see the soft green glow from a rooftop on Mars. But that won't happen. When these guys drop their payloads, it'll sound like a bass drum larger than Rhode Island.

This is a Sea Knight chopper, also for the Marines, and this is a Super Stallion; it can carry 155-mm howitzers or trucks and is the biggest chopper in the known universe. This is a Cobra gunship, our personal favorite here in the 1st Division because they tell us where the enemy is and sometimes they shoot him first so we don't have to.

And this is a Huey, which you all know and love. Flying in one is like flying in a tin breadbox while somebody beats it with a sledgehammer. Plus it has no doors so you can see exactly who is trying to kill you. The only armor it has is up front under the pilot's feet, which is why the rest of us all sit on our helmets or on someone else.

These are the missiles—the Hellfire, the TOW, and the Seawolf, the Sparrow, the Harpoon, the Patriot, the Hawk, and the Tomahawk, and these are Scuds, and this is something called the Al Hussein—he's Saddam's brother or something like that. The Scud carries two thousand pounds of explosives and is accurate to within this solar system. If you are hit by one you can console yourself with the thought that it was purely accidental.

This is an Iraqi Fulcrum, a serious warplane, and this is a Fishbed MiG, also known as the Iraqi version of the Kamikaze because the only thing this plane is sure to kill is the pilot. This is a Foxbat. If you see one, it will probably already have killed you and all your buddies.

Here is a videotape of an A-10 Thunderbolt. We call them Warthogs and here is a Warthog killing a tank. It will come in at five hundred feet until it gets close and then it pops up over the horizon line and fires off a Maverick laser and TV-guided missile, which, as you can see, can turn a tank into punker jewelry in a half second.

Here we have some raghead choppers. This is a Hind and these are Gazelles and these are Super Frelons and they all belong to the bad guys so you can kill these too, please.

And all of these are land mines. Here's the Cardoen directional, like our Claymores, lethal out to fifty feet in a sixty-degree arc, C4 powered, wire detonated, and here's the OZM, a Russian "bouncing Betty," designed to pop up to your groin level before blowing your dreams of grandchildren all over your chest, and here's the Valsella antitank, and the PMN antipersonnel, another gift from the Russians, and here's the TM-64, which, if you step on it, will scatter most of what used to be you over a circle fifty feet wide.

This is the cost to Uncle Sam of everything you guys are going to carry or wear in Saudi, a total of fifteen hundred dollars for every grunt. This is the projected cost of pounding the Iraqis into tapioca for one day, a total of a hundred twenty-five million bucks, so make sure every day counts, right?

These are Jordanians. They are allies of ours who hate us and love Saddam. And these are Syrians. They drive the very same tanks as the Iraqis but we're gonna stick an orange triangle on their T-72s so you can tell the difference. The Syrians are the guys who blew up those Marines in Beirut. They are now our allies as well, so if you see some, don't shoot them unless you can make it look like an accident. These are the Brits and these are the kinds of tanks they drive. These are the French and these are the other countries who are sending troops or nurses to help us fight this war—the Turks, the Australians, the Senegalese, some New Zealanders, the Italians, the Bangladeshis . . . write this stuff down, men, there's a quiz later . . . the Canadians . . . none of these people are combat arms so basically it's going to be us and the Brits and the French, but memorize the rest in case Wolochek wants to ask you.

Oh, yeah, this is a video of a shamal, a sandstorm like we're going to run into in Saudi. It can give you a wall of flying sand ten thousand feet high, it can move at forty miles an hour over a path sixty miles wide and a hundred miles deep. The sand—here's some from the Intel guys, feel that—hey, Mosby, wake up—it's just like talcum powder and it *will* screw up your rifles and your SAWs and it'll foul the infantry fighting vehicle, or IFV, filters, and by the way it's too fine to use for sandbagging so the Airlift Command is flying in sand from North Africa for that.

It's November, so the heat will be down to around a hundred degrees during the day and seventy by nightfall. So far, a lot has gone wrong over there. The field radios with the metal handles get too hot to hold so we have to wrap them in burlap. All the humvees need to have their tire pressure reduced because they're blowing up. The rubber around the tanker goggles melts in the heat. We don't have enough filters to go around so we're going to have to steal them from other units. Batteries are exploding. Rifle magazines are warping and can't be inserted in the chamber. Barrels overheat and lose their accuracy. Rounds cook off without warning. The water—and you all have to drink around ten bottles a day—sucks and sometimes it gives you dysentery. The night-vision goggles, or NVGs, work okay but the terrain is so flat that the Apache pilots can't see a dune coming up.

The ground is full of scorpions and horned vipers and lizards and rats. You can't go anywhere near the big Saudi towns, partly because there aren't any and even if you got there, no one will talk to you.

This is a BMO, a black moving object. That's what grunts are calling Saudi women. You can tell a Saudi woman because she will be dressed like John Gotti's grandmother and will not under any circumstances allow you to take her bowling. As far as you are concerned, Saudi women do not exist.

This is a beer. Kiss it good-bye. The Saudis have no penalty for murder but they cut hands off for theft, which will give you a clue to their sense of priorities. The Saudis do no work. All their work is done for them by Palestinians and Filipinos. Sort of like California. The Saudis are Muslims—Wahabi Muslims—so they don't drink and they don't dance and they don't fool around with girls, unless we're talking about princes, of which there are about thirty thousand in-country, and Saudi princes do pretty much whatever they want but they'll never admit it to you because you are an infidel and all Muslims have sworn holy oaths to drink the blood of all infidels but they have kindly agreed to wait until we've tossed the Iraqis out of Kuwait.

This is a picture of a Kuwaiti princeling. He is doing the frug in a disco in Paris. He will not be joining you in the war. Think of him as Jody, only he spells it Jahdi. He thinks you are infidel trash and will be grateful for the return of his Mercedes provided you don't get blood on his *dishdasha* or ask to meet his sister.

We will have around thirty thousand women in Saudi. The Saudis do not like women. They will be rude to our women. You will do nothing about this. You will tug your forelock and say, Yes, sir, Mr. Raghead, and you will sing three choruses of the Saudi Arabian fight song, which is "Onward Christian Soldiers."

This is a picture of Baghdad Betty. She is Hussein's answer to Tokyo Rose. You don't know who Tokyo Rose was? Never mind.

In Saudi they have different names for everything, so I hear.

The sun is called Big Red, I think you can see why.

This is Bob, he's an Iraqi soldier. I guess the mustache is a religious thing, or they all love the Marx brothers. If somebody tells you they CNXed the war—that's *canked*—it means they canceled it, and I wouldn't believe them. Here we have golden BBs, which are, as you can see, antiaircraft fire. This is a slide of a grunt in his MOPP, his Mission-Oriented Protective Suit, which you are all going to learn to hate. It is supposed to protect you from nuclear and biological weapons, and it works, so I'm told, but you have to walk around looking like an extra from *The Fly*. And, for some reason that has so far escaped us back in the U.S., the grunts over there are calling the war the Hoo-Yah and they go around screaming out Hoo-Yah without warning at all hours of the day and night.

This is something called Saudi Champagne. It's made of 7UP and apple juice. You can bet no Saudi kinglet is ever gonna taste this shit, but *you* will. *Semper gumby,* as the jarheads say. Always flexible.

And this is Saddam Hussein. He is not now and has never been eleven bravo. He actually *is* as mean and stupid as he looks, which is rare in life. He wants everyone to die for Iraq and Allah. If you get a chance, make him the first one to go. . . .

They'd watched several hours of Iraqi combat footage from the war with Iran. Skinny young Iraqis and Iranians being bussed to the front, given a three-hour lecture on the uses and abuses of an AK47 and an RPG by a senior raghead trooper who wasn't going anywhere *near* the front, thank you very much, and then they bundled the kids off to the war zone where they promptly got themselves drilled through the left eye and ground into road kill under the treads of somebody else's tank. It had been a war of fanatics, and that was Crane's least favorite kind of war. Although fanatics did have one advantage, in Crane's experience. You could always get them to do something stupid.

Aside from all the tactical briefings and the memory testing, Crane and DerHorst and the other sergeants had also tried to attend to the concerns of the married troops, many of whom would be leaving young wives with newborn babies stuck in trailer parks and flats all over Ogden and Junction City and Manhattan, families with credit problems and domestic difficulties. Wolochek, who didn't actually have to *do* anything about these problems himself, liked to quote from a West Point handbook, something about the problems of Command being the problems of those you command. Which for Wolochek was a theoretical reality and for Crane a real reality.

A buck private pulled in maybe seven hundred dollars a month. By the time they cleared boot at Benning and made PFC, they got a raise to between nine hundred and a thousand dollars. A corporal made around eleven hundred dollars a month. Having no brains and an uncertain grip on reality, these kids promptly married their current sweetheart and sentenced themselves to a term of indentured penury.

Since there were no facilities for married grunts on base at Fort Riley, the newlyweds had to find off-base accommodation in one of the nearby towns. All the landlords gouged and there were damn few jobs for the missus, who was anyway either pregnant or working hard on it, so home was a rat's-ass walk-up over a stripper bar, a trailer in Junction City, or a shotgun shack somewhere in the boondocks. The 1st had Personnel Support Services people, and the Officers' Wives Organization did what they could, but Crane and DerHorst, Huckaby, Shabazz, Noshaug, and Fanand, along with Felz from Quartermaster Stores, had found themselves tending to everything from a Saudi-bound trooper with an eviction notice to a trooper with a homesick wife and a female trooper whose husband was in jail and unable to take care of her two-year-old who, by the way, had asthma and was on a special diet for juvenile diabetes.

For Crane, it was a rat-fuck from the get-go.

Kids nineteen years old had wives who were sixteen and babies ten weeks old. Of the two hundred and four troopers in Baker Company, one hundred and thirteen were married and most of those had one or more children. They were going to be in Saudi with half their minds on what was going on at home—was the rent being made, was the baby all right? This did not make for a good combat soldier. And when they were deployed in Saudi, each and every one of them would come to *hate* mail from home, or their once-a-tour ATT Phone Home opportunity, because all that trooper was going to hear was more bad news.

As far as Crane was concerned, soldiers should NEVER be allowed to marry. Soldiers should have to turn their reproductive organs in at the induction center and pick them up again after their combat days were over.

The 1st was going to move twelve thousand pieces of equipment and seven thousand troopers to Saudi, most of whom had joined the Army thinking of it as a job, something to help with the business of raising a family, something to get them out of a rural limbo or a downtown ghetto, but suddenly reality was dawning. They were soldiers and they were going to war. This morning. Now.

Crane walked down the line, looking at the faces of the kids in Baker Company, thinking about what Shabazz had said about Kuwaiti oil and Exxon.

Here was Duane Mitchell, a black boot only a few weeks out of Benning, thinner now, and harder, and Mitchell's good buddy, another city kid named Davis. Mitchell's skin was as smooth and brown as a gunstock and he had a good smile. Crane liked the kid and hoped he'd stay in the infantry, but Mitchell had already applied for one of the computer specialties. A lot of the black kids from the northeastern cities were doing that, going for tech courses rather than staying in the combat arms. Crane didn't blame them. In spite of what the Army said, there wasn't much of a market for combat riflemen in the private sector. Mitchell smiled at Crane as he passed, part of a crowd of black troopers. Even in the infantry, the races tended to keep to themselves.

Combat would change all that. For a while.

Darryl Mosby, a tall hard-boned white kid from Richmond, was sitting at the end of a line of troopers with his rifle between his knees, working at the bolt. Crane liked the kid, who had come in on the Army Reserve Control Group plan. The plan gave him a guaranteed skills-training assignment, what the machine called an MOS, a Military Operational Specialty. Mosby's had been Range Data Specialist in Artillery, but he had washed out of that last year—hadn't taken it seriously, in Crane's view—and now here he was on the tarmac, MOSed as a rifleman, eleven bravo. Combat Infantry.

The thing was, the kid had something. Charisma, a sense of himself. But he just wouldn't go beyond a certain point, like it was all a kind of joke and if you took it too seriously you'd lose your cool or some similar piece of adolescent bullshit. The business of combat infantry was something very serious to Crane. But Mosby had something, and the Army tried to make soldiers out of anything they could get, so Crane had talked it over with Huckaby, Mosby's platoon sergeant. Huckaby and Crane decided to recommend Mosby to the lieutenant, or LT, as a fire-team leader for 4th Squad, 3rd Platoon, Baker Company of the 2nd Battalion.

Each platoon was led by a first lieutenant, usually a greenhorn from some Midwest ROTC program, occasionally a Point graduate, rarely a mustang or field-commissioned noncom. The LT was backed up by a platoon sergeant. In the 1st, the average combat infantry platoon sergeant was in his late twenties, a graduate of the Army noncom school at Fort Leavenworth and the War Fighting College at Fort Bragg. In Baker Company, the four platoon sergeants were Brett Huckaby, the oldest and most experienced, thirty-five, white, single, a very good horseman who rode in the 1st's cavalry squadron on parade days, along with Dave Fanand, twenty-five, a thin white kid from Winnemucca who had come into the Army married and had since developed a family of four, which explained why Fanand was so thin, and Gil Noshaug, an ex-hockey star from Mystic, Connecticut. Huckaby ran 3rd Platoon, Fanand ran 2nd, and Noshaug 1st.

The 4th Platoon belonged to Achmed Shabazz, who had rubbed everybody raw with black power slogans until they got to the NTC in the Mojave, where he had shown a clear and even temper and a wonderful talent for keeping his LT from looking like a complete asshole. Now Crane and DerHorst had Shabazz marked for a promotion to staff sergeant as long as he didn't screw up in Saudi. Since Shabazz was the 1st's only actual live Muslim sergeant, they had him running religious orientation lectures for the troops to keep them from mortally offending a Saudi once they deployed.

Each platoon's roughly forty soldiers were broken down into rifle squads of around eleven each, commanded by a corporal. Inside the rifle squad, the infantry tactic was to run two fire teams under the command of a senior rifleman. The fire team was made up of two riflemen with M16A2s, one man assigned to the M249 SAW, the fire-team machine gun, and the fourth man equipped with the M203 grenade launcher. A fire-team leader was responsible for keeping his troopers in the fight no matter how hairy it got, for seeing to it that the team acted in unison with the other fire team in covering and Overwatch assaults, and for keeping the SAW and the grenade launchers manned at all times in the event of casualties.

Leadership ability was a prime consideration, and Mosby had the aura. If Mosby did okay in Saudi, he'd come back with stripes and maybe even make squad leader.

He was in for four years, Montgomery Bill qualified, so he was due to muster out in three years with over twenty-five thousand dollars to pay for a college education. Mosby's father was a guidance counselor for the Board of Education in Richmond. When Mosby had decided to join the Army, his father had shaken his hand, and when the day came for Darryl to report to the induction center, the old man had driven him there and watched him get on the bus to Fort Benning, crying, standing alone by the side of the road.

The name Mosby had attracted Crane's attention because there had been a John Singleton Mosby in the Confederate cavalry, and there was even a street on the base named after him. The kid didn't seem to know for sure if he was related to that Mosby, but the possibility was there and Crane was still doing some digging, just for his own interest.

Mosby was typical of the young men and women in the 1st Division, in the entire Army for that matter: intelligent but disconnected, maybe a little lazy, coming from an unhappy background with little confidence in getting a college scholarship and no real prospects in a recession, kids who were looking at a life in fast food or day labor. Crane hadn't yet figured out how to get Mosby to take his life seriously, to really work at being a soldier. Crane stopped in front of him and watched Mosby working at his ejection slide.

"What's the problem, Mosby?"

Mosby ducked his head and raised his shoulders. "Just rechecking the gear, Sergeant."

"How many times have you checked it since we left Riley?"

"A few."

"So you know it's okay, right? Look, son, you just relax, don't worry about your gear. The other guys see you poking at it, they think you're nervous. You be still, they'll be quiet too."

Mosby nodded and set the rifle aside, his face reddening.

"Sergeant, can I ask you something?"

"Sure."

"Word is, we're only going so Bush can get more money for the armed forces."

Crane looked at the kid, trying to see a trace of John Singleton Mosby. Maybe in the cheekbones and the eyes, the bony ridge above the eyes. Sooner or later, every soldier wants to know why he's going to go get killed. These were cynical times.

"Mosby, you know better than that."

Like hell he did, but so what?

"So why are we going, Sergeant? Aren't we just going to fight a bunch of ragheads that we were giving weapons and money to last year, just so they'd fight the Iranians? And now we're supposed to go over there, leave the kids and everyone, Polanyi's wife is gonna have a kid and he's not gonna be here, gotta go over there and take the tanks and the missiles away from Hussein and it's all something we could have avoided, that didn't have to happen?"

Crane looked at the kid for a while. Maybe it was a good question. Jesus. It was an excellent question.

"We're infantry, kid. Eleven bravo. Combat Arms. We fight. That's what infantry does." Nice, Crane. Now give him a cookie.

The other kids in the squad were silent now, listening hard. There weren't many sergeants who allowed this kind of talk. Crane wasn't happy about it either but he felt that sometimes it wasn't enough just to say, Hey it's orders, so shut the hell up, boot.

The hardest part of leadership, as Crane saw it, was finding the right way to bullshit your troops and still keep some traces of your self-respect. A leader—even a noncom—has to tell the grunts what they want to hear, tell them the *way* they want to hear it, but he better not tell them what they don't know, what the Army keeps a buried truth deep in its soul: we fuck up, our enemies fuck up, our allies fuck up.

And when the military fucks up, it happens in huge and spectacular ways—like Grenada or the *Indianapolis* sinking or Operation Tiger in the Second World War or Pearl Harbor; or Hamburger Hill or Khe Sanh or getting the Americal and the Special Forces guys *out* of Kham Duc after dropping them *in* to a slaughterhouse; LZ Bitch and the Big Red at Xa Cam My in '66— Christ, the list goes on. How do you tell Mosby what he wants to hear when all you want to do is tell him the truth?

But if you tell him the actual truth about combat, about military life, first, he won't believe you, and, second, if he does, he'll get up and start running for the bus station. Crane put on his sergeant's face with a feeling like a man selling a kid a poisoned Sno-Kone.

"Okay, in a way, you're right. This didn't have to happen. Neither did Vietnam have to happen, or you could say neither did we have to go into Panama, since everybody knows Noriega was working for the CIA anyway, and maybe those med students in Grenada weren't in all that much trouble. So what else is new? Nobody goes to war until the civilians have fucked things up so bad they have to send in the Army. It's been that way forever, and you guys are all volunteers, you *picked* Combat Arms. You could have picked Range Data like Mosby here—sorry, Mosby—or you could have picked Accounting or any one of three hundred and fifty other MOS routes, but you all picked the Combat Arms and now here you are, eleven bravo. That's an honorable thing to be, and it's something you'll always carry, so that when you leave the Army, no matter where you go, you'll always know who you are, what you've done. Maybe this one coulda been missed. But it wasn't. Maybe there were a bunch we *did* miss, thanks to the politicians. We never did go fight in Nicaragua. We never had to fight the Russians. We found a way to get around Cuba. We dodged a lot of stupid wars. Shit. Maybe *all* wars are stupid. They fought the First World War, killed maybe ten million people, and not one of the commanders could tell you *why*. Now we got one we can't dodge, and so here we go, this is where we all earn our pay. It was like that in Vietnam, and it's like that now. Sooner or later, someone has to fight."

Damn fine speech, Crane. So basically, going to war is seasonal, kind of like cyclones. Every now and then, you get sucked into one? That's the way to motivate your troops? The kids were still working on it. Mosby spoke for all of them.

"You never talk about Vietnam, do you?"

"No, son. Not much."

"How come? All the guys, they've read up on the afteractions. About what our guys did over there, about Abilene and the Triangle. Some of the guys were asking why you never say anything about it?"

Crane looked down at the kid's face, seeing the bones under his skin and the strain. He was aware of other troops, aware of their attention. At the back of his skull a home movie started showing up on the pink wet bone, a hammer head rising in yellow light, the smell of fish.

"I don't know why. I guess it just seems like it was a long time back. Everything was different then. The Army was different. Why? Is there something you want to know about?"

Mosby was silent. Polanyi, one of Mosby's fire-team members, a pale pink kid from Salina, Kansas, said, "What was it like, Sergeant? What was a firefight like?"

"You been through it yourself, Polanyi. At the Training Center."

Part of the war-gaming that went on in the Mojave involved combat simulations using the MILES, the Multiple Integrated Laser Engagement System. As the tankers and the infantry fighting vehicles raced around the terrain and the dismounted troopers went through their combat maneuvers, practicing fire-team tactics, Overwatch and Bounding Overwatch movement, all the infantry fire-team skills, simulated laser fire from the OpFor units would come out of the dark. It would hit the sensor on a trooper's MILES kit, and the sensor would indicate a kill. Usually, the kid would sit down, look down at the sensor flashing on his helmet, and with this kind of half-embarrassed, half-stunned expression, look up at

Crane and say, Man, I'm dead, like it was a game of touch football, and Crane would check the indicator and say, Yes, son, you're dead.

War games, they called it. Red team, blue team, winning, losing. The thing for Crane was that every hit made him cringe, because he knew what a real hit was like, how it turned a young man into meat, how he pissed in his pants and dropped in a kind of boneless way, how the really bad ones were very quiet, the way the lips changed as they died, the color leaving the cheeks and the forehead. You could see death coming over the face like a kind of pale blue stain, and the eyes changing. Polanyi wouldn't let it go.

"Sergeant? Whaddya think? What is it like?"

Crane came back to Polanyi's face. And Mosby. How old was Mosby? Maybe twenty-two? Crane thought about what it would feel like to write his father a letter, tell the old man how his son had done one hell of a job over here in Saudi, fought like a bearcat, stopped a round with his forehead, died for the cause, which was keeping some raghead princeling knee-deep in Evian water and liquid assets. The kids were still pushing it.

"That was a war game. We mean, what's it really like?"

There was no answer to that, at least nothing that would help these kids right now. Crane had done all right in combat. He'd kept his head most of the time, missed the really stupid deaths, like the way Weir died.

This was in '65, they'd just shipped in and now they were diddy-bopping all loosey-goosey and strung out on a lock-and-load patrol and they'd walked right into an ambush. A VC unit had the whole zone zeroed in. Mortar rounds were coming in from south of the perimeter. The whole thing was going sour in a hurry. Guys were down on their bellies, trying to put out some fire. Crane had had the M60 machine gun in those early days and the sergeant kept yelling at him, Keep the 60 working, keep that sector suppressed, and Crane's partner was jammed in behind this termite mound but he must have had his boot out, because suddenly the toe explodes in meat and bone chips and the guy—Weir—he yelps and swears and sits up to look at his foot.

In the middle of the screaming and the sound of the incoming AK fire and the LT shouting for air cover and the mortar rounds slamming into their position and everybody yelling and firing, Oh, *fart*, Weir had said, a little-kid swear word, and then he'd sat up and grabbed his foot and there was a soft little *whack* sound and there was a hole in the top of his helmet and Weir flew backward. Crane looked down at Weir, trying to make sense of what had happened to the guy, and then he saw a little red hole above Weir's left eye. It looked like a pimple or maybe a mole. Then blood began to pump out of it in a thin red jet and that was the first dead friend Crane collected in Vietnam.

Polanyi and Mosby and the rest were waiting, and it made Crane angry, all that trust and confidence.

"What I believe, I think you guys are better trained and better drilled than any of us were when we went to Indochina. I think, what'll happen is, when the time comes, you'll do what you've been trained to do, you'll do what comes out of habit and reflex. Nothing you're gonna run into will be any different than what you saw at the NTC. All the OpFor tactics, even the desert—the creosote bushes and the snakes. Only difference is, maybe the Iraqis won't be as good as the OpFor troops you war-gamed with. Probably not. Like the guy said, hard training, easy combat. Easy training, hard combat. I think that this time our government is serious about winning the war. I think they're gonna give us enough troops and gear to do the job. I think you'll do fine."

Orso, a heavy-shouldered Italian kid from Columbus, spoke up from the rear of the group. "Word is, we're gonna be there forever, like we were with the Russians in Germany. Just sit there staring at each other for years, another Cold War like in Germany. They say we'll get stuck there for like two years."

Crane had already considered that possibility, and it was a real one. Most of the administration advisors were stuffed full of Cold War strategy. That was why they had misread Hussein in the first place. Crane could see them all getting sucked into a permanent posting in Saudi.

"Orso, why don't you just worry about today and let the commander worry about next year? Even if you're right—which I'm not saying—there's no way any of you will have to stay outposted for more than a few months. Okay? Anyway, my feeling, we'll go in there, root him out soon enough.''

Polanyi wouldn't leave it. Crane knew the signs and braced himself for the inevitable boot question.

''But what's it like to kill someone, Sergeant?''

The rest of the squad groaned and shifted, but they were listening. Crane had never tried to be a buddy to the troops. And whenever some civilian asked him that question, he'd say to the guy, Well, what you should do, you should get out there, kill someone for yourself. Then you'll know.

The trouble was, the 1st was cherry all over again. With the exception of a few lifer sergeants and the upper-echelon commanders, not one of the line troops in the 1st had ever seen actual combat, and sure as hell none of the platoon LTs had any, except for Mahaffey, who had been with an Airborne brigade in Grenada, an action Crane tended to see as more of a scout-troop cluster fuck than an illustration of modern warfare.

But then, thinking about it one night over a Miller back at Harry's Uptown, it had come to Crane that *every* war was fought by inexperienced civilians just a few weeks into uniform. Very few grunts were dumb enough to *stay* eleven bravo from one war to the next—present company excluded—so the majority of the front-line combat troops in any war were going to be recently inducted civilians. Even the brass rolled over so often that there were very few combat-experienced officers down at the brigade or battalion level, where combat experience really counted. Upper-level brass usually marched into the next war backward, their eyes firmly fixed on the last war. By the time they got turned around—look at what happened to the 1st at Villers-Cotterêts in World War I— most of their soldiers were dead or terminally pissed off.

In Vietnam, the insanity of the three-hundred-and-seventy-day DEROS rule made certain that there was a constant turnover of experienced troops. Lucky was the line unit that managed to keep a hard core of combat vets together for longer than four or five months. Since DEROS was staggered, with FNGs arriving every month and vets shipping out—horizontally sometimes—life at the platoon level consisted of an ever-diminishing cadre of guys who knew each other well, who had a history, who understood what each guy was capable of and what he'd do in a fight, and a widening circle of new guys distrusted and excluded by the cadre, until, after a long time, each platoon had maybe one or two guys who had been together for a full tour.

Not so for Mister Charles. He was in for the duration. It was death or glory for Mister Charles. Some of the dinks they had captured during Junction City had been fighting for Uncle Ho and Giap for fifteen years.

And when one of the two hardcore guys in the platoon got popped, the last survivor pulled back so far that *he* was the outsider, the angel of darkness, a fugazy night walker with eyes so far back in his head that talking to him was like talking into the muzzle of a .60-caliber.

Crane had finally been ordered out of the bush by a colonel who had choppered in to their fire base near Ben Cat in '69 and seen Crane come in through the wire looking like an Apache, his uniform in rags, unshaven, fifty pounds underweight. The look in his eyes had moved the man back twenty feet, until he bumped into his ADC and remembered his rank.

All of which meant that, once again, the civilians had to learn about the bush all over again, on their own. And what they had to learn in Vietnam was something called small-unit tactics, war based on close-in contact at the fire-team level, which was a very tricky kind of war.

In small-unit tactics, there were a few simple rules of engagement. You had maybe five guys in your fire team who knew instinctively which way everybody was going to go in a fight: a guy with the M60 machine gun to lay down suppressing fire, and his loader to keep *him* alive; a man on the M79, the short-barreled shotgun-looking grenade launcher to take out enemy machine guns and RPG teams; and the riflemen to maneuver at the flanks, get around the enemy, and kill him with aimed or grazing fire.

And all of this had to be done *within* the tactical maneuvering of the rest of the squads, with the platoon in general, and done without talk, automatically, so that the man on the 60 knew exactly how long it would take his flanking team to get in position, where they'd be, and when they were going to open up. It was a kind of gunpowder quadrille performed in silence, in deep bush, in the middle of booby traps and trip wires and snakes and hornets— nobody ever talked about those goddamned Vietnamese *hornets*— and if one FNG made the wrong move, they all got lit up and wasted.

Better to lose the FNG—or shoot him outright, which happened sometimes, late in the war, or so everybody said. And this was just a skirmish, Harass and Interdict, Advance to Contact, get your ANGLICO guy to call in Navy shells, bring in a Phantom and roast the dinks.

Now the *ambush*, that was a whole different thing.

And in the middle of your learning curve, MACV would drop in a couple of new guys—wide-eyed Bambi-looking cherries you hated on sight—and the whole goddam thing would start over again, with more raw civilians. And the brass—they dropped into the war, most of them, for no more than six months, long enough to get some trigger time, or at least to *hear* about it, and then they were back on the Braniff jet to Fort Sill or Fort Dix or, the *best*, Fort Monroe with their CIB and a wide grin, and the company had a *new* commander, another *civilian*, who didn't know combat and rarely had the balls to admit it, and *never* talked to the grunts directly. They said Schwarzkopf, the Commander in Chief, was different, had done two full tours, and some of the other brass had done good time in-country, but far too many of them, in Crane's experience, were in and out as fast as they could manage it, and that was the general grunt opinion.

Same then, same now. They were trying, with this new COHORT policy—COHesion, Operational Readiness, and Training—trying to keep some kind of unit cohesion, but all in all it was same shit, different war.

And, as usual, the troops had very little contact with the brass, so there was no one left for them to ask but the sergeants. Wolochek was like most of the New Modern Army captains, a good manager with a real solid work ethic, but all officers were taught to keep their distance from the enlisted men—Army regs demanded no fraternization—so all of the Baker Company platoon LTs were more or less in Wolochek's camp over there on his side of the class line and they kept their reserve around the gentlemen rankers.

About combat, it had been Crane's experience that no amount of talk actually helped a trooper when the time came, but these were his boys, on their way to a strange war.

Crane didn't want to tell them that it wasn't the firefight that ruined you, made you so frightened you wanted to crawl back into the earth, made men cry and shit themselves. No, what did that was artillery, getting shelled. Mortars. Lying there with your face in the mud, lying on your hands so that when the concussion comes up through the earth it doesn't explode your heart inside your chest. Hearing guys around you screaming, hearing men blow apart, feeling the ground jump and the air around you turn to molasses, that was the purest distillation of blind, crawling, helpless terror. You lay there and felt like a cockroach on a kitchen floor, the boot coming down, nothing going on in your head but numbers spinning on a wheel, roulette, dice. Somebody else get it please, somebody else, my buddy, my mother, my kids, but not me, not me yet.

No, Crane wasn't going to tell them about *that*.

He looked at their faces, angry with them for what they needed from him, angry with himself for his meanness. He had to give them something.

Someone was blowing a whistle and now the Hercules had its engines firing, the big props strobing in the sideways sunrise, and the officers were fanning out across the tarmac.

"Okay, Polanyi . . . the first thing, you think you're gonna be scared, maybe freeze up. Embarrass yourself in front of your buddies. Only you don't. I don't know why. But most guys, when the shit starts, you're into it so fast you don't have *time* to lock up. Your training kicks in, you put out rounds, you back up your buddies, you see you're not alone, and that first feeling, what it is is relief. What it's like, you see a guy in your iron and you don't think, you just squeeze off a burst, and he goes down, and usually there are more guys coming up, or you're taking a lot of fire, bits

of brush and dirt are flying up all around you, your ears are ringing and you're getting deaf, but you keep firing, maybe take down
a few more guys, see them go down, time stretches out so that a
minute can go by, it'll seem like an hour, or you'll be in a fight,
think it was over in a second and find out you been in it three
hours. And then suddenly it's all over, and *that's* when you get to
think about it, and maybe you can walk over, see the guy you
killed. You look down at him, look at the holes in him, see what
the rounds can do, and you feel a little sick, feel like you're gonna
throw up, but mainly you feel alive, you feel, Hey, I did okay, I
didn't choke, and you look back down at him and you say to
yourself, Better you than me, asshole.''

They all smiled and grinned and laughed, as if they knew what
he meant. But they didn't. Not yet, anyway. Crane smiled back at
them, as if he felt the same way, but he didn't, and as he walked
away toward the end of the troop file, he started thinking—
again—about how much of his life in the Army called for this sort
of well-intentioned bullshit.

Maybe "lying" was a better word.

Crane's grandfather had had an uncle back in Lake Placid—his
name was Harding or Hardinger, Crane could never remember
it—but the guy had apparently gone up as a conscript back in
1917, had eventually become part of what was then known as the
American Expeditionary Force, and he had gone to France with
the AEF. They got off the troopship and marched into Paris behind Blackjack Pershing and when they reached Lafayette's tomb,
Pershing had renamed the AEF the 1st Division, and that was the
birthday of the 1st Infantry Division.

So this man, Hardinger, let's say, sent back letters about the
campaigning, about St.-Mihiel and Villers-Cotterêts and the assaults around Berzy-le-Sec in 1918, and Crane's grandfather had
kept them all, and Crane's dad used to read them aloud to Crane
and his brother when they were kids.

At the time, listening to his father's low, whiskey-grating voice
while the snow piled up all around in the Adirondacks, Crane
thought that this Army thing, it sounded pretty good, lots of travel
and glory, as well as job security, and he liked the sound of the

name, the 1st Division, and the look of that patch, the big red numeral 1 against an olive-drab background.

That was the start of the Army experience for Crane, and whenever he had to bullshit the grunts about what they were doing, he found himself thinking about the difference between what his uncle's letters had talked about and the *real* Army Crane had met as soon as he reached boot camp. Because what the *real* Army was about—at least for a puke FNG at Benning—was chickenshit.

At least, chickenshit was what they called it at boot, although now the new kids were calling it "ball busting" or "dogging out," but whatever you called it, it was what made the life of a barracks soldier a kind of low-rent, low-grade, lunatic, nitpicking hell, because no matter how hard you tried, there was *always* going to be some desk jockey noncom who would take a personal dislike to *you* and dedicate his entire career to busting your personal balls.

For a kid, an American kid, raised on the idea of fairness—even if he rarely experienced it—the whole thing about ball busting came as a brutal awakening.

Crane's troubles started around the question of kit inspection. Each of the enlisted pukes in Crane's boot company had been issued a set of personal items—toothbrush, shaving cream, comb, brushes, scissors, files—all OD, or olive drab, and there was a precise military regulation that governed the *exact* way this kit had to be maintained and displayed. Each morning there'd be an inspection of the barracks by a sergeant, who would go down the ranks of the pukes—each puke in his white skivvies and standing on top of his footlocker, elbows in, forearms level, hands extended palm down, fingers together, barefoot—and the sergeant or the DI would study each and every element of the puke's kit and personal appearance.

Crane had been raised in a semimilitary family so he had a fairly high standard of personal neatness, and he kept his kit in perfect condition, but there was one DI who took a dislike to Crane—something about Crane's ears offended him or the color of his eyes, whatever it was Crane knew the man hated him—and he'd always find some microscopic flaw in Crane's kit. When he saw it, the DI's face would redden, and he'd seem to swell up with disgust and outrage, and Crane would be down on his face doing sets of military fifties while the assistant DIs stood over him screaming and the senior DI threw Crane's kit all over the barracks.

This happened sixteen times, until Crane tumbled to the secret. After that, and for every night he remained in boot, he kept *two* separate kits, one he'd actually *use* and the other one he would show at inspections. He also learned the trick of laying out his kit and making his cot up according to regs the night before an inspection—do it by the numbers, measure everything with a ruler—have the whole array gleaming, mathematical.

Then he'd sleep on the floor beside the cot.

They all did that for the last five weeks of boot.

And when he was at Bragg and Fort Sill and other bases for his AIT, Advanced Individual Training, he saw to it that there was an area of the barracks that no soldier ever walked on. They all kept it spotless, shining and buffed to a satin finish, and whenever a noncom wanted to bust their balls about the hardwood floor, they'd make sure what he looked at was this one special section. Drove the sons of bitches crazy, although they had to know what was going on. Chickenshit.

There was chickenshit about religion too—nobody *ever* said he wasn't religious, and everybody went to whatever church he had listed on his intake forms, and there was ball busting about sideburns—couldn't have them—and mustaches—some noncoms *insisted* on them and others hated them—and there were always the officers who dogged you out for not properly saluting them while you were overtaking them on a walkway; the Army has very exact rules about how a soldier salutes and what he says when he does and any variation was likely to draw fire. You had to come abreast of the officer, salute exactly right, and say, "By your leave, sir," and hold the salute until the officer says, "Carry on," and returns the salute. . . . It went on and on, it was dizzying and maddening, like a horde of gnats, and every one a stinger.

There were literally hundreds of rules and regs you had to think about, and a breach of any one of them—real or imaginary, it made no difference—could get your day pass jerked or your home leave canceled, your pay docked, or see you jogging around the parade square with a full pack on and your M14 on your raised arms.

The whole idea of dogging out a grunt seemed to be to impress upon him his absolute worthlessness as a human being, to get him to accept that his bosses had the power of life and death over him, and that he could be busted back to puke for *anything* he did, because there were so many rules that it was impossible to be in compliance with all of them at any given time. All a noncom or an officer had to do, if he wanted to fuck with you big time, was to flip through the manual for a minute or two, come up with some piece of inane Army bullshit, and your ass was toast. You could be a grown man—come back from Vietnam with two bronzes and two stars on your CIB, even a purple—and there would come a day, you'd piss off some rear-echelon motherfucker, maybe some pencil neck out of OCS—Officer Candidate Schools—and this pogue could *ruin* you: kill your pension, get you assigned to Ultima Thule, bust you back to PFC, make your every waking moment a grinding clockwork monotony. . . . Crane had this theory, that one of the reasons the Army had so much of this dogging-out ball-busting bullshit was that it made the average grunt so goddam cranky that he'd go into combat just for the chance to get even.

It had been Crane's experience that there was only one place in the whole goddam Army where you were out of reach of the Army's endless petty bullshit, and that was on the line. In combat.

And the further out there you were, the less chickenshit you ran into. There had been precious few combat consolations, but that was definitely one of them.

And now here he was, looking Polanyi and Mosby in the eyes and handing them a line about how it was in a firefight, as if *talking* about a firefight would do the kids any good. . . . Maybe Crane was becoming *part* of the chickenshit factor.

Well, all he really knew was that the closer he stayed to an eleven-bravo MOS, the more he liked himself, and as a sergeant it was his job to keep kids like Mosby and his crowd combat ready, because there was one thing that would always be true: There was no dogging on the line. That part was very, very real. If he was part of the problem, too fucking bad. Life's a complex business, and if you try to make sense out of it, you'll trip over something nasty and fuck up beyond recognition.

A flurry of shouts and a shrill blast brought his head up as he reached the wheel chocks of one of the Airlift Hercs.

Wolochek was blowing his whistle and the LTs were scurrying around, the troops struggling to their feet. The big rear gates of the Hercules were opening with a slow hydraulic whine. The engines were blasting hot air and kerosene across the tarmac, making dust devils and whipping at everyone's BDUs. The grunts put their heads down and lined up in company formation, two lines abreast, platoon by platoon and squad by squad. Crane watched Mosby lead his fire team into line, saw them blend into a long line of soldiers so that it was hard to pick them out. There were the platoon sergeants—Huckaby, pale and intense; and over by him stood Shabazz with his Beretta slung low and a SAW over his shoulder, the homey at war; and in the back were Fanand, the worrier, and Noshaug, who'd rather be sailing. At the top of the ramp, the loadmaster came up to look at the file, her clipboard in her hand.

Across the field, the Armored guys were maneuvering a column of IFVs into the nose gate of a C-5 Galaxy. The Abrams tanks and the rest of their heavy armor were going by sea. They'd link up with it all in Saudi in about two weeks. The sound of engines and the smell of kerosene and gasoline and dust and the developing roar of a division mobilizing rolled up and over Crane, beating on his chest and buffeting his face. People were laughing, shouting, somebody was calling a cadence, boots were shuffling and bumping on the tarmac and then clanking up the load ramps. Crane watched the men disappear into the Airlift transports, into the yellowish half-light inside the belly of the Hercules.

Man, he thought, somebody ought to be playing a bugle.

Crane was one of the last men to board his Hercules. He strapped himself into a canvas seat and set his feet up on the running board of a humvee. It was one of the Headquarters humvees, configured to carry a .50-caliber machine gun and all kinds of Motorola radio gear. Crane looked into the driver's compartment and saw the Motorola logo on the handset. In Vietnam all the radios were Motorola radios, the Prick-25 and the long-range sets. Some things never changed. At least they weren't Sonys.

The Hercules started to roll forward. Crane looked sideways down the huge loading chamber, down a line of company humvees under their black cargo nets, and saw about seventy troopers, half of Baker Company. The inside of the Hercules smelled of gas and rubber and—Christ—the loadmaster's perfume. She was a couple of seats up from Crane, a short, compact brown-haired woman, maybe in her midtwenties. She was flipping through a sheet of computer print, checking cargo manifests against the humvees. She looked intense and very tired. Loadmasters from Military Airlift Command were working thirty to forty hours at a stretch. A lot of the MAC pilots were women as well. Just like in World War II. This Herc had just come back from delivering a load of Marines out of Kaneohe Bay in Hawaii, and now it was headed back into the rising day with a load of infantry. Crane watched her for a long time, thinking about women and the Army, about women and modern life.

Now the Hercules was full of sound and wind and the engines were howling. Speech—thought—was impossible. The cargo bay was like a beaten bass drum and the wheels were slamming over cracks in the concrete runway, and then the plane tilted suddenly up, everybody leaned toward the cabin, Crane's humvee shifted an inch inside its tie-downs, there was a bouncing bang as the landing gear came up, and they were banking to the right. Out of the tiny porthole, Crane could see the green earth of Kansas rolling away, and beyond the sweet grass he saw the lights of Topeka, and the sun glinting off a silver ribbon of water, the Republican River, lying against the blue-green grassland. The loadmaster unbuckled and stepped up to the cockpit door. It opened and she stood there in the doorway for a while, silhouetted in the rising sunlight, an aura of auburn fire around her head. Beyond her the sun burned a deep and angry red.

———

Sometime during the eighteen-hour flight to Saudi, Crane woke from a restless dream and saw a row of strobe lights in the gathering night. An escort jet was refueling in midair. Just off to port Crane couldn't see the Starlifter or the Hercules ahead and above them, but the turbulence from it buffeted the airframe. Midair refueling.

How the hell they could do that in twilight was something Crane decided not to think about. Hours later, in the middle of the night, they landed on a stretch of nowhere desert in the middle of Saudi Arabia, coming down through wind and dust onto a runway lined with Army gear and Air Force hutments. The latrines in the plane were reeking, everybody was tired and scratchy, their ALICE belts cutting into their chests and their collars chafing. The Hercules slammed down hard. All the gear shifted and rocked and all the troopers cheered weakly, the sound lost under the waterfall roar of the braking turboprops. Already the platoon leaders were unbuckling and stretching, the troopers fumbling with their packs and rifles. Everyone in the cargo bay was nearly deaf and their ears were ringing. Everyone felt mildly concussed. Stunned.

In a few minutes they were at the disembarkation point and the Hercules came to a lurching stop. The loadmaster, whose name Crane never found out, walked past the shuffling troopers and hit the gate lever. There was a low whining, grinding sound as the two huge clamshell gates pulled back and suddenly the plane was full of heat, massive, overwhelming, alien as the surface of Mars. Beyond the open bay doors, the airstrip was a tangle of trucks and off-loading tanks, arc lights and half-tracks and people in every kind of service gear. An Air Force crewman in blue overalls stuck his head into the load bay and grinned up at the troopers.

"Hey, this one's fulla grunts! Hello, boys and girls! On behalf of the United States Air Force and the Royal House of Saud, welcome to Operation Desert Shield!"

One of the grunts by the cargo bay doors grinned at the man and said something Crane couldn't hear.

The airman, who had a huge white handlebar mustache,

laughed and waved the man's attention to an enormous hand-painted sign nailed to a plywood equipment hut. Several halogen runway lamps had been focused on the sign so it could be read from a long way off.

The sign read:

WELCOME TO SAUDI ARABIA

THE HOME OF WALL-TO-WALL

FUCK-ALL!!

For some reason, the sign made Crane feel a number of different emotions, and by the time they were up and stretched and starting to get off the Hercules—into a cloud of blowing sand and stinging gnats and into a kind of heat Crane hadn't felt since Bangkok in 1966—Crane had sort of figured out that what he was feeling was that he had come home.

CHAPTER SIX

HIRED GUNS

WESTERN SAUDI DESERT, JANUARY 1991

Crane came back to the hootch he shared with DerHorst, Felz, and Baumgart to find the three of them betting on a lizard race. They had the cots shoved back and the gear piled up and Der-Horst was prodding his lizard, Norman, in the flank with the point of his bayonet. Felz's lizard, Lance, was ambling across the plywood floor of the hootch with his tongue flickering in and out and a look on his face that reminded Crane of Carla's father. Baumgart's lizard—Crane had forgotten its name—was under Crane's cot and showed no real interest in taking part in the festivities. DerHorst looked up as Crane came back from his run and grinned hugely.

"Potatoes, Dee. Actual potatoes! Felz got them from his brother in the four-twelve." He prodded Norman again and huffed at the animal.

Felz, a bald-headed master sergeant from company HQ, overweight and just about the *pinkest* man Crane had ever seen, touched his finger to his lips. "It's a secret. The grunts find out, they'll want some."

"For jack? You must be out of your fucking skull. Wolochek finds you with jack, he'll rip you apart. This is Saudi, not a bivouac in JC."

Baumgart groaned at Crane, his lean black face seamed and corroded with childhood acne, his fuzzy gray hair shaved to a thin mist of white over his bullet-shaped head. "This ain't the goddam Peace Corps."

Crane looked at him. "Yes, it is."

Captain Wolochek was too straight-arrow to try to make anything alcoholic out of potatoes, but a lot of the grunts were privately convinced that some of the brass in the KTO had some Johnnie Walker stashed. They were supposed to be getting it from some Saudi troops down the line. The Saudis loved their Johnnie Walker Black. It was bullshit, but typical army bullshit. If anybody was drinking, they weren't sharing it with the Combat Arms.

DerHorst and Crane had been down to King Khalid Military City in December, scouting for some kind of ersatz military turkey for a big Christmas dinner, and Crane had seen some Saudi and Kuwaiti officers drinking whiskey in a private club while a couple of Filipino hookers danced on the top of a pool table. It turned out that a good time could be had in Saudi, but you had to be an officer or a Saudi prince. Crane didn't like Saudi princes. The way he saw it, all that oil made the richest ones greasy. And hypocrisy was the second-largest Saudi resource.

Since a lot of Saudi officers *were* princes of the royal house, anybody who got close to certain ones could count on some diversionary delights involving Johnnie Walker and Filipino women, no matter what the mullahs thought about it.

On the same visit, Crane had seen two Wahabi Muslims spit on a female trooper from the 24th Infantry as she walked by them on her way down to the suq. She was in full BDUs and had been carrying her M16 but they walked right up to her and spat in her face, saying something ugly in a dialect that sounded like a goat choking on a plug of tobacco. Crane had stepped in just as the trooper was unlimbering her rifle with a look on her face that would have scared their sandals off if they had any sense at all.

Crane gave the mullahs a serious snarl, shoving them down the alleyway. They cursed and spat at him, gargling some awesome raghead curses and promising death and dismemberment to all infidel whores and their infidel pimps. Crane felt his generalized dislike of the Saudis turning into active animosity.

He offered the trooper a cloth. She was in tears and her face was bright red with rage.

"Why the *hell* are we putting up with these assholes?"

Crane had grinned at her, ignoring the people gathered around, ignoring the obvious disapproval of the crowd. The locals were looking at them as if they were something a camel had just spit up, their hardwood faces blank and their small black eyes glittering. Islam. It was one of the world's great fighting religions. Like all fighting religions, the thing it did best was make good haters out of the peasantry. Looking around at the crowd, Crane began to see why there were so few Islamic stand-up comics. He brushed some wet spit off her collar and started to walk her away.

"Don't ask me. I just work here. Hey, look at it this way. Hussein doesn't move, you're gonna get to kill a whole mess of them sometime soon."

She was maybe twenty, the name on her BDU read Curphey.

"Where you from, Curphey?"

"Maine, Sergeant. I wish I was back there. I don't get why we have to put up with all this shit, no beer, they get to spit on me, and all we can do is say, Hey, thank you for the privilege of allowing us to die for your rat's-ass country."

"Onward Christian Soldiers, right?"

Curphey had laughed at that, looking around them at the people in the suq, the dark angry faces, the black eyes and the skin like dry lumber, and the women watching from the cool dark of the shops and alleyways.

"Where's your platoon?"

She tilted her head to the left. "Over there. I was trying to find some batteries."

Batteries. That was another thing about this war. The hardest thing to find in all of Saudi was a double-A battery. Every trooper in the Area of Operations had a Walkman or a video camera and they all ran on double-As.

Crane had walked her back to her buddies, more soldier kids with an air of school break around them; Crane could see them at a sock hop or a rave or whatever they called school dances now. They were an escort for their company executive officer, who was nowhere around. Crane had a theory but he kept it to himself. The trooper's mates gathered around her, a press of gabbling kids in desert camo, their reddened skin and watery eyes showing signs of the dreaded Saudi two-step, known to the grunts of Baker as Walt Dysentery. Crane talked with them for a moment, watching Curphey get herself together, then he said good-bye.

The incident had stayed with him, part of the general FUBAR factor of this butthead AO. It was blindingly clear to every soldier and airman in the country that the Saudi people looked down on them, thought of them as defiled pig eaters, infidel subhumans. It was a best-kept war secret, but clearly the Saudis saw the grunts as expendable mercenary warriors. You could see it in every face. There wasn't a single operational trooper in the entire AO who didn't resent being told how to live by a Saudi goat fondler—who would be at this very moment hogtied across a barrel of crude oil while a platoon of unzipped Iraqi soldiers lined up behind him if the U.S. Army and the rest of the forces weren't there to protect his virginity.

Crane—and everybody else with a functioning brain—knew damn well *why* the U.S. was there. Saudi Arabia existed *because* of the United States. The U.S. government had made a conscious decision to use the Saudis as front men for their oil interests worldwide, even to the extent of allowing the once-powerful American oil-production industry to go belly-up in the seventies through artificially low OPEC oil prices. The U.S. kept the House of Saud in power, and the House of Saud kept the price of oil right where the U.S. wanted it—not so high as to tick off the voters, but not so low as to cut into the carbon-based economy of the West. All you had to do was look around at the Saudi forces; all their gear was American, their operational protocol was strictly U.S. Army War College, and every bit of their military hardware and communications technology was a direct copy of American military designs. It was one of the war's unspoken truths that the duplication of war-fighting technique was intentional. When push came to shove-it-up-a-raghead's-butt, all the U.S. forces had to do was ease the Saudi techies out of the way, sit down at the consoles and the controls, and jump-start the war. Keeping the Saudi soldiers around was strictly public relations, and every soldier in the region from Turkey to Qatar knew it.

Except the goddam mullahs. And the U.S. press people, who were, in Crane's opinion, the most gullible, compliant, and downright militarily *ignorant* clowns he'd ever come across. There were something like three thousand of them in Saudi right now, and fewer than fifty of them knew the difference between ballistics and ballroom dancing. It was no wonder Bush and Cheney held them in contempt. So did most of the field commanders and all of the eleven-bravo troopers.

Which made it very hard to keep the morale up, and even harder as the endless boredom and the endless visual monotony of the terrain and the endless Army make-work bullshit piled up on everyone.

Crane watched Felz and DerHorst and Baumgart, Felz stamping his boot trying to get Lance to run faster, Baumgart poking around under a cot, DerHorst leaning back in his cot and looking out the plastic window.

DerHorst felt Crane's look and smiled thinly.

"So . . . think he'll move?"

"Homer Simpson?" which was their slang for Hussein.

"No, *Lance*. Of *course* Homer."

"Today was the deadline. I don't think Hussein gets it. I think he thinks we'll fade."

"Been the pattern for a while, Dee."

DerHorst had missed Vietnam, but he was a lifer like Crane, well into his late thirties now and likely to be a noncom for the rest of his hitch. But he was a good soldier, had that vaguely Jesuit-priest manner that comes over lifers, if they don't collapse into drink and low living, which many of them did. If you stayed in the Army long enough, you either simplified and became a kind of military monk, or you ran quietly to seed in your quarters while the world rolled by on its way to the future. Crane wasn't sure which way he was going yet.

"You know what's going on right now?" he said. "Why do you think Wolochek's in such a tizzy? They got the Warthogs fired up right now. Our perimeter artillery and our TAC-Ms—the long-range missiles—are at Red. This thing kicks off in a few hours and everybody but Homer knows it. Bush has his fur all ruffled over this one. Remember, the guy was a fighter pilot himself, fought at Midway, didn't he?"

"Bomber, I thought, but yeah. A long time ago."

"You don't forget something like that."

"The boots asking you about all this?"

"Oh, yeah. Mosby and his crowd, they got into it a bit back at Forbes Field in November. And now and then the newer ones will ask, or the guys with kids and families back in JC. I figure, all that shit belongs to Shabazz and Noshaug and Huckaby. Why? They ask you?"

DerHorst grimaced as Felz's lizard scampered up his chest and onto the hootch wall. Felz and Baumgart laughed and went back to fiddling with their television reception.

"No, they don't. I don't have that kind of connection with them. Maybe I'm not old enough. Anyway, it don't pay to get too chummy with them. They'll use it on you when you can least afford it."

"Maybe. Damn, they seem so young to me."

"They are young. They always are. You're the one who's getting old, Dee. . . . You know, I never asked you. I hope you don't take this wrong, but how come you're still in? You got a full pension coming, plus all your buy-out, you got no family, the Army owes you a lot of pension, bonuses. You gotta be looking at a fair whack of cash plus loan guarantees. But here you are, on your ass in Wall-to-Wall Fuck-All, pulling down a large twenty-four hundred a month plus a hundred and ten per month for combat pay, baby-sitting a bunch of bored troopers and getting pissed on by every Saudi cart humper and goat boinker in the AO."

"Goat boinker?"

"You know what I mean. I'm serious, man. I can't even under-stand why I'm the sergeant major and you're not. You have all the qualifications but you're still at first sergeant. That's crap. There's lots of positions for sergeants major in other divisions, other operations. Why stay?"

Crane looked around the patchwork hootch, at Felz and Baumgart trying to get CNN on the Sony, at the piles of gear, the boxes full of packaged meals and cherry Coke, the M16s and the M60s, the 9-mills in their holsters, took in the smell of men in close quarters and the damp alien air that was rolling in through the rickety door, saw it all under the flickering light from the overhead bulb.

"I got nowhere else to go, Pete. I'm not a soldier, what am I?"

"Yeah, but you'd still be *in*! Nobody wants to be a civvie. I mean, who gives a shit about them, they're never gonna be *operational*! But the Army's a big corporation, man. I think of it like a big spiderweb, you could have gone anywhere in it, gone into the War College, become an instructor at Leavenworth, you coulda gone to Washington, got political. You should have rank now, shoulda been a mustang back in Vietnam. You could have had all of it."

"I could have moved, but I couldn't stay eleven bravo."

"Shit! *Nobody* stays eleven bravo. That's just where you start. You know how it works. It's the Great Game."

"The Great Game's for officers only."

"Not with guys like you. You had some diversity in your sheet. War-fighting studies. Weasel your way into a D.C. posting. Connect with the brass. *Use* that Star, the CIB. You know where the levers are. Go pull some. I sure plan on it. I get some combat under my belt, I'm outta here. I got my sheet in for Intel, get assigned to TRADOC at Fort Monroe, get to the Pentagon, make myself useful, see how the wind blows. . . ."

"Yeah, you'll make Jedi Knight around the same time I win the Preakness. Smell the coffee, Pete. You're not Point. You're not even rank. You're just another grunt sergeant like me."

"Not for long, my friend. And Wolochek says you could go anywhere too, that you knew DePuy from the war, that he'd have snapped you up in a flash. You were one of the first in back then, you fought under him, hell, didn't the guy pin your star on you at Long Binh? Wolochek says all you had to do was write DePuy and bang, you're on the yellow brick road."

"I spent my time at the Staff College, back in '72, when they were asking all the grunts, What went wrong, my son, all that stuff that General Abrams was doing. I told them everything I knew and they said, Thank you, son, now fuck off. You figure you're gonna get to the Puzzle Factory or swim the moat at Fort Monroe on the undying gratitude of a brass monkey, I got a telemarketing job for you. Tell me, your wife, her name Muffy or Blaine? Have you *ever* played touch football at Hyannis Port? Or ridden to the hounds in Virginia? Ever owned a handmade Purdy? Word up, boy. The corporation keeps those jobs for its own, the Point, and all those Ivy League cluster-fuck kindergartens. Here's a basic fact for you, maybe you don't know. How many guys from Harvard got blown away in Vietnam? Come on, how many?"

DerHorst was silent for a moment. "Man, I don't know . . . a hundred, maybe?"

"Twelve."

"Twelve?"

"That's right. Twelve guys from Harvard. I read this article once, the guy was the Secretary of the Navy—what the hell was his name? Webb! Webb wrote that of all the guys who graduated out of Princeton and Harvard and MIT during the Vietnam War, something like *thirty thousand* guys, only *twenty* died in-country. Twenty! Now, you come from where is it, Buttwad, Idaho?"

"That's *Benewah,* dammit!"

"Whatever . . . and how many guys from Buttwad High got their names on a plaque in the local high school, presuming there *is* a high school in Buttwad?"

"Jeez, I get the point."

"Whatever it was, I'll bet it was more than twelve. And yeah, that's the point. It's the *Point* point. Guys like us, we're bullet stoppers for the brass, Kevlar that can mow the lawn and drive the wife to Wal-Mart in between wars."

"I still ain't heard my answer."

Crane wasn't happy about this. This was the kind of stuff Carla was onto him about, how he could do better, how he could get into his own business, develop outside interests. And Crane knew that was all pipe smoke. His day was done. He was too old and too long a noncom to even think about the Great Game.

The Great Game . . . he'd heard all about it in southeast Asia. Every junior LT with some pedigree had it all worked out, like a very complicated polka with the Army playing the fat chick in the dirndl.

The players started out at the Point, if they had the grades or the connections—usually a local congressman who had a nomination to spare—and if the LT can't get to the Point he goes to Officer Candidate School or ROTC on campus, and once he's in the machine he signs up for Combat Arms—nothing else, not training units, not Accounting or Finance Corps, not Quartermaster or Police Corps and sure as hell not Ordnance—only the Combat Arms would do. Artillery, Armor, or Infantry. Maybe Engineers, but better not. Do very, very well, graduate high, get noticed. Then Ranger, or maybe Airborne—back in the sixties the path to Valhalla was to be in the 11th Air Assault, because that unit was the core cadre that formed the 1st Air Cavalry, and anyone who had been in Air Cav in the Indochina War had that special light around him, and they took care of one another later. Next step was tricky—lead a platoon, make command of a line company at the front, get a good evaluation, or OER—and the attention of the colonel. Then get some Staff time. Whatever the Staff time was, it had to be Operations, which was S3, and not Personnel, which was S1, or Intelligence, definitely not Intelligence, which was S2, because very few S2s were real combat vets. Most of them were specialists from Support branches who had a hard time getting noticed, although there were exceptions. Stay away from Logistics, the S4 spot, because Logistics was a career blaster, charged with getting materiel and gear and food up to the line, work nobody noticed until you fucked up, and then you were toast.

Next our runner splits the war zone—being killed interferes with your long-term career goals—and goes to a university somewhere, on Army funds, and gets a graduate degree in anything sexy, preferably at a name college—State University of Western Hogfondler would not do it—and then gets posted back to an

ROTC spot as a trainer. If the man is good—or the woman—the runner goes from there to the Golden Palace—the Command and General Staff College at Fort Leavenworth—and after that, chicken wings on your boards, lots of gold braid, command at the battalion or brigade level—you could see the stars from there. . . .

Crane ran all through it in a New York minute and knew in his heart he had never even been on the starting line for that race. Some noncoms made it, but they were always "mustang"—lifted from the ranks—and no field officer would trust him to pick out the right oyster fork or do a decent quadrille at the ball. . . . What the hell did DerHorst want him to do, anyway? It was all over for him, and he was going to have to look at that, because he couldn't stay Army forever.

"Okay," he said, looking down at DerHorst, "lemme ask you, you get to Fort Monroe, get rank, whatever. What's that all about, at the bottom?"

"Hey, it's about war, about making this Army better and better, about fighting wars better."

Crane looked out the window over DerHorst's head. It was starting to rain.

"You really think like that—about making the Army better?"

"Most of the time."

"How do you feel about this war, so far?"

"That's a big question, Dee."

"You're a big guy."

"Well, don't ask me about the Big Picture. I think the same thing you think about that. It's a military fever dream. It's the Hoo-Yah and Hussein's the Wicked Witch. The whole AO belongs to Cold War spookazoids playing Risk or hide-the-floppy with little plastic models on some big game board. War-gamer wonks and situation freaks who couldn't run a flank maneuver without stepping on their dicks. The operational troops, that's a different story."

"Yeah, but if you were already at Fort Monroe, would you still feel like you were *part* of it?"

"Part of what?"

"Christ, Pete—somebody's got to stay and *fight*. Somebody's got to be *operational*! And that's what I am, I'm operational."

"So we're back to all that eleven-bravo shit."

"If it's shit to you, my friend, then you have the problem."

"That's not what I meant. But the Combat Arms, that's just the beginning. From there, you go anywhere in the corporation. You got that CIB there, that's your ticket to ride, Dee!"

"*If* you're an officer. Anyway, there were a lot of guys I knew, being eleven bravo was as far as they got. That's what I am, eleven bravo. The rest is politics. If you're not fighting, you're cargo. We're fighters."

"Hardcore, huh? You shoulda been a Marine."

"Couldn't get my head in the jar. Let's leave this, okay? Place is depressing enough."

DerHorst studied him for a bit, and then sighed and looked out the smeared-over plastic sheet at the base camp, sodden and gray in the fading twilight under a low sky full of ragged clouds.

"Depressing? Maybe. But this is where I get my Combat Infantry Badge, just like yours. This is my war, Dee."

"Maybe, but it's not your country."

"Thank Christ."

———

After sixty-six days in the Saudi desert, Crane and his hootchmates, the rest of Baker Company, the rest of the 1st Division, hell, the entire United States Army, had come to a couple of conclusions about the place.

First of all, if there was anywhere in the world that had more nothing than this place, nobody wanted to see it. Saudi Arabia had more kinds of absolute *nothing* than anyplace else in the world. Saudi was *empty* beyond belief, Saudi had more *empty* per square mile than Kathie Lee Gifford's cortex. Operationally, it was so damn empty that the night-vision goggles couldn't tell a sand dune from a dry wash. The landscape was so undifferentiated that the chopper pilots were having a hell of a time finding their way around using military maps, and many times they had to rely on the Global Positioning System and SatNav functions just to get to a target and back home, let alone *hit* the damned thing.

And secondly, there was only one thing worse than November in Saudi, and that was January in Saudi.

The 1st was spread all over a sector sixteen miles south of the Kuwaiti border, deployed in a miles-wide entanglement of troop quarters, motor pools, tank parks, artillery parks, latrines, mess halls, HQ huts, medical tents, football fields, baseball diamonds, barbecue pits, malt shops, garages, PX shacks, airstrips, chopper pods, weapons bays, ranges, pits . . . from the air the sector looked like the world's biggest trailer park after a hurricane. All around the forward perimeter, barriers of concertina wire and motion sensors and tank traps ran in a ragged zigzag line for miles across the flattest, most sorry-looking landscape in the world.

Most of the Baker Company troopers had expected a kind of Foreign Legion movie set, with rolling dunes of sand, maybe a palm-lined oasis or two, lots of Arab nomads in blue robes offering women and hashish to the infidels in the suqs, here and there a big mud fort like in that *Beau Geste* movie with Gary Cooper. What they got was a wind-scraped panorama of scrubland the color of vomit, rats the size of poodles, clouds of gnats, and more of that wall-to-wall fuck-all than any sane person could handle. It was hard to like a place where the major feature of the landscape was the horizon line.

The horizon.

Somewhere to the north, beyond the concertina wire, out in the far distance where the haze rippled and writhed and the land seemed to fade away under a sky the color of a bruise, legions of blood-drinking Iraqi fanatics were sitting around in their bunkers waiting for the infidels to come strolling into their kill zones. It was enough to drive a trooper to drink, and of course there wasn't any. As war zones ran, Saudi was the uttermost pit of rotten and everybody in the cantonment was behaving like dogs.

Wolochek and the rest of the brass were always uprange in the rear, talking over logistics with the rest of their West Point buddies, most of whom looked like yuppie investment bankers to Crane. The day-to-day life of the post was run by the Baker Company XO, or executive officer, First Lieutenant Ackisson, a squeaky-green black youngster who had been in ROTC at Kansas State less than a year ago, and the various platoon lieutenants— Mahaffey, the Airborne grunt who'd seen some action in Grenada, Petrie, Seafferman, and Rossberg, and under them the sergeants, Noshaug and Shabazz and Huckaby and . . . the new one . . . Crane could never remember his name, a black kid from Boston. Fanand had lasted about two weeks in Saudi and then the dysentery had taken him out. Now Dave Fanand was in a base hospital in Germany and this black kid—Duvall! Duvall had taken over Fanand's platoon.

The XO and the platoon lieutenants were all good kids but once Wolochek had handed out the Orders of the Day, which came over the secure fax every morning from the lieutenant colonel of the battalion, it was pretty much up to the sergeants to execute them while the LTs stood by and nodded approvingly. Crane was happy that the LTs had enough sense to do that. Life in a platoon could get very ugly very fast if you got saddled with a cherry LT who didn't understand how cherry he was.

The entire sector was up by six in the morning, each squad and platoon in formation in front of their hutments, Huckaby, Noshaug, Shabazz, and Duvall to the fore and flanks, platoon LTs at center front, all troopers turned out in gray tee shirts and shorts, everyone carrying his weapon and his gas mask in a canvas bag. DerHorst and Lt. Ackisson, in their "chips suits," would stroll out to the center of the parade and the color guard would raise the Stars and Stripes while someone played a tape recording of reveille.

DerHorst would read the Orders of the Day, Lt. Ackisson would look stern and confirm them, DerHorst would call the roll, and then it was Ackisson's turn to say something uplifting about the war effort.

Since Ackisson was a Baptist, what he usually did was read something from the Old Testament in his high young voice, and then the watch would retire to their breakfasts, and then the company would come left-about into column formation and kick into a two-mile jog around the perimeter. Crane, at the right rear of Mosby's platoon, would sing out the cadence—these days the troops liked the one that ran, "If I die in a combat zone, box me up and ship me home, pin my medals on my chest, tell my mom I done my best, bury my body six feet down, till you hear it hit the ground"—actually a Marine cadence, but it seemed to catch the spirit of the place—and Baker Company would stretch out in a long gray line, shuffling and rolling over the hard ocher dust while the tankers fired up their Abramses in the armor parks and the smell of kerosene and JP5 fuel rose up into the morning sky.

The 1st troopers had been given two weeks to "acclimatize" when they reached Saudi, around the same length of time it took the Navy to ship their armor in from Stateside. The tankers and the IFV drivers had been bussed down to the ports to pick up their vehicles, and tank transporters had been used to bring the armor up to forward dispersal areas. Once in the forward AOs, the tanks and the engineer battalions had been employed building up revetments and perimeter defenses. The usual quartermaster screw-up about gear meant that for the first few days in Saudi, a lot of the grunts had to sleep in their tanks and IFVs while somebody figured out where the hell the tents had got to. Once they arrived, the days settled down into a kind of routine.

There was a morning alert, everybody in formation, tanks up and ready, all grunts with their IFVs, humvees out. Then they'd break for chow, do every kind of daily maintenance that the sergeants could dream up, and run the squads through their paces.

There was a lot of combat drill, working out the bugs with the gear—fewer of them now that the heat had backed off. The biggest problem now was dust, a powder-thin lime dust that seemed to work its way into every seam and armor crack. Getting ready for a drill involved cleaning intake filters and wiping off sensors, lenses, lamps, almost every piece of tactical gear.

Then it was out into the badlands to run formation drills, to make sure the locator systems were working. Communications were always breaking down, and the grunts were having to work hard at seat-of-the-pants navigation because, sure as hell, the SatNav gear would screw up just when you needed it most. A *big* part of that was making sure every trooper understood the uses and abuses of the TI420 GPS, the Texas Instruments Global Positioning System, a hand-held satellite-communications system that placed the troops and the armor in precise positions, or at least, within three hundred feet. Given the staggering emptiness of the region, the complete absence of any kind of landmark reference, these Walkman-sized GPS units would be critical to troop coordination and combined-fire ops once the land war had started. Crane had struggled with the damn things himself until he was an expert with them, and he made sure that everyone under his command knew all there was to know about the GPS systems. Crane had a feeling that the KTO would be a very tricky place for any unit that strayed outside its assigned sectors.

There were too many hotshot chopper and Warthog pilots up there, aching for a kill, and too many fire-and-forget systems in the arsenal. A bunch of guys lost in an IFV would look like a rabbit in the road to a stand-off fighter twenty miles out. Crane intended to lose no one to friendly fire. In southeast Asia, he had seen far more deaths caused by friendly fire than you'd ever see in the afteraction reports. It was his private opinion—and the opinion of a lot of operational troopers—that friendly-fire deaths ran as high as ten to fifteen percent in real combat, but the official line was two percent.

Bullshit. And the Gulf looked like exactly the kind of place where friendly-fire incidents were bound to happen. The terrain was too undifferentiated, and the high-tech systems too twitchy. Add to that mix a lot of green troops and the SatNav GPS rigs that were just a little too sensitive, and you were in a very exposed position. Somewhere in this theater someone was going to wander off and get himself turned into a landmark-sized crater and a mention in next year's training manual.

After the small-unit drills and the lectures and the maintenance details, usually about three in the afternoon, they'd break for whatever recreation the troops could find—football, baseball, poker, listening to the armed forces 'net or to shortwave radios, working on personal hootches to make them livable, organizing lizard races, videotaping each other in the latrines; for some insane reason, the military supplier who had designed the fiberglass latrine stations had made the toilet frame so tall that nobody sitting on the can could reach the floorboards. Since a lot of guys had some sort of low-grade dysentery, this miscalculation about the latrines became one of the more irritating aspects of Desert Shield.

Which, as far as Crane was concerned, was typical Army.

Then the day would end with another full-up buttoned-down alert, the posting of guards, some kind of individual mess service, and so to bed, or at least, to your hootch, to swat gnats, sweep the silica out of your sheets, listen to music, write a letter—Crane even wrote Carla—and, eventually, to sleep. Crane never noticed it at the time, but each and every night he was in Saudi he slept like a stone, a solid, serene, and seamless night of unbroken and dreamless rest.

In November the heat had been brutal, over a hundred by dawn, but gradually that had changed and now, in January, the weather was chilly and the rain that fell was gritty and foul tasting. The only good thing about the onset of winter was that the two-mile run was easier to take.

After the run, the sergeants and the squad leaders would lead the company in a half hour of calisthenics and then they'd take the roll again and dismiss for breakfast.

Breakfast was taken in the company mess tent, long lines of troopers in their BDUs straggling past tables where cooks from the support battalions would dish up creamed corn and scrambled eggs and dry toast, washed down with cups of bitter dark coffee and suprisingly good orange juice. Other days they'd get T-rations, or tray rats, in which something that pretended to be chicken cacciatore and potatoes in butter sauce would float in a green-bean swamp. Tray rats came in twenty varieties and were a hell of a lot better than the chili-mac monstrosities delivered up out of massive steel cauldrons by the Service Support Group.

Some of the troopers had learned how to scrounge the best of the MREs, the Meals Ready to Eat, and they'd skip the company breakfast and eat back in their homemade hootches, listening to armed forces radio or watching CNN on the occasional television set. They'd been in Saudi long enough to build reasonably comfortable hootches out of scrap plywood and packing crates, four to five soldiers to a hootch, so there was a fair amount of domestic comfort around. It made the Saudi winter easier to take and went a long way toward keeping the morale up.

Back on the twenty-fourth of December the sergeants had thrown a huge Christmas dinner for Baker Company in the field hospital tent. They'd had the turkey-loaf dinners that Crane and DerHorst had scrounged in King Khalid Military City—what the troops called "the Emerald City"—and mashed potatoes, cranberry sauce, and stuffing. The brass had arranged for a band and they'd sat around singing carols and swilling near beer and for a little while everybody had managed to forget how much they hated Saudi Arabia and every living raghead within a thousand miles.

Felz had played Santa Claus and the Army Personnel Service Corps had brought in video cameras so everybody could make a fifteen-minute videogram to send back to their wives and families. Mosby and Orso had set up some mikes and Polanyi had borrowed some instruments from the division bandmaster, so later that night they'd listened to Mosby and Orso play pretty good blues. Then some female troops from HQ Company and Div Arty—Division Artillery—had shown up and a dance got going and sometime during the night Crane figured a lot of young kids found a way to make each other feel okay about Christmas. It had been a good time, a welcome break from the mindless routine of camp life.

Most days, after the water break—each trooper was *required* to down three to four gallons every day—the company would break up into work details, equipment maintenance, field exercises of some sort, although no one was allowed to actually approach the Kuwaiti border.

Usually it was latrine duty or policing the grounds, building more hutments or off-loading the endless flatbeds of supplies and gear that rolled into the camp twenty-four hours a day. The food shipments alone took a platoon-sized work detail all day every day to unload, cartons and cartons of heat-resistant chocolate bars or freeze-dried meat, dehydrated scrambled eggs, and the T-rats.

Crane had been told that the daily grocery bill for the U.S. forces in Saudi ran to five million dollars. One thing he knew, none of that was beer.

Since Baker was Combat Infantry, they had no females, and the flatbed trucks were often driven by females from engineer or support battalions, so off-loading flatbed shipments was a popular assignment. It was weird for the eleven-bravo troops to see women so close to the front, but here they were, pushing eighteen-wheelers downrange from the hundred scattered airfields around the desert.

Crane found it hard to get used to, seeing girls no older than high school cheerleaders lugging their M16s, wearing Beretta 9-mms slung low like gunfighters, ear-to-ear grins on their faces, adrenalized by the long-haul driving and the war-zone intensity, laughing and flirting with the troopers surrounding them.

The New American Army, thought Crane.

He could see the day coming when any woman who could qualify would be eligible for the Combat Arms. Crane knew it was coming, that there was no way to stop it. But he felt it was a bad idea, no matter what the politicians said.

In '69, four years in and a month from being ordered out by a colonel at Ben Cat, Crane had pulled some handles and gone up to I Corps to look for a friend who'd been in boot with him at Fort Benning. One thing led to another and he'd finally found the guy in a mobile surgical unit at Camp Radcliff in An Khe. There was a nurse in the same tent, also in bad shape.

An Khe was a big Air Cav base up north, in the middle of a terraced plateau about twenty miles wide, cut down the center by Route 19 from Qui Nhon to Pleiku, near the legendary Mang Mang Pass.

Crane's buddy had stepped on a shit-caked pungi stick while on an LRRP, a Long Range Recon Patrol, under the Deo Mang approaches. By the time he'd been medevacked out, he had some gangrene, so they sent a nurse along with the extraction chopper to give him early treatment, see if they could save the leg.

But the medevac Huey had taken AK fire and the rotor got clipped and they'd gone down in the bush again, Crane's buddy, the nurse, and the crew chief. The VC had watched them go down and had come up hard on their zone—AKs and RPGs, a real hot assault. Crane's buddy—Gorman—and the crew chief and the nurse had put out a lot of fire while they tried to get a new extraction and some air cover. For a while it had looked like they'd be overrun. Gorman knew the area, knew that the VC they were dealing with here were real bastards, into cutting and mutilation, and he found himself thinking about putting one into the nurse, take her out fast, so she wouldn't have to go through something very bad. It was the first time Gorman had ever thought about something like that.

Crane had listened to Gorman's story and thought about it hard. Air cover had come in—a Phantom from Yankee Station offshore—and they'd laid some napalm down right on top of the VC unit. They'd gotten out, but the image had stayed.

Crane figured, yes, women could probably fight. Other armies used them, the Israelis. But it would take a long time to change the men who served with them, especially the men of Crane's generation. They'd always try to cover for the women, no matter how stupid it was. They'd take fire or do some bullshit heroic thing, try to keep a woman safe. A thing like that, it would break the concentration of a fire team, put a lot of strange vibrations into a clear situation. And how many women actually *wanted* to get into combat, anyway? Most of the pressure was coming from fighter pilots, women who knew they could fly as well and fight as well as the men, women who wanted to get the same access to promotions.

But there was a hell of a difference between air war and ground war, between a Tomcat or a Harrier and bayonet work six inches in. Few women were asking for that. Even fewer could do it.

Crane knew it was going to happen. There were enough people back home, feminist activists who would never get within a thousand miles of combat, but who would make damn sure some *other* woman would get her chance to go die for the cause of female equality. But he didn't want to be there when it did. Whatever happened, it was going to be ugly as hell.

Crane stood and watched the troops playing around the flatbed. They were pretty good troops, the men and the women. They were different somehow from the guys he'd served with in Vietnam. These kids, they'd taken a look at the world, seen the situation, and said, "Give me a *job*, please." They were a long way from the sullen and slovenly draftees he'd had to deal with in III Corps. Most of these kids were smarter and healthier and all of them were committed to the job, to finding something in the Army they couldn't get outside. Well, they were about to get it.

Crane had listened to the talk around the HQ today and he knew that tomorrow—tonight—all of this waiting around was going to end. Hussein had come to the end of the line and he wasn't moving. The word was, Hussein figured the U.S. couldn't fight anyway. Hussein knew all about the Vietnam syndrome. He was making international policy based on the goddam Vietnam syndrome, the asshole. Hussein was going to sit there on Kuwait like a hog on a corn pile. Hell, he probably had the place stripped clean by now anyway, aside from the few Kuwaitis his troops hadn't raped or shot. Or both.

So it looked like the Air Force was going to kick it off any second. They'd send in Tomcats and Intruders and Tornadoes, take out the radar and the antiaircraft. Bomb the living shit out of every Iraqi installation in Kuwait and Iraq. Do it again and again. Crane figured maybe a month, maybe less.

But sooner or later, you were going to have to go in there, take the ground away. And the Army was going to do it with Huckaby, Noshaug, Shabazz, and Duvall, with Mosby and Orso and Polanyi and all of the other kids in Baker Company. With *his* kids. And Crane was going to have to be there, watch the kids go in, lead them in, and probably watch a lot of them die. Maybe die himself.

And DerHorst wanted his Combat Infantry Badge, his CIB. Crane hoped that a CIB was *all* DerHorst would get.

The kids? It was a first for him, thinking about the troops like that. Carla had always wanted kids, that had been part of her problem with him, but Crane had dodged the issue, not saying yes, not saying no.

Now he realized, it didn't matter what he wanted. He had them anyway. In Vietnam, he'd been only a year or two older than most of the kids he served with. Now he was forty-nine, exactly old enough to be a father to one of these troops.

The thought rocked him. The hell with taking a woman into combat. How about going to war with your children?

That night came on clear and cold. Crane was doing a perimeter cruise, checking on the wire guards. The base was buttoned down for the night, most of the troops in their hootches, listening to music or watching CNN on their portables. The base was a wide plain of huts and weapons parks, soft yellow light coming from the seams in the walls or glowing through the plastic windscreens of the hootches. Above, a strange field of stars showed through a ragged cloud cover. Over in the tank battalion a crew chief was revving one of the Abrams engines, but, with the exception of the artillery companies, most of the base was silent, waiting. The word was out now and everybody was quiet, as if the whole base was holding its breath and listening. Sometime during the night, orders would come down from HQ and the 1st Infantry gun parks— battalions of the 5th Artillery and the 3rd Air Defense Artillery— would fire some of the first shells in the Gulf War twenty miles downrange into opposing Iraqi positions. The rest of the division was at Defense Condition Red.

Out at the perimeter wire Crane pulled his humvee over beside one of the guard posts. The night air was damp and chilly as a graveyard fence. The trooper challenged him as he opened the door and Crane gave his name and rank. It was Mitchell and his friend Davis. Mitchell was shaping up nicely, a "strack" soldier with brains and a good attitude.

Out beyond the post, the terrain was shadowed and unreal, a vast gray emptiness as flat as mercury on a plate, stretching away into a luminous distance. A soft light lay on it, like a fine silver dust. There was no moon but the stars were clear and hard as shattered glass.

"Anything yet, Mitchell?"

"Nothing out there, Sergeant. I been using the night-vision goggles and all the motion sensors are quiet. Had something a while back in sector four but it was too small to be anything."

"A rat, likely."

They stood looking out into the desert for a while. Crane had no idea of exactly when the air campaign was going to start, but it had to be soon. All over the theater the air crews would be working on the jets. On the carriers, the *Midway* and the *Wisconsin,* Tomcats would have been fired up a while back. There'd be Intruders loaded with Harpoons and HARM missiles idling at King Khalid and other bases all over Saudi. The B-52s would already have taken off from Diego Garcia. The Airborne Warning and Control System, known as AWACS, and reconfigured Hercs would be on station over the gulf. And somewhere out there in front of them, Army Special Forces teams were already in position around Iraqi forward radar stations.

Every single target would have been analyzed and a weapons assignment developed. They'd blow the forward radar, either by a Special Forces operation or with smart bombs, missiles, whatever it took. Kill the radar and then come in from everywhere, out of the night, timed to hit their targets all at the same time, and first on the list would be the Iraqi Air Force.

So far, the 1st hadn't seen a single Iraqi fighter, but once the air war kicked off, the 1st would have Kiowas and Apaches in the air, and AWACS cover, and fighter protection, waiting for an Iraqi retaliatory strike. The best information was that it would get hot very soon, that the 1st would take long-range artillery fire, maybe some Scuds, certainly strafing runs and missile attacks from Foxbats and Fulcrums.

Right now, it was as quiet as the base ever got. Even the tanks had shut down and now there was only that generalized murmur of compressors and generators and air conditioners and electronics spread out across the camp.

Crane patted Mitchell on the shoulder and turned to walk back to his humvee. Out of the corner of his eye he saw a red flare far away on the northern horizon.

Mitchell and Davis saw it too and they all stood there watching it flare and fade. In a little while they heard a faint rumble, like very distant thunder. Back behind them they heard the camp come to life, some whistles blowing, troopers heading for their ready stations. Some of the tanks were coughing into life. Boots crunched and scrabbled, voices called out. Far away in the north, there were more red flares, and now yellow, and suddenly a thin streamer of green fire rose up from the land.

Golden BBs. Tracer fire. Antiaircraft fire.

Now from the south they heard the sound of jets. Suddenly they were overhead, invisible, the roar of their engines hammering the earth. Five, maybe six, they could see the blue fire of their after-burners as they barreled over into Kuwait, moving at over a thousand miles an hour.

More jets thundered up out of the south, heading into Kuwait. The ground rattled and shook with their passage. Troopers were cheering and running. Out in the north the terrain started to light up with fire and the distant rumbling became constant, punctuated with the solid thud of heavy bombs and the sharper crack of missile impacts. Most of the troops were running up to the perimeter line now, shouting and cheering.

The night sky was full of the sound of jets going north, a rising, hammering roar that deafened and shook, an almost continuous sound that vibrated through the earth and ripped at the air.

Christ, thought Crane, watching the night sky light up in the north. Better you than me.

Mitchell was inside the post, digging around in his gear. He came back outside with a small Sony portable television. He set it on top of Crane's humvee and about fifty troops gathered in, pushing and shoving, as CNN got their shit together and the air war came to the undivided attention of Peter Arnett and the rest of the press corps in downtown Baghdad. It was a surreal moment for Crane, standing there in the middle of the Saudi desert, the night sky full of thunder and aircraft, a war going on fifteen klicks away, surrounded by kids from all over the U.S., watching rockets and missiles slam home in downtown Baghdad. Arnett was saying something about missiles, about not seeing any jets. Arnett didn't get it yet, hadn't heard about the stand-off capability of the Eagle and the British Tornado and the Stealth fighter-bombers. You never saw the jet that killed you. It was fifteen miles away. Behind Arnett the Baghdad skyline was a pulsing green field of bright lines and intersecting webs of antiaircraft fire and hot red flares of impacting bombs. It looked like hell's videogame.

Yeah, thought Crane. Kill them all.

Drop a nuke on them. Turn the whole region into black glass.

Maybe I won't have to take one of these kids into combat. Maybe this will do the trick, send Hussein a wake-up call. It was a nice thought. Crane managed to hold on to it for about an hour.

They spent the rest of the night watching fighter sorties and artillery volleys, and, in the rare silences, listening to the far-off muted thunder of aerial bombardment. It was a sound you could feel deep in your chest and sometimes they thought they could smell a whiff of burning, of cordite and gasoline in flames.

Crane and the off-duty troops stood by the perimeter fence, on top of the sandbagged entrenchments and the .50-caliber positions, like spectators at a Fourth of July picnic. For most of the cherry troopers around him, this was something like a celebration. But for Crane, it was an arc light raid, a Buff, or B-52, mission over the jungle, and in spite of the rain and the building chill in all his bones, he felt a kind of heat rising in his belly and a very old feeling came back to him like a remembrance of his youth. Crane felt something close to but not quite happiness. Crane felt the *size* of the thing they were inside, the guns and the planes and the thousands of men under arms here in this desolate landscape, the war rising up around them like a sandstorm or a Kansas tornado.

Later he described it as a feeling of peace, of being where he should be, of being a part of a long chain of lives, and in that moment knowing that if he died in this war—if he had died in Vietnam—that part of him would never die, and that was why he was still in the Army and still eleven bravo.

CHAPTER SEVEN

PUNTS

The next morning, brutally early, Crane heard a sound that took him back more than twenty years, a rhythmic beating, drumming sound getting louder and louder. He looked out past Felz's bright pink neck as they crowded the hootch door. A Huey chopper with MAC markings was landing in the company parade square, its cargo bay wide open, a helmeted crew chief leaning on the sling-loaded M60. Behind him Captain Wolochek was staring out at Crane's hootch, his thin West Pointer face bright with windburn and enthusiasm. A crowd of people in flak jackets and brand-new chocolate-chip fatigues was pushing against the restraining net.

Crane heard Baumgart's voice in his left ear. "Oh, shit, it's the JIB rats!"

"JIB rats?"

Felz looked at Crane over his shoulder.

"PAOs from the Joint Information Bureau. The PUNTS! The PUNTS have come to Hell."

"What're PUNTS?"

Wolochek was out now and striding purposefully toward Crane's

114

hootch door, followed by a string of people, men and women, and a couple of guys manhandling a video camera and some lights.

DerHorst stepped out of the platoon latrine across the lane and watched the crowd closing in on them.

"Hey, Pete," said Baumgart. "The PUNTS are here!"

"What the hell are PUNTS?" said DerHorst, louder, losing his patience.

Baumgart seemed to get a little larger. His grin tugged at both jug ears.

"PUNTS. People of Utterly No Tactical Significance."

"Oh," said DerHorst, turning around to go back into the latrine. "You mean the press guys. Tell them I have infectious dysentery, okay?"

Wolochek had reached Crane by now. Crane stepped out of the hootch and saluted, trying to straighten his tee shirt and BDU pants. He had shaving cream on his left cheek. Wolochek smiled and returned the salute, giving everyone his best middle-management attitude.

"Ladies and gentlemen, I'd like you to meet our resident combat expert, First Sergeant Dee Crane. Sergeant Crane is a Vietnam combat vet and one of our foremost infantry troopers."

Crane, being a lifer, did not say the first thing that came to mind. He looked around at the reporters—all of them flushed and giddy from the chopper ride, their faces bright and eager, a couple of older reporters trying to look bored and cynical, some talking head he recognized from the ABC affiliate in Wichita—and it came to him that he definitely should have bought some stock in Banana Republic. He wiped at the soap on his face and tried to work up what he hoped was a charming corporate smile.

"Well, sir, as these folks can see, this is a forward position here"—he swept his arm up and toward the north—"so much of the duty is combat readiness. We keep the soldiers in training, carry out various drills, conduct perimeter patrols. And of course, the armor requires a lot of maintenance—"

One of the bored-looking older reporters cut in, shoving a Pearlcorder in Crane's face.

"Sergeant, the word is these Abrams of yours are a military disaster, that they stall out in dust storms, can't take the heat. Would you say that's a fair statement?"

"No, sir, I'd say that's bullshit."

The man's face twisted a bit and he shut off the Pearlcorder, looking at Wolochek for some kind of backup. Wolochek's face was impassive. The reporter came back to Crane.

"There was a lot of talk about the Abrams before this war, and you're an experienced tanker—"

"Actually, sir, I'm Infantry. The tankers are—"

"Well, it's all Army, I mean, the First is a tank division."

"Elements of the First are armored, sir. But this unit is mechanized infantry. We fight with tanker support, or we maneuver in IFVs and deploy to achieve various tactical effects that—"

"Maybe, but the Abrams—"

"The M One is working out fine here, sir. We had some trouble with the filters and we changed them and now they're just fine."

Someone else broke in, a woman in her late twenties, dark haired, with a thin and aggressive face that looked as if it was locked into a permanent pout. Her accent very upstate New York, it made Crane think of home for the first time in weeks. She was wearing a brand-new Army-issue flak jacket over her tan Banana Republic jungle suit. She had one of those stupid-looking Tilley hats jammed down over her head.

"Sergeant, how do you feel about having to die for Zionist imperialism?"

"For *what?*"

"It's a known fact that the Zionist forces in Washington are behind this effort to crush the Arab—"

The other reporters were groaning but she pressed on, raising her voice against the murmurs and the rising morning wind from the desert.

"Crush the growth of Arab solidarity by destroying Iraq, and your men are going to get killed trying to do that—"

"None of my men are going to get killed, lady."

"Sergeant, you're facing one of the world's best armies, dug in behind concrete bunkers and hardened steel—determined fighters who will resist Zionist aggression—"

Crane was looking over her shoulder at Wolochek. Wolochek was talking into his cellular phone, his face hidden by his helmet.

"They're sand berms, ma'am."

"What?"

"The Iraqis downrange here are dug in behind sand, ma'am. Not concrete."

"Well, my point is—the Iraqi positions are very strong, and—"

Crane was kicking at the sand under his feet, piling it up in a small mound. "See that, lady?"

They all looked down at the sand mound.

"Yes, and—"

Crane stepped back and drove his boot through the mound, sending sand and lumps of dirt flying into the air. Some of it bounced off her flak jacket and her tan pants. She stepped back, her face in a knot.

"That's the difference between concrete and sand. Come the day, we're gonna go through those poor bastards just like that."

"Bravado won't help you when—"

"Any other questions, people?"

They all started up at once.

"Is it true that your infrared night-vision scopes won't work in the daytime?"

"No, sir, and we don't *need* them in the daytime."

"What happens to all the expended shell casings? Do they just get left there, or does someone pick them up?"

"Someone picks up every last one of them and mails them back to the manufacturer for a refund."

"How do you feel about not having any beer over here?"

"Cranky."

"Can we meet some female soldiers?"

"Not right here. Baker is eleven bravo. There are no female eleven bravos."

"Is that fair?"

"I don't know, ma'am."

"Women make up fifty-two percent of the American population. Doesn't it seem unfair to you that they are not allowed full access to all aspects of a military career?"

"Well, that's a little out of my AO, ma'am. Not everybody *wants* to get into Combat Arms. Not everybody can do it. Most of the recruits we get, they're choosing any MOS but Combat Arms. We have more female Range Data Specialists than males. Is that fair? Range Data is a sure-fire job getter after you DEROS. All that technical stuff, and most of the people in it are either women or black. Is that okay? Is that discrimination? It's a matter of what somebody wants to do, and what they *can* do. I don't think we should be using the Army for lab work. That's not what an army is for."

"The Army represents the people, Sergeant."

"The Army fights wars, ma'am. The rest is PR."

"Would you like to see more women in combat positions?"

Christ, lady . . . give it a rest. Crane heard that little internal growl that his temper made when somebody woke it up. He gave her a big smile.

"I'd like to see more women in all kinds of positions."

They were all closing in now, all speaking at once.

"When do you think the ground war will start?"

"Any minute now."

"Do you think the time of the infantry soldier is past? Shouldn't we just let the Air Force take care of Saddam?"

"The only ground you hold in a war is the ground an infantry soldier is standing on. You don't hold territory by flying over it and dropping bombs on it. All that can do is make the territory dangerous for your enemy, and as soon as you *stop* bombing it, he's back. To *win* a war, you have to control the land, and that means infantry. Sooner or later, a grunt has to go in and take it for you."

"Are your men ready to fight the Iraqis on the ground, Sergeant?"

"They are. They are very ready."

"How do you attack a tank? Do your men surround one and shoot it down, like, shoot for the engine or the radiator?"

Christ.

"Well, sir, the Bradleys are armed with TOW missiles, they're wire guided and pretty effective, but we use a combined assault doctrine against tanks, pretty much bring in whatever we want, Warthogs with Maverick missiles that can hit a tank from twenty-five miles out. But the main thing here, it's tank-to-tank, and the M Ones have a very good sighting system, their laser range finders are computer linked, and they each carry forty rounds of HESH and HEAT shot—"

"What do those letters mean?"

"HESH is High-Explosive Squash Head, that's a shell, and there's shot—which is High-Explosive Antitank. The HEAT rounds are discarding sabots—"

"What are sabots?"

"A sabot is a casing around the core of the shot which makes the shot fit the barrel of the gun. When the round is fired, the sabot flakes off in flight, discards, leaving the core of the shot, which is made of depleted uranium—"

"My God, it's a nuclear weapon?"

"No, sir. Depleted uranium is just the hardest kind of metal we can make. The core is very streamlined—no more than a few inches long, about an inch and a half wide, but it has great speed and penetrating power."

"What happens when one of these rounds hits an enemy tank?"

Crane considered telling him the literal truth, which was that it made a kind of putrid black paste out of every living thing inside the tank, that no real tanker ever went near a destroyed tank because the smell coming from the inside of that tank was something you never forgot, a combination of burned pork and rotten meat. And the way you knew one of the tanks in your command had been hit, you heard a brief click on the radio carrier wave as the tank's electronics incinerated, and the microphone in the commander's helmet incinerated. But he didn't.

"It's usually a kill, sir. The enemy tank is destroyed."

"How many times can one of these M Ones fire?"

"Their maximum rate of fire is twelve rounds a minute."

"What's the likelihood of a kill at that rate?"

"It's not likely that the tankers would acquire that many targets in a minute, but if they did, I'd say their accuracy rate is close to one hundred percent for aimed fire."

"In the Iran-Iraq War, the Iranians used motor scooters against tanks, didn't they? A driver and a guy with a shoulder-mounted antitank gun. What if the Iraqis do that to you? I mean, each tank is like three million dollars, isn't it? And how much is a Honda?"

"It's the job of the infantry to protect the tankers from individual tank killers. We are right there alongside the tankers, and that is part of our job."

"All these boys, they look so young."

"Yes, ma'am. Soldiers are usually pretty young."

"But you're not, Sergeant. Why are you still in the Army?"

Good question. None of your fucking business. But a good question.

"I guess I just got caught up in it, ma'am."

"I guess you're like a father to these soldiers, would you say that?"

This from the older reporter, the talking head from Wichita.

"No, sir. These soldiers don't need a father. They need a sergeant."

"Are you allowed to have pets here, Sergeant?"

"Only lice. But they have to be cleared by security. Wanna meet mine?"

"What has the Army done to help prevent the spread of AIDS over here?"

Crane stared at the reporter.

"I guess that's what the bio-warfare suits are for."

"Does the Army supply condoms?"

Jeez.

"Yes, they do, but only in olive drab and camouflage."

"Are we prepared for this war to go ballistic, Sergeant?"

"I'm not sure I follow, sir."

"You know, when a missile takes off? Goes ballistic?"

"When something 'goes ballistic,' sir, that means that its power source or propellant has ceased and the object is now falling. As in gravity driven. If something goes ballistic, it means that it is falling along a trajectory. Or not. Like when a plane crashes, the Air Force says that the plane 'vertically deployed into the terrain.' That's what ballistic means. So, in answer to your question, if this war goes ballistic, I'll try to get out from under it."

Crane knew he was fucking with the guy, but so what? The guy was a PUNT, they were every last one of them completely *non*-operational. If Bob came over the wire right now, they'd all be grabbing their dicks and crying for their mothers. Fuck 'em. Fuck them all.

"Is it true that the Marines are better fighters than the Army?"

"Until a war starts, yes."

"How does this war compare to Vietnam, Sergeant?"

"Vietnam was way off to the left and further south."

"That's not a serious answer, Sergeant."

"No, sir, I'm sorry. Vietnam was a counterinsurgency war, fought by small units in the bush, with limited air cover and limited goals. Desert Storm is a large-scale multidivision multiforce combined op with full air superiority and open terrain, and a clearly defined OpFor—Opposing Force—and a clearly defined goal, the departure of Iraqi forces from the Kuwaiti Theater of Operations. Vietnam was fought with conscript forces and had limited domestic backing. This operation has the full backing of the American people and is being fought with an all-volunteer Army. Does that help you, sir?"

"What's a counterinsurgency war, sir?"

"You don't have to call me sir, ma'am. I'm a noncom. Counterinsurgency war is, I guess you'd call it guerrilla warfare. Your enemy is native to the territory, he hides in the civilian population, he uses terror and infiltration, he won't close with large units, fights hit-and-run, ambushes, fades back into the bush. It's a war of attrition, ma'am."

"Which kind is worse, Sergeant?"

"More men get killed in large multiunit operations. The First and Second World Wars were combined-forces ops. In Vietnam, over ten years, we lost fifty-eight thousand men. In the taking of Okinawa, we lost forty-seven thousand men. In the Third Battle of Ypres, the total loss—the KIA—was a half million men. A million

Russians died in the Kiev pocket in 1941. The First Infantry Division was only in the First World War for about eighteen months and we had twenty-three thousand casualties. The First was in combat in World War Two for . . . four hundred and forty-three days and nights, and we had twenty-one thousand killed and wounded. We were in Vietnam for almost five years, and we had two thousand guys killed in action. The First World War was obviously the worst kind of war, because it was a long tactical war of intensification, of increasing violence, like the Civil War. On September seventeenth in 1862 over twenty-six thousand Union and Confederate soldiers died in one day. That place was known as Antietam. It was the bloodiest day in our history."

"You're something of a historian, Sergeant. Do all the noncommissioned officers in your unit know this sort of thing?"

What a question. . . . Only a civilian would ask it.

"The First is my home, sir. We all make it a point to know these things. That's how a guy remembers who he is, and it's how the division remembers *you*, if something happens."

"So it's like, ah, a team spirit thing?"

"Nobody dies playing volleyball, sir."

"Do you hate the Iraqis, Sergeant?"

"Not yet."

"When will you?"

"When I lose a soldier."

"You said you didn't think that would happen."

"It won't."

"How do you know that?"

"I won't let it happen."

"Are you personally ready to kill an Iraqi if you have to?"

"If I'm not, I've been collecting my pay under false pretenses."

"You've been in actual combat, Sergeant? In Vietnam?"

Crane braced himself. He nodded.

"Did you hate the enemy then?"

"Yes, sir. I did."

"Doesn't hating the enemy interfere with your job as a soldier?"

"My job as a soldier is to find the enemy, close with him, and kill him." Crane didn't feel like saying that *nobody* who had actually fought in Vietnam had a detached attitude. If the war hadn't been personal, a thing of hatred and corrosive anger, then you were either In the Rear with the Gear—a REMF—or you hadn't gone to Vietnam at all. Any time Crane heard some guy say he was sorry about the VC and that it hadn't been personal, he knew he was drinking with someone who had never been in a firefight.

"Yes. So, strong emotions like hatred, wouldn't that be unprofessional? Make you lose your control? Endanger your troops?"

"You ever been in combat, sir?"

"I covered the Panama operation, Sergeant. I've seen war."

"Seeing a war isn't like being in one."

"What's the difference? I was right there on the front line, right beside the soldiers. I was in danger too."

"Did you carry a weapon?"

"No. That wouldn't—that wasn't my job."

Crane studied the man's jutting florid face. Guys like this were why Crane hated the press and especially hated war reporters. They were usually more macho than any soldier, radiated "tougher than thou," saw themselves as On the Edge. All that Hemingway bullshit. What do you say to guys like that? For Crane, war reporters were vultures. Vampires. They lived on your blood, could hardly wait to see you spill it, get in there, get their boots in it, tell themselves they were hard guys, right in the dark heart of the thing. The guy wouldn't leave it alone. And now Crane saw the *big* question shaping up behind the guy's eyes, saw the sick and hectic flicker in his head.

"What's it like to kill, Sergeant?"

Crane thought about pulling out his 9-mill and showing him. He felt his right arm tighten.

Then, in a burst of dirty thunder, a flight of Warthogs hammered through their airspace, pushing north. In the north, a string of golden pearls rose into the sky, wavering, searching for targets. Then a low deep rhythmic booming seemed to rise up from the ground and the air turned thick with concussion.

"What's that, Sergeant?"

"Arc light, sir. B-fifty-two strikes."

"Are we using nuclear bombers on the Iraqis, sir?"

"No, sir. That's gravity ordnance."

"What's gravity ordnance?"

"Iron bombs."

"What guides them?"

"When what you're aiming at is the earth, it's hard to miss."

"So it's indiscriminate bombing, then?" said the anti-Zionist.

"No, ma'am. We're definitely discriminating."

"Against defenseless Iraqis."

"Yep."

"That's hardly fair."

"Nope. I'll cry all night. Wanna watch me?"

"What's your name, Sergeant?"

"Crane. Dee Crane. I have it tattooed on my dick. Would you like to see it?" He reached for the buttons on his BDUs. Wolochek was suddenly in the middle.

"Thanks a lot, Sergeant. I'll take it from here."

"Thank you, sir. May I retire, sir?"

Wolochek sent him a blistering look. Crane felt it on the back of his head as he walked away. Another flight of jets thundered by, going north. The air seemed to thicken and coil and the ground turned into a drumhead as something deep and terrible rumbled through it. Crane looked up and saw a small diamond of light through the tattered clouds. Another Buff. More arc light. Behind him the chatter of the press pool faded. Crane felt light-headed, crazily manic. An intense joy pierced him and the muscles in his belly tingled and burned.

What does it feel like to kill, Sergeant?

Hard to describe, sir.

Let me show you.

CHAPTER EIGHT

THE BUFFS

It was like living under a bridge in the middle of the longest lousiest January in upstate New York history. For two weeks now, the sky had been low down and greasy gray, sopping wet and dripping steadily down on the 1st Division huddled in hootches and tents and garages, a dreary and relentless rain. Sixteen of the troopers had dysentery and everyone else was just waiting for a turn. Others suffered from persistent coughs and mild fevers. Troopers were spending more time in the latrines than in their hootches. In the night the sound of a thousand men hacking and coughing and snuffling was a continuous low-level background murmur. The air reeked of cordite and oil, and visibility was down to a couple of hundred yards. The days started out cold and dim and stayed that way, and the nights were long and full of distant thunder from the B-52 strikes and the fighter missions.

The sector controlled by the 1st was part of the gateway lane used by all coalition aircraft returning from bombing missions, so the sound of jets was almost constant during the night. The tank crews were being kept at it, firing up and idling their Abramses, checking the weapons systems, practicing column and echelon for-

125

mations along with IFVs and humvees from the 16th. Under that there was the constant drone of compressors and generators and the reek of camp cooking and the damp smell of thousands of men and women in close quarters, and the wet-wool smell of the desert itself.

Crane had given up trying to sleep through the B-52 runs as had almost everyone else in the country. The Baker Company LTs, Ackisson, Petrie, Seafferman, and Rossberg, had started up a low-stakes poker game in their hootch, and they spent most of their off-hours in it, drinking Cherry Coke and Jolt cola and passing around bits of military scrip. In the weariness of waiting, the lines were drawn between the officers and the enlisted men, with the noncoms coming down on the enlisted side. Shabazz and Noshaug and Duvall had taken a hootch together about fifty feet from Crane's quarters. Huckaby, still missing Fanand, who had been his hootchmate, was living alone in their old hootch across the square.

Crane and the other noncoms, including all the platoon sergeants from Baker, would gather together by one of the sandbag .50-caliber machine-gun positions on the northern perimeter, share some Kool-Aid, and watch in silence as the bombs fell from seven miles up onto Iraqi troop concentrations across the line.

It was a holy sight, with some of the same resonances that you got if you stood in the doorway of a cathedral and looked down the nave at the vaulted dome. The Buffs were the war gods; invisible, towering, relentless, cold.

Each Buff could deliver eighteen two-thousand-pound gravity bombs or a higher number of lighter ordnance. They'd fly way up there beyond the clouds and the stink of the oil well fires, six or seven miles up in a night sky so clean and cold and full of stars it hurt the infantry just to think about it. There'd be three in each shell, flying maybe all the way from Diego Garcia or even from England. They had a range of seventy-five hundred miles—half the world—and were each over a hundred and sixty feet long with a wingspan of one hundred and eighty-five feet. White on the belly and mottled gray on top, like sharks, they were the original angels of darkness, the bringer of nuclear fire, as elemental as an earthquake in the imaginations of a ground trooper.

If there was anything in the wide world of war that marked off the uttermost distance between two kinds of terror, it was the seven miles that lay between the men of the 1st Infantry and those SAC B-52s way up there in the night sky. When a stick would hit ground, the concussion could be felt like a soft blow in the chest fifty miles away, especially in this damp winter air. Underfoot, the earth would tremble and vibrate—seem to liquefy—and then the sound would come, a low growling rumble, rising and falling in the wind, with a bass drum percussion under it, as deep as the bones of the earth.

Standing out there on the line, under the lowering sky, each trooper was alone in that moment, staring out at the northern border and seeing in his mind what it would be like to be *under* those bombs, to know that there was nothing he could do to stop them in their long fall, feeling his muscles tense, knowing that just overhead, just above the roof of his hootch, a two-thousand-pound iron bomb full of explosives was just about to smash him fifty yards into the earth, turn him into pink mist for the wind to take. You could almost feel sorry for Bob and his buddies over there. Almost.

They'd had arc light missions in Vietnam, in the Trapezoid and the Song Be corridor, the Triangle, Thunder Road. They sounded exactly like these B-52 missions in Kuwait and Iraq. It gave him a weird sense of vertigo, and if he closed his eyes, he'd be back there on the veranda of the Peacock Bar or in Vhin Drin Bau on the Plain of Jars, his nose full of the scent of cigarette smoke and jasmine and cold beer, and there would be that same sound, the low snake of sound roiling and rumbling down from the green mountains to the northeast and the faint far-off flicker of white light.

It was a sound he loved, a sound that made him feel part of something immense, part of a power that lived inside that low and eternal distant thunder, a power that could pound a whole nation into the mud, a power to keep you safe.

He heard a short sniffle next to him and turned to see the pale wet face of Captain Wolochek surrounded by a streaming poncho. He was standing next to him in the dark, watching the arc light missions up in Kuwait.

"Hello, Dee. Hell of a show, isn't it?"

"That it is, sir."

"You know, they say the *Missouri* is shelling right now. From twenty miles away, something like that. First time since Korea."

"Yes, sir. I saw her once, in Norfolk. Amazing ship."

Wolochek was silent for a while. His nose was red and running and he looked about twenty years old, a skinny kid from Washington State.

"All of this . . . in a way, we're lucky."

"How come, sir?"

"To be inside something this . . . it's historic. This is our nation, this is America. The most powerful nation on earth. This is a time, we'll tell all our kids. Not many men live to be a part of something like this."

Crane looked at Wolochek and saw to his surprise that Wolochek was crying. At least, his eyes were wet. Maybe it was just a cold or the rain. Crane felt a strange intimacy and also an acute embarrassment. He looked back at the skyline. Out there beyond the banked clouds and the rain-swept terrain, they could just make out a brief white billowing light that lit up the underside of the storm front.

Wolochek snuffled again and wiped his face with his woolen gloves.

"We'll go in soon, Dee. Baker looks good. Ackisson has the junior LTs all strack. The boys look good." He looked over at Shabazz and Noshaug and Duvall, smiled at them, an officer's smile, thin and distant. "Your men look good. The colonel asked me to tell you."

"They are, sir. They'll do well."

More silence. DerHorst and Felz were watching them from a few yards away. Huckaby had appeared from somewhere and Noshaug and Shabazz and Duvall were edging away from the brass, hiding their cans of cola, afraid that Wolochek was going to ask to share one. But Wolochek wasn't watching them. He was looking at the B-52 strikes in the distance.

"You ever go in after something like that, Dee?"

"Yes, sir. They once called in a B-52 as close air support, it was in Two Corps, during the Tet counteroffensive."

"Did it work?"

Crane thought it over.

"That was jungle, sir. Wet mud."

"I know that, Dee."

"No, sir. It didn't. We needed air bursts for that, but the strike was too close. So the ground bursts went up and the mud took most of the concussion. A Spooky, maybe a whole flight of Spookies, or an air-burst Daisy Cutter, that might have done the job. But Charlie was dug in deep. Soon as the bombing stopped, Charlie came out and shot us up pretty good."

"Yeah . . . same as in the St.-Mihiel Salient."

Crane remembered it, but he let Wolochek tell it.

"We were there, you know? I mean us, the Big Red. The Krauts had held that piece of terrain since 1914. We went in on September eleventh, 1918. The Allies spent a week. Second biggest artillery barrage in the history of war. Tons of shells into the German lines. But that was mud too, and the shells blew up but the concussion, the shrapnel, was lost in the mud. So when we got there, the Krauts were all ready. We took it anyway, but it was hard. Same thing happened in the Argonne. You can't put too much faith in Arty, nor in the Buffs up there. Sooner or later, it's gonna be a grunt has to go in there."

Crane braced himself for the lecture. All of this was doctrine developed at Fort Monroe, part of the rethinking of military strategy that arose out of the world-class cluster-fuck disasters of the Indochina War. Creighton Abrams had been Chief of Staff in those days, and he pegged William DePuy, a 1st Infantry commander, to do the reworking. The assignment involved rewriting military operational guidelines—what the Army called Training and Doctrine Command, TRADOC for short.

Although strategic doctrine was the responsibility of the Army War College, the operational tactics the Army would use to achieve the government's strategic aims were often worked out by officers assigned to TRADOC at Fort Monroe and the Command and Gen-

eral Staff College at Fort Leavenworth, back in Kansas. DePuy's
main contribution to TRADOC development had been to remind
the pin pushers in the War College that Vietnam had shown them
all how god-awful the combined-service operational guidelines actually were. Incompatible radio frequencies. Screwed-up support
assignments. Operational inconsistencies. Greed and power grabbing and every kind of career-blasting venality.

Interservice rivalry had caused a lot of needless deaths, and the
worst of the rivalries was between the Army and the Air Force,
because deep in its sky blue heart, the Air Force nurtured the
obsession that the U.S. didn't actually need an army. Why take
the ground in a war when you could simply fly over it and blow
everything on it and under it into plasma? In the infantry, this was
known as the barrage theory, and it was an old artillery obsession.
Crane remembered the theory of barrage from noncom school.

In the First World War, the science of mass killing had made a
kind of quantum leap, as the generals drew, however glacially, the
appropriate inferences from the rising slag heap of the dead. The
Industrial Age had arrived on the battlefield, and war was now
going to be more a matter of increasing mechanical *intensity* and
less one of massed columns wheeling by the numbers, cavalry
flanking runs, concentrated musketry in a British square. Maxim,
Krupp, and Browning had changed all that. So it was decided that
artillery would provide cover—the French word for "barrage"
means "toll bar" or "barrier"—for infantry advances, would, in
the surgical sense, "prep the site" for a military operation.

The idea was—still is—that a coordinated delivery of combined
shells and explosives, advanced by the numbers up the terrain
toward the enemy position, would clear the way for the infantry,
would *shield* the infantry, and would very likely destroy the enemy's
will to resist. In the Argonne, as at Villers-Cotterêts, the infantry
assault was timed to begin shortly after the artillery barrage had
ended. As a matter of operational fact, the sooner the infantry got
themselves into the enemy lines once the barrage had lifted, the
better. Crane had heard about the battle for Hamburger Hill in
Vietnam, an Airborne Greasy Grass, and they'd all seen the old
black-and-white films of the Somme. Unfortunately, it's in areas

such as this—matters of timing, estimates of troop readiness, calculating for luck of all kinds—that military planners have the poorest records. Battlefield maneuver is a very complicated affair, rather like trying to herd lemmings, and the one thing that you can always count on is not that *something* will go wrong, but that nearly *everything* will foul up to some degree or another. FUBAR is just a modern word for what Napoleon used to call the "Fog of War."

It's the army that *reacts* best to these random disasters that usually wins the struggle. Eventually. Or so TRADOC maintained.

Throughout the First World War, and in many ways in every war to follow, including the one Crane was in right now, an artillery barrage consisted of massed guns firing in unison. Field artillery—eighteen-pounders and five-inch howitzers—fired shrapnel and high explosives out to around six thousand yards. Medium artillery—called Arty in military slang—fired sixty-pound shells out to ten thousand yards. And heavy howitzers lobbed rounds ranging from one hundred pounds to fourteen-hundred-pound shells at a very high angle of descent out to eleven thousand yards.

Wire cutting was the basic intent of the shelling in the First World War. Berm destruction was the aim in the Gulf. And the collapse of trench walls, the ruin of revetments, the eruption of bunkers and bodies. The rain of combined shot, shell, shrapnel, wire-cutting ordnance, heavy howitzer shells, all of the torrent of heavy metal and hot iron was part of a cold mechanical calculation. So many tons of iron equalled such and such proportion of physical effect. This is the kind of thing they study at war colleges and naval academies. There are textbooks and logarithms and tables and charts that make it seem an exact science. The idea is, keep it up long enough, and you cannot fail to have destroyed—or seriously impaired—a tactically useful amount of men, materiel, fortifications, supplies, weapons, revetments, communications, horses, ordnance, wagons, kitchens, tunnels, latrines, goats, cabbage patches, Revolutionary Guard Divisions, barbed-wire entanglements . . . whatever.

Then you *lift* the barrage—like a tollgate bar—and send in the infantry, who overrun the enemy lines—bayoneting and shooting as they go—and you have a breakthrough, you are into the enemy's flank or in his rear echelons, which are poorly protected, and if you do it right, and follow it up with good lines of supply, you have a rout! The enemy flies before you in disarray, and, in time, if you set your cavalry snarling at his heels, in panic.

This was doctrine at the time, and in many ways it still is. There are many officers in the modern military establishment—in particular old-line SAC commanders in the Air Force—who believe that the time of the infantry is over, that air power and tactical nuclear weapons are all that a country needs to pursue its imperatives in the global arena.

What Crane remembered from his last war, and what DePuy had tried to get the rest of the services to realize, was that, unfortunately for the assaulting infantry, the real effects of combined Arty—or smart bombs and Cruise missiles and "gravity ordnance"—were never quite as planned.

As soon as the barrage or the bombing was halted, everyone knew that an assault was coming. The sooner the assault was launched, the better chances it had for success in what was then known as "the race for the parapet," and the kill rate depended on the distances.

But what about all that iron rain?

The answer was in the earth itself. The aim of gunnery is to deliver a preordained number of shells into every square yard of the beaten zone—the area where the shells are aimed to fall. In one of the great shelling exchanges of the war, at the Somme, the British had about forty thousand men working for about a week to fire thirty thousand *tons* of shells into the German lines, into an area thirty thousand yards wide and about one thousand yards deep.

They did a fine job.

Every thousand square yards of that beaten zone got an average of thirty shells fired into it, for a total of around two million shells. Yet when the barrage was lifted—it went on day and night for a week—and the infantry came out to race for the enemy parapet, the Germans popped up on their fire steps and decimated the advancing troops in their thousands. By the end of the second day on the Somme, over *sixty thousand men* had been killed, almost a half million British soldiers had been wounded, and another two hundred thousand French soldiers. Even today, almost a century later, the Germans are still evasive about the number of men they lost. But if you walk the territory, you can still come across a bone or a fragment of brass. The country around the Somme River is, in many ways, the world's largest ossuary.

Every modern soldier with the slightest sense of history knows that the infantry assaults along the Allied front composed the largest slaughter of armed men in the history of the planet, and the loss of life has never been equalled, not at Dresden or Hiroshima, and may *never* be matched in the time of man.

So, as Crane's instructor had put it, what went wrong?

First of all, of the two million shells launched into the German lines, almost half were shrapnel, shells loaded with steel balls, and most of these steel balls were fired into mud, exploding at or below ground level. Their cumulative effect was—stunningly—minimal.

As any infantryman knows, what kills is high explosive. Concussion and brute ripping force. Concussion to blow out your lungs or to shred your arteries, to cause a thousand ruptures in your spine and in your brain, and brute explosive force to squash you flat or take you apart in pieces or to smear you like a red stain across a revetment.

So the defenders survived and came out of their holes in time to take part in the final foot race to the machine-gun positions.

And since the attackers usually had to cover at least a hundred feet—sometimes yards—of blasted earth, and the Germans had only to scramble out of their bunkers and run a few feet to reach their own fire steps, the results can be seen on the walls of little churches and on the pediments of statues in every small town in America. It was, quietly stated, more an erasure than a slaughter.

So much for the Artillery delusion. And now they were hearing the same thing from Air Force generals—leave the Gulf War to the Strategic Air Command, to Cruise missiles and stand-off smart bombs. Let the Air Force bring the enemy to his knees. It was the same old myth in a brand-new package. Ground belonged to the infantry; that would never change.

Wolochek had been silent for a long time. They stood there in the half-light, looking skyward, surrounded by the murmurs and muted hum of the military camp. Crane watched Wolochek's face in the flickering light of faraway fires.

After a time, Crane said what they were both thinking. "Well, sir, thing is, you can't wait around. We should get in there, hit them as soon as the bombs stop. They'll be dug in and stunned. Our trouble is, we always give them a chance, let them get their balance back."

"So hit fast. Never let up, is that it?"

"They'll be there, sir. Even through all that."

Wolochek was quiet again, snuffling a little. "Well, that's Air-Land War, Dee. That's how we do it."

"Yes, sir. That's the plan, at any rate."

Wolochek looked up past the cloud cover. Drops of rain slid across his pale pink cheeks. "On their way home now, I guess."

"Movies and donut dollies."

"Jack Daniel's. Steaks."

"Cold beer."

"Beer . . . that sounds good. Got one?"

"No, sir."

Wolochek was working around some question. Crane said nothing. He'd get there eventually.

"How're the married kids? How's it going with them?"

Okay. Now Crane was getting it.

Wolochek was worried about the Gulf Orphans bill, some goddam Senate initiative to have all military personnel who had kids transferred back to the States. Right now, it was supposed to be applied only to single parents, or to couples who were both in Kuwait, but as far as the Combat Arms troops were concerned, it was a thin-edge ploy to get *anyone* with kids brought back home.

The whole movement had ticked off the lifers almost as much as the attempt, in the early days, by several Reserve members to get themselves exempted from combat deployment. Weren't these people *listening* when they signed up? What the hell did they think all those *guns* were for? They'd joined the goddam *Army,* for chrissake, not the Peace Corps. The press had been full of the protests, and the speeches of their lawyers, and every lifer and every hardcore eleven-bravo member had watched it all in stunned silence. And now this new stunt, the Gulf Orphans bill.

"Our married guys are fine, sir."

"They phoning home?"

"No, sir. Once was enough."

Wolochek laughed. "Usually is . . . you can tell them, that Orphans bill, it was killed in the Senate yesterday."

"That's good."

"Well, you know, nobody wants to see kids lose their parents."

"Yes, sir. And how does your wife feel about losing you?"

Wolochek grinned again.

"Yeah. Can't sanitize the thing. Civilians don't *get* it, do they?"

"It's a war, sir. People die. A soldier gets married and has kids, that's something he should have thought about earlier."

"How's . . . Carla, isn't it?"

"She's fine, sir."

"Good . . . good. About your assault here, have some faith. The boss has a couple of good ideas. You'll see some things, they'll put them in the manuals."

Crane didn't ask what they might be, other than Colonel Hawkins and his thing with the M9 earthmovers—the troops *loved* that idea. But still, somehow, it made him feel better. Wolochek was an officer, no matter how easy he was with the rankers. Officers kept their distance. They had to. In a hard place, you had to make some decisions that were sure to get somebody killed. Getting too friendly with a grunt was strictly against Army protocol. But Wolochek had something. Maybe he was one of those weird guys, never looked that special in peacetime, then when the war comes, they seem to change, they turn into the Medal of Honor winners, get their names on the regimental banner.

Wolochek sighed again and a wave of tiredness came over his face. Three more white flares blossomed out at the edge of the horizon, casting a sick green light up underneath the cloud ceiling. A few seconds later, a massive drumbeat roll thundered up and over the base and a cold wind puffed at their cheeks, another B-52 stick coming down, the hammer of God.

"You know, Dee, if war has a heartbeat, that's what it sounds like."

Crane said nothing, feeling a blend of embarrassment and privilege, a strange amalgam of condescension and respect. Wolochek slapped him on the shoulder.

"Well, anyway, someday we'll remember this, maybe even miss it."

He smiled at Crane, waved to DerHorst and Felz, returned the salutes of the platoon sergeants, and walked away toward his hootch, the poncho dragging in the mud, his BDUs limp and wet, his Kevlar bone dome shiny in the yellow perimeter floods.

Miss it, thought Crane.

That was one of those incredibly bozoidal dumb-fuck things that you usually heard from a noncombatant, or from a four-star general who *had* to talk like that for the press. But the thing about combat—the terrible dark secret—was that a hell of a lot of men who had survived it found that everything that came after it was pale and empty. You could see that at the Wall, vets who had been to see the elephant—been stomped into jelly by the elephant, lost friends, had their hopes and limbs blasted, done things that brought them stony-cold awake at four in the morning, waving away the face of a dead VC floating in the air in front of them . . . and yet . . . in many ways, they *missed* it.

Maybe we'll miss this. I hope so.

I hope the kids are *alive* to miss it, Captain Wolochek. Sir.

High above the heavy gray wet-wool sky the sound of jets came to them like a whisper, a kind of warning wind, and the earth under them seemed to shift and quiver, and far to the north the white flare and a deep bass booming drumroll sounded, and each man and woman along the perimeter wire saw it and felt it and asked the same silent questions, the eternal first-time combat questions.

Am I ready? Did they teach me enough? Did they tell me the truth about fighting? Was my training any damn good at all? Are my officers any good? Will logistics screw up again? Will my .50 jam when I need it most? If I get popped, will they get me out? Will the fast movers blow me out of my shorts by mistake? Will Div Arty shoot us in the back? Do the bosses have their heads shoved up their butts? Does anybody here really know what the hell they're doing? Do I know what the hell I'm doing? Will I choke? Will I fuck up beyond all recognition?

Will I die out here?

CHAPTER NINE

FIREWALK

Back in his hootch that night, Crane lay in his cot and watched Felz playing with his Beretta. Even from ten feet away, Crane could see the marks his pink wet hands were leaving on the black matte sheen of the steel. It was hard to watch. Felz was very bad with steel, and watching him at work made Crane uncomfortable. It wasn't that Felz was a bad noncom, or even a bad soldier. He was in Quartermaster corps, essentially a clerk—MOS 70A10—and if it weren't for clerks and mechanics and about two hundred other noncombatant MOSs, there'd be no Army at all.

But the thing with the steel—watching Felz put his hands all over it—Crane realized it made him shiver, literally sent a shudder of physical pain up his spine where it changed into a rubbery shrieking in his skull like the sound of a kid playing with a balloon.

Lying there on his back, looking at Felz dicking around with his 9-mm, Crane realized that the best way to tell a soldier from a civilian was the way the soldier handled steel. Only a civilian would put his hands all over a weapon, hold it by the barrel or let his sweaty palms rest on the blade of his bayonet—something he'd also seen Felz do—or in any other way show disrespect for the metal.

Years back, his father had taken him to the Weapons Hall at Fort Henry, up in Kingston, Canada. They had all kinds of edged weapons there, and Crane remembered seeing very clearly the palm print of some long-dead recruit on the smoothbore barrel of a muzzle-loader Brown Bess. The gun was perhaps two hundred years old, but there was this dumb boot's hand mark burnt into the brown sheen of the barrel, the timeless residue of one afternoon's sweat and carelessness.

It was ugly, like a mark of disease. And one pass with a chamois could have saved the gun. That kind of thing was hammered into you at boot, and quickly forgotten by almost every MOS outside of the Combat Arms. Well, clerks could afford to forget it. Line infantry, that was something they all had in common, how they recognized each other, even in a strange place far from the war zone. In a way it all came down to steel.

Years back, when he was in Vietnam, he'd taken some R&R in Saigon—the town was still a little jewel then, a colonial relic, with pastel stucco buildings and lacy black wrought-iron balconies, red-tile roofs, and narrow lanes shaded with bougainvillea and jasmine and bamboo, a bit like the French Quarter in New Orleans or the boardwalk in Charleston.

When was this? . . . Well, since Saigon was still a nice place, it must have been early in his tour—'65 or '66. The VC hadn't bombed the My Canh barge restaurant then—or had they? Well, it was a long time back, anyway, and he had been wandering around late at night—okay, then it *was* after Charlie blew up the My Canh, because there was that stupid curfew—no, it had to be later because they ran into some grunts from the 101st, and the 101st didn't get deployed to Vietnam until '67—Jesus, the mind goes, doesn't it?

Now in those days olive drabs and camos were forbidden in the town—at least officially—and there was Crane in clean BDUs dodging the MPs, looking for whatever there was to look for in Saigon on a two-day R&R.

He was diddy-bopping down along Tu Do across the boulevard by the old cathedral and the ministry building, a good way from the river, because all the bars, the Milan and the Bluebird—a MAT team clubhouse where ordinary grunts were non grata—the Sporting Bar, where all the Green Beret and LURP guys hung out, and a hundred little places where you could buy painted smokes and hootch-girls, all of this was crammed down by the Song Saigon, the river, into a tangle of huts and yellow cinder-block buildings set amid tailor shops and souvenir shops and that one big department store—what the hell was its name? Man, you lose things as you age. Once he could have named every ville and byroad from the Dong Nai River down to the Bai Bung Point. Now he had trouble remembering the only goddam department store in Saigon.

Anyway, even up there by the cathedral, Crane could smell the opium and the *nuoc mam* sauce, the reek of bad tobacco. The charcoal smoke floated on the damp air and the low yellow lights hung in the haze like fireflies. He had a warm 33 beer in his hands and he was taking a pull at it when he bumped into someone in OD and his first thought was MP, then, no, a White Mouse, one of the ARVN cops.

But the guy was beefy, solid, too heavyset for a Vietnamese, and as he bounced back off the guy the man said something that wasn't in English or Vietnamese and there was this little leathery slipping sound as the guy pulled out a knife, which he proceeded to wave in Crane's face, back and forth, slowly.

Crane, cross-eyed from the nearness of the thing, saw that it was a kukri, a Gurkha knife, and the way the light shone along the blade was like moonlight on water, and he had the fleeting thought that whatever the guy's problem was, he cared about that knife.

The man behind the knife wasn't a Gurkha—too big for that and anyway Gurkhas only pulled the kukri if they meant to kill and this guy hadn't killed him; also Crane was pretty sure there were no Gurkhas in-country anyway—well, whatever, his temper, which was bush fugazy by now, came racing up into his brain like the rocket's red glare.

Crane stepped—hopped—back and threw the beer away to give himself some fighting room, tugging out the only metal he had, a P38, known as a can opener—and it happened that he stepped back into a cone of light from a streetlamp, where the guy with the knife saw him clearly for the first time.

Boom, his smile was a broad glitter of white, and the guy was saying something in pidgin that sounded like *ta-grrr,* and the knife went away somewhere on the man's belt—Crane watched the knife go away, the guy with his head down, not looking, and Crane thought about drifting the dumb fuck right there, putting him on the ground and kicking some manners into him, scraping his eye out with his P38, but then it was over, the guy was all apologies and bows and that big wide Asian grin, and now they were good buddies, going down Tu Do together toward the river.

The guy turned out to be ROK, a Korean trooper, and what he was saying was *Tiger,* that he was part of the Capital Division known as the Tigers, who had shipped in to cover the highways and ports up in the central coast around Qui Nhon and Tuy Hoa. His name, as far as Crane could work it out, was Moon something, and after a couple of hours down near the Half Moon Bar, Crane was a yard off the ground and Moon was half in the bag.

By now, Crane was calling him Half Moon, although with respect, because the reputation of the ROK troops was starting to build in the war zone—that the ROK were stony killers who liked to leave their enemies staked out and disemboweled, guys who had fought communists in their own country not ten years back and who had come to Vietnam for payback, which they got in spades.

The ROK troops got so much payback that throughout their tour in-country, the safest place to be in Vietnam was anywhere in Binh Dinh Province. Later on, the ROK forces in Vietnam would run close to forty thousand, the largest force commitment in the theater after the U.S., but this night on Tu Do, Half Moon was one of the first Koreans Crane had ever met.

At any rate, they had a pretty good time in spite of the language barrier, falling in with a bunch of Special Forces guys from I Corps, drinking Jack Daniel's in the Sporting Bar, trading lies, and one thing led to another so that after an indeterminate amount of time Crane and Half Moon were staggering down along the docks toward the Canh Hoi neighborhood, singing "Surfing U.S.A." by the Beach Boys, a song which was big in those days back in the world and had become a kind of Marine drinking song up in Cam Ranh Bay.

Now at that time Canh Hoi was not what it became later, a no-go zone for white guys; they called it Soulsville, where the blacks kept their own bars and ran their own rackets and all the hookers were imported Khmer girls and Senegalese orphans, who were darker than Vietnamese and Korean girls. But even then it was a tricky place for white soldiers and still more so for any Asian grunt. Half Moon was new to the place, but Crane had been fully briefed by his platoonmates, and the deeper they got into the Canh Hoi alleyways, the more sober he was getting. Half Moon was saying he was thirsty, so when he saw a kerosene-lit bar set way back from the lane behind a fence made of cane lattice, Crane figured they might as well get off the street and maybe think about coffee and a trishaw back to civilization.

It wasn't a surprise to Crane that the bar was crowded with black troopers, "Blue boys" they called themselves.

"Black power" had really taken hold, imported by black FNGs from . . . Crane was trying to remember the name the blacks had for the United States . . . yes, they called it "the clip side of the big moist."

Black guys loved that trick talk, like Cockney slang. Come to think of it, as the war went on, the blacks developed their own language entirely, as a way of keeping whitey at a distance. Blacks were "cuffees," a "flatbacker" was a Khmer hooker, and a "booly" was an Oreo, a black man who was white on the inside.

So Crane and Half Moon, they stood in the doorway of the place, both full of Bammy-Bow and whiskey courage by that hour, and took it all in while the bar noise stilled and slowed, just like in the movies.

The dim little cave room was full of Screaming Eagle shoulder flashes, which definitely made it at least 1967. The 101st flashes were never subdued—Old Abe, the eagle's name, never hiding his colors. The 101st patches always stood out in Vietnam, a blaze of risky white and black and yellow color that had to draw fire in the boonies—and looking back on the night, the thing Crane remembered most was the way the yellow kerosene light flickered on all that shiny black skin and made little circles of red fire in the wet beer marks on the tabletops and bounced off the polished silk 101st patches on their shoulders.

The greeting was less than warm, a sudden stony silence, no smiles, and the music tinny and scratchy in the background—not something by the Beach Boys, that was damn sure—and Half Moon, now finally awake to the mood of the place, shoved himself clear of Crane and straightened his back as he made his way through the tables toward the high back bar made out of ammo boxes and corrugated iron.

Behind the bar a mama san with a face like dried fruit and dark brown Khmer features watched him in an up-from-under Veronica Lake parody, her hooded eyes touched with a pale yellow glitter. When Half Moon got to the bar he tugged out his Gurkha knife and laid it on the bar top and showed the mama san his teeth, saying something to her in a language she must have understood, because she ducked her head and reached for a porcelain jug and poured out a shot glass of clear liquid. Crane stepped through the tables, not making eye contact, aware of about fifteen black faces tracking him as he crossed the twenty feet to the bar, and he reached Half Moon's side just as Half Moon drained the glass and was setting it down again, and at that point a lean Airborne grunt with all of his facial hair burned off seemed to materialize like black smoke at Half Moon's side and a gray shimmer registered in the yellow light and Half Moon's right sleeve was nailed into the ammo-crate bar top by a candle-blackened Fairbairn knife and two more blue boys were coming up behind Crane.

Three . . . four seconds of perfect stillness . . .

The Airborne Spec 4 with the commando blade drew a breath and started to say something clever and ballsy and then there was a kind of ripping flurry and a huffing sound and the man was bent over backward across the wooden ammo crate with Half Moon's Gurkha blade lying across his shiny wet blue-black skin, the edge pressed in hard enough so that Crane could see the man's carotid pulsing under the skin like a snake moving under leather.

Crane turned to face down the blue boys while running through a number of options. All of them involved a severe loss of blood, the majority of it probably his own. So, having nothing to do, he did it very well, turning back to the mama san and raising Half Moon's shot glass.

"*Khong zau, ba. Toy*—Me—Crane. This man, Half Moon, is a Korean brother. Please ask the nice men not to kill us, and may I have another glass of this *ba-see-day?*"

The Airborne guy stuck against the bar top made a twisting motion with his head and Half Moon eased up on the blade. The man blew out his cheeks.

"*Di-di mau,* peckerwood. This is Tan Town. All Originals only."

"Half Moon doesn't know that. What you make of his knife?"

"It's a Gurkha blade."

"You know about the rule?"

"Yeah—fuck him."

"He has to have some blood before he can put it away."

"Fuck you. He's no Gurkha."

"No. But the knife is." Crane raised the Fairbairn and turned it under the kerosene lamp. "Where'd you get this?"

Behind him, he heard men moving, stepping lightly, and he was aware of the smell of dirty ODs and body heat and whiskey breath.

"From one of the Ozzies."

"Nice blade—you ever use it?"

"Not yet. Tell him to let me up."

"You know the full name for this knife?"

"Yes. Sikes-Fairbairn. Fairbairn-Sikes. Shit. It's some fucking commando knife."

"You know what a misery-cord is, Airborne?"

"Yes."

"What is it?"

"Mercy. A knife for mercy killing."

"What's a forte?"

"Shit . . . it's the strong part of a blade, you parry with the forte."

"And what's the name of my friend's knife?"

"It's a kukri. That's Nepalese for snake. I got one in my pants bigger than this. Tell him to let me up, my back hurts."

Crane looked around at the men in the hootch, and back at Half Moon, whose broad face was set and calm, his hands steady.

"You know a lot about blades, Airborne."

"Fuck you, Sylvester."

Crane patted Half Moon's shoulder. "Let him up, Half Moon. I think he's a soldier."

Half Moon lifted the blade away from the man's neck and stepped back. Crane held up his left hand, palm out, offering it to Half Moon. After a few seconds, Half Moon smiled at Crane and drew the edge of the blade across Crane's palm, slicing the callused skin. Crane let the blood run down his wrist and saw some droplets hit the wooden bar top. In his adrenalized state, each droplet looked like a gravity bomb and each strike flared up in the kerosene yellow glow like a burst of napalm. Half Moon took a piece of cotton out of his pocket and wiped the blade carefully, bringing the shine up again, his head down, ignoring the press of blue boys.

Finally, somebody from the back said, "Fuck this, booly. Save it for the Zipperheads," and the men went back to their tables. Airborne rubbed his neck and stood for a long moment, considering what was required of him, what was the right way out of this. Half Moon ignored him, and said something to the *ba roc* behind the bar.

After a time, the air seemed to change and Airborne nodded at the mama san. She set a glass of *ba-see-day* in front of him. He drained it, made a face, and said, "Ask him why he carries a Gurkha blade."

Half Moon finished polishing the blade and said, in a densely accented Korean-American pidgin, "Ask *him* why he carry," and pointed to the Fairbairn.

Airborne took his blade from Crane's hand and held it up to

the light. He kept his hands off the blade. It was a slender tapered blade with a ridged haft and thin steel hilts. In the half-light, it looked like a crucifix. Moon's kukri was a very different knife, almost a short sword, with a narrow foible widening into a broad down-hooked delta-shaped forte, heavy and solid and made for chopping.

"Why'd the Ozzie give you his knife?"

Airborne sipped at his glass of rice whiskey and pulled a face.

"We did some stuff together. I showed him the bush."

"Where?"

Airborne grinned at him, his singed eyes strange in the glimmering light. "I could tell you, but—"

"Then you'd have to kill me."

Airborne's smile went away, and a silence settled over them, but it wasn't a difficult silence. Young grunts in-country liked to flare up and look like man-killers, but a lot of it was strictly theater. Most real beefs got settled hand-to-hand or were broken up by very large and cranky MPs from MACV—the Military Assistance Command in Saigon.

So they talked away the anger the way young men sometimes can, and began to see each other as codefendants in a world of shit, and more *ba-see-day* got poured while Half Moon talked about his Gurkha friend in an accent so thick no one had any idea what he was saying, and that was the first night that Crane got that sweet-sad connected feeling with soldiers who were not part of his own unit, and he knew himself a part of the same machine that bound them all together, that made them all soldiers.

As he lay there in his cot a thousand years later and halfway around the planet, stuck in Saudi, he wondered what it was that made him so much like a long-dead Korean grunt and fifteen Airborne blue boys—two of whom stayed in-country as long as Crane and came to be good friends, so that Crane could feel even shittier than normal when he heard they got shot to bits on May 11, in '69, trying to get up Hill 937, later known as Hamburger Hill—and so unreachably alienated from this fat pink clerk across the room, sitting there in all his baby-soft blindness, playing with his 9-mm dick.

Well, it was obvious if you gave it some thought, which Crane eventually did. The difference was training, and the relentless drop-forge hammering the Army put you through, every waking shift.

Now the clerks and the cooks and the motor-pool mechs, they sooner or later turned into clock punchers with one eye on their discharge date, but it wasn't that way for eleven bravos. Every grunt in the Combat Arms was shoved under that drop-forge at least eight hours a day, from his first day staring down the DI's throat as he told you precisely where you fit in on the evolutionary scale—below soap scum and above Jane Fonda, but not much— to Advanced Individual Training, and then to your in-country orientation at Long Binh, and more training when you reached a line company—if you lived—and on and on endlessly for every month of your hitch. . . .

After a while, he closed his eyes. Just before he fell asleep, he saw a narrow country road running by a field of cut wheat; the sun was hot on his shoulders, he was running, and each time his foot came down he felt the jolt up his spine while the sun burned overhead like a white phosphor flare and someone called a relentless and unmerciful cadence for a stretch of time that ran straight and clear all the way to the horizon line, and everyone around him wished the man an early death, and so did Crane, although the voice was his own.

———

The first time Crane saw it, Fort Irwin looked like a place that had been asked a lot of hard questions by a sadistic god but the place had refused to answer so the god beat the living shit out of it and left it for dead. The base was a collection of huts and trailers and hangars at the south end of the Tiefort range. It was a thousand square miles of rock and dry wash and blue sawtooth ranges, with shallow salt valleys in between that were eroded and channeled with runoff water. Stony arroyos climbed up to dead ends, and canyons and slopes radiated to all compass points, covered with stunted ocher and purple creosote bushes and joshua trees and yucca plants, not one of which had the juice to get higher than three feet. As a kind of compensation, they all grew tough enough to puncture a humvee tire, foul a half-track tread, or trip a man flat. Everywhere you looked there was desolation and sudden basalt eruptions, pillars and buttes and mesas wrapped in purple haze, or shining ocher and red and sulphur yellow under a sun that seemed to float about a hundred feet over your head.

The place had a strange prehistoric power, the way you feel in an old cathedral or walking an ancient battlefield, and any recruit with a bit of imagination could look around and see the world the way it was a hundred thousand years ago. There were ghosts and shadows everywhere, and something always seemed to be moving just at the edge of your vision.

In short, Fort Irwin was the kind of place a lizard would save up to retire in, so of course it was exactly the place the post-Vietnam Army went to lose weight, toughen up, pay for its sins. Do penance and purify itself.

In the worst stretch of this high-desert wasteland, the Army established the National Training Center, on the site of an abandoned artillery and antiaircraft training camp. Fort Irwin had been an active camp during the Second World War. It had been abandoned—but not forgotten, because the Army never forgets anything—in 1951.

Positioned somewhere between Death Valley and the China Lake Naval Weapons Center, the cantonment is a war gamer's daydream. Edwards Air Force Base is seventy miles to the south and west. Twenty-nine Palms Marine Corps Base is off to the southeast about fifty miles. The closest town is Barstow, California, thirty-five miles away. Los Angeles is on the far side of the San Gabriel Mountains, almost two hundred miles away. The camp is surrounded by ranges of granite and volcanic upsurges and alkali flats, occasionally relieved by black lava beds, quake fissures, and glacial moraines. There are six salt lake beds, each one dotted with wrought-iron bushes and alkali sinks, and one airfield called—oddly—Bicycle Lake.

The climate is the invisible mirror of the landscape, every bit as uncompromising—peaking at a hundred and thirty on some bad summer days, bottoming out at subzero nights in January or February. Winds come up out of nowhere and reach sixty miles an hour. Sand can blow hard enough to strip the paint off a shed or skin a mule in a morning. When the rain comes, the stony ground can't hold it, so it runs off in sudden torrents, carrying rocks and gravel and hapless snakes along with it, filling the gulleys and washes in a roiling tumult of mud and confusion. The terrain favors defense, especially in the valley floors, many of which are ridged with low dry washes across their entire breadth, chief among them being an attacker's grief factory called the Washboard.

From the low slopes above, these valleys look like corrugated iron, a rippled field of ditches and ridges that are high enough to conceal a tank and slow down any kind of armored assault across the flanks.

The chief attraction of the zone is that the Army and the Air Force can cook off major ordnance, tear-ass around the terrain in heavy armor, conduct live-fire exercises until the main gun warps into a pretzel, do pop-up-and-plaster Cobra sweeps, chew the living guts out of the landscape with every kind of vehicle known to the war gods, and generally make all sorts of bone-shattering noise until the wee hours of the morning and not one civilian will ever call up the MPs and whine about it. Because there aren't any. And if any civilians wanted to go there, they couldn't, because there's only one road in and the Army makes damn sure no outsider ever comes up it unless it's just to say, Oh, goodness me, so sorry, and do a U-turn under the muzzle of a sandbagged .50.

But the main feature of the terrain, and the reason the Army sends its combat divisions there, is the OpFor.

———

After Vietnam, the U.S. Army commanders realized that the biggest mistake they had made in the conduct of the war was to let SAC flyboys and Cold War civilian spooks like Robert McNamara tell them how to run it. Not that they hadn't done a lot of screwing up on their own, in matters such as the DEROS issue, rotating single troopers in and out of the war zone like toddlers on a merry-go-round, and the draft itself, which pulled the poor and the ghetto blacks into the war by the tens of thousands while leaving mainly white middle-class kids safely back in the World.

But the single most destructive thing the Army did was listen to high-level spooks and Ivy League number crunchers, all of whom had swallowed entirely the self-serving SAC mantra that modern wars could be won by high-altitude carpet bombing and realpolitik chess moves of "signaling" and "positioning" and "containment."

Mainly, they all believed that the threat of nuclear Armageddon had made a classic ground war impossible, that any armed confrontation had the potential to escalate all the way to the nuclear level, that the world communist conspiracy was indivisible, and that any localized communist incursion was more or less a branch plant franchise run by the firm of Marx, Kosygin, and Mousie Dung.

Therefore, their reasoning went, since actually holding ground is not only strategically unnecessary but tactically vexing, the infantry was, essentially, obsolete. Clausewitz and Bismarck were out. Langley was in. The National Security Council was the new Vatican. Think globally. Carpet bomb locally.

This is not to suggest that the threat from the Warsaw Pact forces was chimerical. The nose-to-nose was a grim reality that shaped the lives of an entire generation. But soldiers know that sometimes it's not enough to *look* like you're ready to fight. Sometimes it's necessary to show up and prove it, and if you're going to show up, then do it with absolute conviction and commitment. Real combat is not a signaling exercise, and anyone who thinks it is needs to spend some time in the beaten zone.

But containment was the received wisdom generated by upper-echelon think tankers such as Robert McNamara. As Secretary of Defense in the Kennedy and the Johnson administrations, Robert McNamara, a graduate of the Harvard Business School, kick-started his double-breasted version of war with the Gulf of Tonkin presentation to Congress in 1964, then backed the use of SAC strikes against North Vietnam, and lobbied to get Westmoreland's troop count raised in 1966. He was a hawk among hawks, pound for pound the best life-taking, man-killing dink buster in the entire administration.

In the summer of 1966, in the best tradition of Cold War spooks everywhere, McNamara pulled together a group of CIA and National Security "specialists" at Dana Hall, a prep school for girls in Wellesley, Massachusetts. The idea behind the meeting was to come up with the McNamara Line, a concept suggested to the Secretary of Defense by another Harvard professor, Robert Fisher, of the Harvard Law School.

Fisher's idea was to erect a "surveillance wall" in the north of I Corps, along the DMZ, composed of top-secret high-tech devices that would prevent the resupply of the VC cadres in the south and "strangle" the war. Some of the ideas this group came up with kept the senior noncoms in Crane's mess laughing for years.

For example, they wanted to sow an area twelve miles by sixty with over a million gravel mines and button bomblets, triggered to explode whenever an enemy soldier stepped on one. The resulting detonation would be picked up by patrols of low-flying Spads and BAT planes, who would vector in Spooky and gunship assaults.

The trouble with that idea was that the bomblets tended to explode when *anything* stepped on them, so a hell of a lot of the Spooky and gunship runs were targeted in on some poor Mung tribesman with his foot blown into a tree or a herd of very confused oxen whose leader had just blown her nose off while nuzzling a shrub.

Then they came up with urine sniffers, electrical detectors designed to locate the VC by the smell of their urine, evidently forgetting that almost every ox and water buffalo in Vietnam put out more piss per pound than a hundred VC, and—one of Crane's favorites—an infiltration of specially equipped bedbugs, each with a tiny electrode glued on its back which would start to emit a radio frequency when the bedbug found a VC to sleep with.

They also decided to train pigeons to carry impact bombs, but no one could get the pigeons to tell the difference between NVA tanks and U.S. tanks. And, of course—the pièce de résistance of this whole spookazoidal cluster fuck at Dana Hall—a motion-detector monitor disguised as a pile of dog shit, which worked perfectly as a metaphor for everything that was wrong with Harvard but was as operationally useless as a sponge-rubber bayonet. No one had bothered to ask if there actually *were* any dogs in the jungle out there.

Of course, by the time the McNamara Line and all of the rest of his NSC-CIA scams went awry, the man himself had Seen the Light, like Saul on the road to the White House, and was at that point campaigning for an end to the war, saying that "the picture of the world's greatest superpower . . . trying to pound a tiny backward nation into submission on an issue whose merits are hotly disputed is not a pretty one."

His May 1967 report on the war, which is on file at the noncom school in Fort Leavenworth, Kansas, was a typical Harvard Business School term paper, in which he offered graphs to show that the typical VC firefight was initiated by the VC over eighty percent of the time and that their "rate of losses" could be held to two thousand a week "regardless of U.S. Force Level upgrades." There were statistics and "erosion tables" and "mortality coefficients" and a raft of other MBA-style prognostications. His conclusion was that the war was unwinnable. It was all there in the charts and the graphs.

Crane figured it was about then that the actual combat soldiers in the Joint Chiefs boardroom pulled their heads out of their asses and started to wonder why they were listening to clipboard-and-slide-rule wonks like McNamara and Fisher in the first place. Too bad that by then "the unwinnable war" had already killed a lot of good men.

But when the true magnitude of the defeat sank in, the brass, under DuPuy and Abrams, made a secret vow never again to let civilians tell them how to run a war. Including civilians who worked in the Air Force disguised as SAC generals.

And they needed a place to go where you'd never expect to find a Harvard MBA. They needed a place where they could recall all the old truths about war, about Clausewitz and Bismarck and Lee, about Lines of Supply, and Hasty Defenses, Bounding Overwatch,

Movement to Contact, and Recon in Force, and the "Fog of War." Because while they were all getting pulled in up to their elbows in the tar-baby tangle of southeast Asia, the second most powerful military force on the planet was sitting on its massive armored ass a few blocks from Checkpoint Charlie, and the U.S. Army was in no shape to fight it.

The trouble was, there was no way to relearn Warsaw Pact AirLand tactics without sending the 3rd Armored off into East Germany to rile up the Soviets. So they came up with an excellent idea.

They built their own Soviet Army.

In the early 1980s, the best intelligence estimates of the war-fighting capabilities of the Russian Army put them at about forty-five tank divisions, six paratroop divisions, an indeterminate number of helicopter assault divisions—possibly nine—and fifteen field gun and artillery divisions, all bound together under the control of a unified central command.

They could field fifty thousand tanks, twenty-four thousand artillery elements, seventy thousand armored personnel carriers and recon units, four thousand helicopters, and a varying number of support and logistical units, all of which added up to a manpower force of eight million men. This calculation left out the missile forces and didn't take into account the morale and training levels of the Warsaw Pact forces, an important consideration but one that was hard to translate into fighting potential. At the War College, they decided to assume that the Russians could fight well when pushed to it, a conclusion that the German general Paulus would have agreed with, particularly on the second day of February in 1943, when he surrendered an entire army to the Russians after the collapse of the Siege of Stalingrad. Ewald Kleist, the German commander, barely got his own forces across the Don before the Russians came down on him as well, so the lessons were learned and they were not forgotten at Fort Leavenworth. The Russians were a global force, and when they had to, they fought as well and as cruelly as any force in history.

Against this huge military machine, the United States could field seventeen Army divisions and three Marine divisions, along with

Allied units such as the British and the French, the Germans, and the Canadians, all of whom are respected and professional soldiers.

Since the general rule of war is that it takes a three-to-one advantage for attackers to overrun defenders, and the NATO forces were defensive forces, the belief at the time was that, after suffering initial trip-wire losses, the Allies would eventually beat the Warsaw Pact advance and wring a kind of victory out of the bloody ruin of what had been Europe.

Army manuals describe the Soviet assault doctrine as a kind of cast-iron lava flow, a massive broad-front advance using combined forces—AirLand Battle—as well as every kind of technological and biological obscenity that the white-suit boffins could conjure up in the basement.

NATO forces are, theoretically, skilled in reactive and maneuver warfare—concentrating their greatest power at the most vulnerable points, breaking through into the rear areas, executing sudden flank attacks with combined air and artillery and tank assaults backed up with mechanized infantry. As the phrase runs, they expect to get inside the enemy decision cycle, let loose the dogs of war, and generally fuck them up big time.

The kicker in all of this is that fast-maneuver warfare is very hard to supply. Ask von Rundstedt and von Manteuffel, whose massive combined arms assault through the Ardennes had the Americans on the run in 1944—until the 5th Panzers ran out of gas about a hundred and fifty miles later, where they were promptly enveloped and erased by an Allied counterattack.

To get the enemy on the run is a consummation devoutly to be wished. To *keep* him on the run takes more than courage and speed. It takes a brilliantly executed and highly coordinated tour de force of that one military quality most often neglected by practically everyone—logistics.

It's the job of Military Logistics to see to it that the tanks have gas to run on and plastic piping, called fascines, to dump into tank traps and Engineers to drag ruined hulks off to the side of the advance. Logistics gets shells to the Artillery and parts to the Air Assault wing. Logistics sees to it that radios have replacement parts, that the troops have ammunition and food and extra toilet paper and bug spray and MOPP suits and new filters for their gas masks and mobile surgical hospitals closer to the front than Perth Amboy.

If you think of a war as a giant bark chipper that eats up just about everything a city like Pittsburgh could use over the Memorial Day weekend, and eats it up in the time it takes to read this, you get some idea of the importance—and the degree of difficulty—that effective logistics requires.

Now, if you imagine that while you are shoving all this stuff into the business end of the bark chipper, five million extremely energetic and adrenalized sons of bitches are dropping bombs on you and shooting you up with artillery and gassing you to your knees and setting fire to your pants, you begin to grasp the magnitude of the problem facing the U.S. Army at the close of the Vietnam War. Because, having worked very hard at losing an insane and civvy-driven war of counterinsurgency against a neolithic but impassioned enemy, the Army found itself too misdirected and demoralized to muscle in on a Girl Scout's cookie route, let alone run a decent AirLand Battle against something as huge and unstoppable as the Soviet Army. This made the Joint Chiefs of Staff very uneasy, and that is why General DuPuy and General Abrams and everyone else at the War College slept very badly through most of the late 1970s.

This is not to discount such war-game exercises as Operation Certain Strike or, the grand old mother of them all, the annual REFORGER combined-forces exercises in Germany. But these exercises bear as much resemblance to a real war as an evening of Bavarian slap dancing resembles a performance of *The Ring of the Nibelung.*

Crane and significant elements of the 1st Infantry Division joined their prepositioned armored units at Danger Forward in Germany to take part in the 1991 REFORGER maneuvers, and it was, in Crane's view, an engaging but basically useless two-week period of tag, he-said-she-said, and hide-the-bunny.

In REFORGER, as in all of the standard Army war games, Army commanders, mindful of their performance evaluation reports and the good opinion of their bosses, will gleefully roar past a paper "obstacle" defended by blank-firing "enemies" while an umpire with a clipboard waves his arms and tells them they've all been "killed" by a probability calculation based on hit-to-kill ratios worked out on some NATO mainframe in Stuttgart. Tankers play rock music and drink Coca-Cola while they chew up acres of German rutabaga fields and the farmers sit by the side of the track, adding up their Crop Damage Rebate sheets. Captains and majors get into fistfights at crossroads while the grunts lollygag around in the village square, chatting up the local fräuleins and trading unit patches. Choppers hammer past in peacetime formations, looking for topless sunbathers and harassing herds of goats. Infantry platoons walk a mile into the Schwarzwald and have a picnic while the radio 'net boils and buzzes with cross talk. Near-apoplectic umpires try to shout a rifle squad dead while they stolidly ignore him and proceed to blank-fire an enemy post into theoretical smithereens. Generals descend to the level of kids playing cowboys and Indians, screaming, I shot you first, and No you didn't, you were already dead, and Did too, Did not, Did too, so there!

And then the entire three-ring circus comes down to a statistical analysis of whose convoy got how many trucks through how many kilometers of terrain while how many troopers got "degraded by unseen biological agents" or "administratively killed" by pissed-off umpires.

Crane had seen real combat, as had many of the senior officers in the Big Red, and it was their private opinion that REFORGER operations taught a general officer the very best way to cover his ass on his OER and suck up to his bosses, but as a lesson in real war, they were marginally better than adultery and not quite as instructive as setting a badger on fire and chasing it into the nurses' quarters.

———

Every soldier, or at least every good noncom and most good officers, knows the standard by which a unit performance is judged. The standard is called the Seven Operating Systems:

1. COMMAND AND CONTROL
   Troop leadership
   Facilities—Tactical Operations Centers and alternate command setups
   Communications—electronic and other

2. MANEUVER
   See and understand the battlefield tactically
   Fight according to combined arms doctrine
   Concentrate and deliver sufficient force at the precise point
   Make intelligent use of defender advantages or attack methods
   Take adequate steps for defense against nuclear or biological
   agents

3. FIRE SUPPORT
   Coordination of air units—choppers, surveillance craft,
   bombers
   Artillery—accurate ordnance designation and forward fire
   control
   Mortars—correct unit attachments and platoon initiatives

4. INTELLIGENCE
   Get out in the field and get good deployment information
   Get it back unmuddied and in a usable form, and on time
   Provide experienced combat people to understand the
   meaning of it
   Swift and accurate communication of Intel to TOC and line
   units

5. AIR DEFENSE
   Air forces understand and support battle plan
   Air forces actually show up on time and in the right places

6. MOBILITY
   Operational forces know how to attack and breach obstacles
   Operational forces know the strength and disposition of
   enemy

Operational forces actually get out there and do the job

Operational forces can respond effectively to counterattacks

Operational forces know how to defend and to build obstacles

7. COMBAT SERVICE SUPPORT (Logistics)

Good plans made in efficient Operations Centers

Adequate engineers in place to recover and clear vehicles

Efficient maintenance forces to repair and re-equip all forces

Reliable push (automatic) and pull (requested) resupply methods

Reliable communications and administration of paperwork

Rapid and reliable medical services in forward and rear areas

Any field force that can pull all these skills together stands a good chance of carrying the day. Any breakdown in one of these areas can endanger the entire mission. A breakdown in three or more will deliver unto the commanding officer his worst nightmare.

Aware of all these problems, the Army responded by creating the National Training Center at Fort Irwin, along with subsequent similar training centers in Georgia and North Carolina, huge militarized zones where the seven fundamental combat principles could be learned in something as close to real combat as safety allowed. And the key to the lesson was the OpFor.

The Opposing Forces are a full-time in-residence brigade-strength enemy force, equipped the way the Warsaw Pact forces are equipped, fighting according to Soviet doctrine, and highly skilled in all the combat basics.

At the NTC, the OpFor is composed of tankers and mechanized infantry drawn from line units around the nation. Usually two battalions, these designated forces remain in residence at Fort Irwin year-round, and several times a year they engage visiting armored and infantry units in almost-real maneuver warfare in the thousand-square-mile arena of Fort Irwin.

They field modified versions of the Sheridan tank, disguised to look like Soviet T-72s, as well as BMPs and every other kind of vehicle found in a modern Soviet rifle regiment. The officers and men wear dark green uniforms and berets, they're highly trained and aggressive, and they usually kick the hell out of the visitors in a series of extremely active and scary engagements that re-create the basic combat scenarios of Force-on-Force confrontations, from a low-risk reconnaissance—called Advance to Contact, which often results in a Deliberate Attack the next day, against OpFor positions, and then a Defend in Sector, where the visitors try to stand off an OpFor armored assault, and then a visitor counterattack against entrenched OpFor units in the field.

All of these operations take place out there in the desert, in the daylight and at night, under every kind of weather condition, in the stone canyons, up the slopes and around the buttes and through the narrow draws and dry washes of the Mojave Desert, in real time, with real physical risks and triumphs. The only way the NTC differs from real combat is in the use of MILES combat-simulated firing devices.

Every piece of gear, from trucks to tanks and artillery tracks, carries a MILES sensor, which combines a laser-beam detector and a yellow flasher. When a unit is "hit" by the—often invisible—laser beam of a concealed enemy, it flashes. If, according to the MILES unit's computer, the incoming strikes are accurate enough or concentrated enough for a kill, the yellow flasher turns to a steady light. The "kill" is registered on a central computer mainframe at the HQ trailer. There's no argument and no evasion. Umpires in the field can actually "kill" a unit if they see the need, using a hand-held "God gun" to activate the MILES detector.

Individual grunts wear a MILES sensor on their helmets and BDUs. If the trooper is being shot at, he hears an intermittent high-pitched beeping. If the microchip inside the MILES calculates that he's been hit often enough, or by something massive enough, to "kill" him, his MILES sensor starts to howl continually, and the central computer lists him as "dead." He's out, and again, there's no argument about it.

The visitors are also MILES equipped, and the same rules apply to their hits on OpFor MILES gear. Even the M1 Abrams and the .50s and the squad weapons have MILES firing simulators on their muzzles. The idea behind the MILES firing simulators is to re-create as closely as possible the conditions of live combat, the chaos and the massive movements, the hasty decisions that cost lives, and the sudden assaults that cut platoons to ribbons and shatter whole battalions in a few ugly minutes.

The rules of engagement at the NTC treat the OpFor army as if it were the kind of army the Russians would field if they weren't frequently incompetent. In other words, the OpFor's main gun of the big T-72 main battle tank has a loading mechanism that never ever slams shut unexpectedly, nipping the loader's arm off just below the elbow. Nor does their auto-loading mechanism ever load the powder bag first, and *then* the round—something that has to be seen to be appreciated, although you better not blink, because the whole tank is about to go up like a rocket and the turret might take your head off as it goes sailing by. The rounds it fires are always fresh and full powered, so they never fizzle out and fall short at a thousand yards. And the OpFor's downsized version, called the T-62, is never troubled by gear shift problems, although in real life the shift, which is manual, has to be hit repeatedly with a sledge—provided for the purpose—to get it into high gear.

The Russian version of the armored personnel carrier, the BTR-60, is actually a mess, running on two gas engines and a drive train made out of old Tinkertoy parts, and one of the two gas engines is usually jammed up by poor maintenance. But at the NTC, the BTR-60 is always assumed to be working at top form and operated by skilled and dedicated men—something else that rarely happens in the real Russian Army, where the rankers are driven like goats by sullen and brutalized noncoms and overseen by officers who think their subordinates are morons who can't be trusted, a sentiment that is often reciprocated. Nor do the OpFor's Russian vehicles ever grind to a halt—or fail to halt spectacularly—because the crew has drained the brake lines and made a kind of vodka substitute out of it.

And the OpFor BMP—the Russian Infantry Fighting Vehicle—never blows up when hit by a tank round even though the armor is magnesium, the same stuff you find in road flares; and the troopers inside are never allowed to burn alive trying to get out of the thing when the diesel tanks, which are handily stored right next to the exit doors, catch fire after taking an RPG round, the way they did with metronomic regularity in Afghanistan.

But the brutal reality of the Russian Army remained, that no matter how many soldiers might be at half strength or half-crocked on brake fluid or carrying an ugly grudge against their officers, the Army itself was mind-numbingly massive, and once it was on the move, the sheer weight of the thing would usually carry the day.

Russian fighting doctrine holds that you never ever reinforce a unit in trouble, that you always reinforce a unit that is succeeding; you never ever slow down on the attack, no matter how many people you are losing; you never stop to bury your dead and you never accept prisoners; and whatever piece of the terrain your objective may be, it never hurts to bomb and shell the living shit out of it for a week or so before you come up over the berm with all your weapons on full auto.

Any force facing the Soviet military machine was in a very bad place, unless it fought very smart, and that was the bottom-line objective of the NTC: to teach the U.S. Army how to fight smart.

———

The 1st Infantry elements did a lot of things during their two-week deployment at the NTC, ranging from CALFEX exercises—Combined Arms Live Fire Exercises, a kind of two-day-long Mad Minute in which every weapon in the battalion, from M1 main guns to the 9-mm Beretta, got fired at various stationary and moving targets—all the way to very complex, and sometimes astoundingly unsuccessful, battalion-sized movements. As entertaining as the CALFEX experience was, Crane's strongest impressions of the NTC program came from the emphasis placed on the first and most important combat skill—reading the terrain.

If you can't read the ground, you'll get chewed up as soon as you try to engage, or you'll get overrun trying to defend. And terrain was one thing they had at Fort Irwin, and they had it in every conceivable variety.

One of the most demanding terrain features of the NTC is created by flash floods. Thousands of years of these sudden torrents of muddy water and gravel have carved up the broad valleys between the mountain ranges, leaving them corrugated and filled with gullies that are sometimes ten or fifteen feet deep. Deep enough to conceal an enemy tank, or a platoon of infantry equipped with tank-killing RPGs, or any number of BMPs armed with Sagger rockets or some BTR personnel carriers with 12.7-mm chain guns.

Crane's unit was assigned an exercise called Movement to Contact, which in this case was a battalion-sized advance in column formation until they reached a broad gap between two mountain ranges. On the far side of this gap lay a three-mile-wide salt flat shaped like a diamond and reaching about ten miles away to the foothills of another range. This broad plain was cut and channeled with river washes until, from a high point, it looked like a sixty-square-mile piece of dusty yellow corduroy. And somewhere in this sector, there was a large enemy MRR—motorized rifle regiment—force in regiment strength, complete with tanks and weapons platforms and dismounted infantry. Crane's battalion had the job of locating these elements, fixing them in place, and developing enough Intelligence about them to determine the best way to engage them. And to do this without revealing the size and disposition of their own force. That was the whole idea behind a Movement to Contact.

The observers decreed that the initial advance had to be carried out at night, under a field of diamond-hard stars in a black immensity, and no moon at all. The advance had not been brilliant.

First of all, the TOC hut was paying more attention to road maps than it was to Logistics, so some of the line companies had food while others had to send a first sergeant back to the supply depot to see if Combat Support Services could get some food up the line before the two A.M. jump-off. Well, it turned out that Supply was run by some civilians, and they didn't *work* on Army time. The depot was closed and nothing the sergeant could say would get them to open up until seven A.M.

That meant some of the troops got fed and went to sleep with a clear idea of the line of march, and other troops waited up until past midnight before somebody said, Oh, hell, let's eat some MREs.

They ate and got practically *no* sleep, which resulted in their waking up at two-thirty in the morning, a half hour after their supposed jump-off time. Two whole companies of Crane's battalion weren't ready to form up in their IFVs and join the tanker column, so the whole advance was delayed while the staffers ran around sorting that out and the colonel boiled and bubbled like a brass kettle in his HQ vehicle.

In the meantime, the tankers were still having trouble with their M1s, which were *not* the M1s they babied and fondled and caressed every day back at Riley. It would be too expensive to ship home-base heavy equipment all the way to the NTC, so the supply cantonment included prepositioned M1s and IFVs and TOWs that were issued to the visitor force on arrival. Fine. But the yard workers were not always up to date with maintenance, and all of the prepositioned gear was getting the hell kicked out of it by successive waves of visitor forces, so by the time the Riley contingent arrived, a lot of the tanks and track vehicles were looking like New York gypsy cabs at the end of a long, nasty winter. Some batteries didn't work and some Engineer vehicles had no parts and some M1s had bad tracks . . . and so on, all of which provided Crane with some brand-new definitions of FUBAR, although there would be every reason to expect that tanks they took over in a real war zone would very likely be in even worse shape, so the exercise was a valid one.

Well, essentially, the fundamental rules of war held true. Whatever could go wrong went wildly, insanely, and gloriously wrong right down the line. Radios didn't work. MILES gear adaptors didn't fit or were improperly installed. Mortar platoon units got lost in the dark. Captains couldn't find their companies. IFVs rolled down the sides of hills and turned over. Then Engineer recovery vehicles rolled down sideways trying to get the IFVs back up the slope. Operators left communications van doors open so that passing choppers could blow fine silicate dust into the open electronics trucks and foul a whole array of fire-control radar, not to mention ruining six pots full of chicken stew.

Up the ladder, the Intel S2s were having trouble getting reports in from their advance scouts because the scouts—humvees and IFVs attached to the Cavalry section—were either operating on the wrong frequency or out of commission or too far off the map to matter. The S4 Logistics officer was back up the line yelling at the supply yard manager, the S3 in charge of operations was at his post in the TOC but concentrating too much on the Movement to Contact problems they were going to face when they got there, not realizing that the battalion might not get there at all. The S1 guy was busy with the reports on the grunts who took a tumble in their IFV, and the colonel was now out of his HQ vehicle and looking for some missing officers. By the time the jump-off hour arrived, the battalion was in no way ready to pull out. None of this surprised Crane, and seemed, in many ways, to justify the entire NTC experience: Let them all find out how screwed up they are now, instead of next year in a real war.

One way or another—and under the scalding wit of their colonel—the battalion finally got into some kind of line formation and began its journey up the long half-mile-wide valley toward the pass, only two hours late.

The convoy formation presents some tactical problems, and they get worse as the landforms close in. Armored units practice various movement techniques, generally classed as Traveling, Traveling Overwatch, and Bounding Overwatch. In the Traveling movement, the five tanks that form a tank platoon will lead the column by about a hundred feet, followed by the company commander in his M1 or, sometimes, in a humvee. Usually the FIST, or fire-support team, trailer will move with the commander, so that artillery fire and aviation assets can be called in as soon as the commander identifies an enemy concentration.

Behind the company commander's section Crane's battalion carried a mechanized platoon in their M113 personnel carriers, usually four in two staggered pairs. Then there was a platoon of four TOWs, followed by mobile artillery and mortar platoon vehicles. The communications van, the MASH vehicle, maintenance and tracked recovery vehicles form a staggered quadrant, followed by a final drag platoon of mechanized infantry, charged with covering the flanks and dealing with an enemy assault from the rear areas.

The trouble with this kind of advance, especially in a narrow canyon, is obvious. Most of the unit firepower is up front, so any advance into fire tends to feed units piecemeal into the grinder. The secret to surviving an attack when you are in column formation is to practice wheeling into an assault line, in effect to herringbone all your guns—from infantry M16s and SAWs and M203s all the way to your main tank guns—right and left down the line, as every unit trains its firepower to the flanks and in front. Do this fast and efficiently and you can survive, even defeat, an ambush by getting out reactive suppressing fire, pinning down the attacker, and getting maneuver units out under covering fire to counterattack and overrun the ambushers.

Dawdle, panic, or fumble even a little, and you'll get cut up into tiny pieces and the local women will come out later to take your underwear.

Of course, you can't wheel from line to assault formation in a canyon, which is why there are so many ambushes in canyons. Even muggers understand this factor. A slightly safer way to travel was Traveling Overwatch, where the column would be led by a tank section, backed up by another tank platoon, with more IFVs and TOWs following up. But Traveling Overwatch meant you traveled buttoned up, or at least you were supposed to, and that meant reduced visibility because of the slitted windows in the M113s and the TOWs. And you were still stuck in a tight place if it came to a fight. It was up to your point people, your scouts and foot patrols, to get up there in the hills and make sure there were no Comanches waiting for you to wander into their kill zone like a herd of buffalo. All of these factors make a Movement to Contact a dangerous and demanding maneuver.

Once an enemy has been located, the basic tactic for assault is Bounding Overwatch. Tanks would maneuver into hull-down positions overlooking the target sector. Infantry platoons would maneuver forward in their IFVs and APCs, under the cover of the main guns and the TOW units, which were usually positioned in another elevated sector, again hull-down and ready to fire. Artillery and mortar platoons would stay to the rear, ready to bring indirect fire to bear in support of the main infantry advance. All the communications and medical vans would beat it to a safe place out of the fire line, protected by elements of infantry and scout forces.

Then it was up to the tankers, your Div Arty, and the TOWs to suppress any enemy fire while the infantry cleared mines and bridged ditches, also keeping up their own suppressing and aimed fire. Units of the infantry would break up into squads and fire teams, covering each other in leapfrog rapid dashes until the enemy had been flanked and shot up thoroughly.

The enemy either surrendered or died, and you moved out to the next enemy concentration to do it all over again.

If you had air cover—choppers, Warthogs, a Spooky or two—so much the better. But the basic idea has not changed in ten thousand years. Whatever the size of the unit, a division or a brigade, a battalion or a company or a platoon, or six guys on a SEAL team crawling up a beach in Malibu, the game was always the same: Show up with the right force equipped properly, find the enemy with your scouts, pin him down with suppressing fire, get your Infantry in there to move under your cover, flank the enemy, bring massive fire down where he's weakest, shake him up, keep his head down, and overrun the position with bayonets fixed. Essentially, it was Go Go Go. Attack. Surround. Destroy. It was the kind of fighting that the Americans did better than anyone, with the possible exception of elite Armored regiments in the British forces, such as the Guards and the Household Cavalry.

That was the kind of thing Crane's men were supposed to do once they reached their objective in the morning. It was the kind of thing they had practiced in small-unit drills in the hill country north of Riley, and on maneuvers in REFORGER. But at the NTC, everything was different and nothing went precisely as planned.

Instead of arriving at their jump-off point in the pass just before dawn, they arrived after the sun was well up. The dust of their arrival was visible for miles and hundreds of IFVs and TOWs and platoons of M1 Abramses churned up the long valley floor and gathered in the pass. The scouts they had lost touch with hours before finally came on the 'net and announced that they had just chased OpFor scout units out of the ridges overlooking the pass, which meant that the OpFor was close and they probably knew the size and intentions of the Big Red column. So that was the end of the Movement to Contact part of the exercise, since the idea behind Movement to Contact is to find and fix the enemy with the smallest portion of your force, allowing the rest of your elements to get into position and coordinate a sudden and combined assault. Naturally this all goes to hell if the enemy knows everything you're doing.

So the Big Red was now ordered by the observers to change their FRAGORD—their Fragmentary Operations Order—from Movement to Contact to Deliberate Attack. In other words, it was the job of their task force to come down out of the pass, spread out on the plain in front of them, and root the OpFor out of those gullies and ridges about two miles away. The observers were calling the target sector North Valley.

As with most places the Army finds names for, this one had a hidden significance. The original North Valley was half a world away, near the Turkish city of Sebastopol. Defined by the Fedoukine and the Causeway Heights, the North Valley had been the site of the Charge of the Light Brigade during the Crimean War.

————————

The sun was touching the crests of a chain of peaks ten miles away, tinting them pink and purple. The valley in front of them was filled with shadows, like a huge pool of black water. As Crane sat in one of the Baker Company APCs and worked away at a can of peaches with his P38, he listened to the muted talk of the other sergeants and thought about his career.

Somewhere back down the valley they had just crossed, the colonel was in his TOC giving some thought to the tactical problems presented by this combined arms assault into North Valley. If Crane had taken advantage of the opportunities presented to him by the brass at the end of the Vietnam War, he could have been one of those officers in the TOC, holding rank and making the hard decisions. Instead, here he was in a forward APC filled with kids half his age, every one of whom wondered why he was still a noncom. And maybe this morning was as good an explanation as anything else he could think of.

Down there in front of them was a terrain crammed full of fatal possibilities. If the colonel gave them a battle plan that failed to provide for the special circumstances of this valley, he would lose a lot of men. And if he came up with a good plan, he'd still lose a lot of men. The big difference between officers and noncoms is that officers make command decisions and noncoms see that they become operational realities. In other words, officers set it up so that men will go off and die, and noncoms go along with the men to die right beside them.

Of the two, the command decision is the harder one. That's what the word *commissioned* really means. It means that this soldier carries a specific—and legally valid—commission from the Commander in Chief and the Congress that charges him with the responsibility of leading men into battle.

*Non*commissioned officers, such as sergeants, are not under the same heavy charge. They execute command decisions at the platoon level, but they don't take part in the development of those plans, except in an informal way through advice given to their lieutenants.

Making command decisions was something Crane felt he could never do, and he'd spent all of his years in the United States Army avoiding them. In many ways, he was a failure, a bench sitter. In modern America, ambition was a virtue. Crane was not ambitious, had in fact settled for less than he could have achieved, either in the Army or out in the world. In the still moments before an action, Crane sometimes faced these thoughts, and made no excuses for himself.

About the corrugated landscape before him, Crane had some specific thoughts. The hills around Riley were long and sweeping, covered with sweet grass and vetch and stands of cottonwoods. Like this ridged valley they were facing today, the hills around Riley provided a lot of hiding places, gullies and ditches and riverbanks where a good defender could dig in his tanks and TOW vehicles, set up a series of ambushes down the line of the washes, and wait for the target to wander into their kill zones.

If an attacker was dumb enough to come across those ridges in the standard armored assault, the attack would be broken up by the terrain. As each tank lumbered down the side of the bank, it would be wide open to flank rounds from the hidden defenders. RPGs would kill the fighting vehicles and the TOW launchers. Decent camouflage might hide the defenders from choppers and A-10s, at least long enough to take a few out with their Vulcan 20-mm cannons and whatever SAM or Stinger simulations they could field. Infantry APCs on escort would get enfiladed and erased. And if the attacker tried to skirt the flanks and come straight up the narrow wadis in line formation, his lead elements would be carved up and destroyed with no chance of getting cover fire from the rearward elements. Nasty.

Places like this rugged valley presented a very interesting military puzzle. It was a puzzle Crane knew how to solve because it was a puzzle *only* the infantry could solve. So he waited and ate canned peaches, and listened to his sergeants and platoonmates talk. Shabazz was part of an armor assault platoon, along with Mosby and Polanyi. A lot of other faces were present that would not be around in the Gulf War days, scattered throughout the Army in keeping with the bureaucratic belief that training was something you could catch from other men like the flu. Unlike the British and the Canadians, the U.S. Army was still breaking up and dissipating unit spirit, although they liked to pretend they weren't. But Crane was there, along with quite a few grunts from Baker, and they waited together in a kind of strung-tight humming readiness.

Orders came down a few minutes later. Scouts had determined that the OpFor units were scattered in force throughout most of the valley, with trip-wire patrols out on the ridges and all their heavy armor and weapons dug in hull-down in the washes, waiting for the Big Red to come rumbling into their ambushes.

The colonel's answer to that tactic was to send advance elements of dismounted infantry into the dry washes in front of the main armor assault. The infantry platoons would engage the OpFor tanks and fighting vehicles with LAWS rockets and Dragons, using silence and stealthy approach instead of a wild cavalry leap down the sides of the embankments. If the OpFor vehicles took enough MILES hits from the simulators, they'd be ''killed.'' If they didn't go down under the first infantry attacks, they'd have no choice but to get the hell up and out of the wadi, since going forward or backward along the wadi wouldn't get them out of the infantry line of fire.

And when the OpFor tanks reached the tops of the ridges, the tankers and the field artillery would be waiting for them. Driven into the open, the Big Red could take them out with direct fire and artillery fire called in by the FIST teams and the unit FDCs. It was a good plan, and Crane was happy to hear it, since it was the only plan that would have worked.

They moved off in an hour, spreading out across the valley floor in assault formation, with tank platoons out front and the Baker IFVs in support. The TOW vehicles and the company HQ armored personnel carrier brought up the middle of the second assault line, and the field artillery—Div Arty—units took up Overwatch positions on two elevations about a half mile back from the first of the dry washes. As they got to within a hundred yards of the first wadi, Crane could see OpFor scouts on foot, small green figures slipping backward up the ocher and red stone banks, getting out sporadic MILES fire with little effect.

Return MILES fire from the IFV 25-mm machine guns and the M1s drove the OpFor scouts over the far side of the wash, and they disappeared into the lee sides out of the fire lines. So far only two of their vehicles, an APC and one of the lead Abramses, had shown any MILES hits, their vehicle MILES lights flashing and then shutting off as the onboard microchip calculated insufficient incoming fire to disable the weapon.

Closing in on the first slope of the wadi, Crane knew what the OpFor was doing. It was the same thing Crazy Horse had done to Lieutenant Fetterman and a hundred cavalry troopers in northeastern Wyoming a hundred and thirty years ago: show yourself, make a weak resistance, and fall back toward a prepared ambush site.

The Baker Company men kept up their rate of fire, making sure the scouts got forced out of the rocks and down into the wadi. A

few seconds later, they were up into the rise of gravel and sand
and Crane's troops were dismounting—piling out of their battered old APC in the classic manner, the men with the M203 grenade launchers taking the outside right and left positions,
riflemen next, and the SAW men in support.

Crane was acting squad leader for the NTC deployment. Most
of the squad he led at the NTC would be transferred to other
units by the time of the Gulf War, but Shabazz was there, along
with Mosby—just out of Range Data and very, very green—and
Polanyi, also a raw kid fresh from boot at Benning. Mosby had the
M203 usually, but today Mosby and Polanyi were going to be dealing with the Dragon, a thirty-five-pound wire-guided antitank
rocket launcher that was as much fun to drag around in the field
as a canister vacuum cleaner. Everybody hated the damn thing,
but somebody had to carry it, and Mosby had volunteered. They
were in armor-killer formation today, Mosby and Polanyi with the
Dragon, Crane as squad leader carrying an M16 and two MILES-
fitted LAWS rockets, and another grunt named Hoechner who
carried the M249 SAW—the Squad Automatic Weapon—a recent
replacement of the Vietnam-era M60.

The second team was the support and security team, with Shabazz as team leader, two grunts with M16s, and two grunts with
M203s, which were M16s fitted with grenade launchers under the
barrels. Each man also carried at least two LAWS rockets.

Crane got his men deployed and they began to work their way
up the rocky slope toward the lip of the wadi. No one's MILES
sensor was beeping, so they had taken no hits.

Mosby and Polanyi reached the top of the wadi and stopped to
wait for their Overwatch team to catch up. Crane edged up to the
lip, feeling his age, trying to breathe softly. All down the wadi line,
other squads of infantry had reached the lip of the wadi banks.
The sun was now high enough in the sky that light was reaching
the crests of the ridges, but the washes were still in shadow. Looking down into the first wash over the iron sites of his M16, Crane
saw creosote bushes dotting a thirty-foot slope of boulders and
rocky fissures. The MILES laser gear made the site image useless,
and he missed the feeling that he could mark a target with tracers

to show his fire team where to shoot. But it still felt like combat, and the men at the crest with him were adrenalized and tight.

Crane put a SAW man on point with a maneuver team, keeping the second fire team back to provide cover fire. Mosby and Polanyi were the team's antitank force, so they held back with the cover team. There was no radio contact, for security reasons. Isolated from other maneuver units, working their way down the wadi slopes, Crane felt the return of an old combat reality, the sense that the war has come down to you and the ten other men in your rifle squad.

Fifteen minutes of careful squad movement went by. Then up at point, the rifleman raised his M16 overhead, then dropped into a crouch with his weapon held rigidly in the firing position. Crane's heart blipped. In silence, the rifle team came up into a hasty defense position. Crane moved up to the point guard and looked in the direction of the man's aim. . . .

Fifty feet up the wadi there was a large tangle of creosote bushes and branches. Hard as it was to tell living vegetation from dead here, these bushes looked exceptionally dry and parched. Even in the dim light, there was something odd about them. Crane pivoted and signaled for Mosby and Polanyi to bring up the Dragon. They did, slipping and sliding and bouncing as they came.

The Dragon was a pain in the ass to deal with, a two-part system made up of a detachable and reusable optical tracker, which weighed about six pounds, and the actual rocket round, which weighed twenty-six pounds including the wire bail and launcher rig. The Dragon looked like a big sewer pipe with a cone-shaped bulge at the rear. It had a backblast that could kill out to sixty yards, which produced a huge cloud of white smoke, marking you as a target immediately. And you had to hold the entire shoulder-mounted monstrosity steady for several seconds after you fired because the optics were linked to the rocket by the trailing wire, and you had to keep the target in your optics until the round hit home.

Naturally, in the meantime, the target or his support team was firing back at you, having marked you by your smoke cloud. Who-

ever called the thing a Dragon got that part right. By the time
Mosby and Polanyi had been in the field with the system for an
hour, they understood why the Dragon was the single most-often-
reported-lost piece of gear they carried. At least this time they
could fire it as a MILES weapon and not have to deal with all the
volcanics of the piece.

Mosby saw the tangle as soon as he came up. His young face
was bright red from effort, and his eyes were wide.

"That's a probable OpFor ambush," said Crane in a voiceless
whisper. "We're going to engage it. Support team will maneuver
and flush. If we blow something heavy, you engage it with the
Dragon. Okay?"

"Yes, sir," said Mosby, "I mean, Sergeant."

Polanyi started to say something. His MILES beeper went off
and a light flashed on his helmet. He literally screamed.

"Christ," said Crane. "We're taking fire."

Suddenly there was incoming laser fire from several sectors to
their front of right. Over on their left flank, three of Shabazz's
security team were sitting down with horrified looks on their faces,
their MILES beepers shrieking like car alarms. Crane got out some
return fire. Mosby had dropped the Dragon to look at Polanyi.

Polanyi looked up at Crane, tears in his eyes.

"Am I hit, Sergeant?"

Crane tried to keep his voice steady, but he was getting some
very old images in the back of his head, and they made him a
little sick.

"You're dead, Polanyi. Mosby, take that extra round, and get
yourself set. The rest of you, get some fire out, protect the
Dragon."

Twenty feet up the line, Shabazz had his support team re-
grouped. The OpFor snipers had gone for his M203 men in the
best tradition of ambushes. Shabazz plucked the launchers out of
the hands of his "dead" men, taking one for himself and giving
the other to the grunt with the M16.

Crane watched Shabazz take a quick look—he was cool and
careful—and then they started to put out fire. The light in the

wadi changed and now they could see the dark green uniforms of an OpFor rifle team, rushing toward them in Overwatch, as a second team covered them with MILES fire from around the tangle.

Then the tangle of brush emitted a burst of blue smoke and a massive roar and started to move out, branches and bushes falling away from it, dust billowing out of the rear. It was an OpFor BMP—actually a Sheridan with a missile rack and a smaller gun fitted. The up-armored BMP was a hard target for a MILES-equipped LAWS, and the NT computer credited it with a 73-mm smoothbore cannon, a Sagger missile, and at least eight infantry in support. As Crane watched, two of Shabazz's team fired their LAWS rockets at it, but the MILES hit indicator light only blipped once. The onboard computer had sensed the incoming LAWS and calculated an inadequate hit.

In the meantime, the BMP was coming up fast, and laser rounds were flickering all over their position. They were about to be overrun in their first combat action at the NTC.

Crane dropped down the arroyo, looking for his radioman, who was supposed to be right behind him. He found the guy sitting on a rock, looking at his helmet flasher. It was a steady yellow.

"I'm dead, Sarge."

"They get your radio?"

The boy shook his head. Crane scooped it up and called tank section. He gave them a fast contact report and asked for fire support. At that moment, Mosby got his Dragon in place and fired at the OpFor BMP.

The BMP hit light flickered on and began a steady flashing. The BMP turret popped open and an OpFor commander stuck his head up. Crane popped a shot at him and saw him duck back inside. The BMP swerved again as two more LAWS hits registered, and then it turned in its tracks and began to climb up out of the wadi on the far side, covered by OpFor skirmishers.

A lot of MILES fire flickered back and forth and three of the OpFor men got MILES hits and started beeping. But the BMP was still moving. Crane fired his second LAWS at the vulnerable rear deck of the BMP, thinking about diesel tanks and Afghanistan. The vehicle cleared the top of the ridge, hesitated, and suddenly the MILES indicator turned from a flash to a steady glow. It was technically a pile of molten steel and cooking men.

The BMP had driven up out of the small-arms fire in the wadi and right into the direct fire zone of an Overwatch M1 main gun. Exactly as the colonel had planned it. Lovely.

Crane and his armor assault team mopped up the surviving OpFor skirmishers and then they called in medevac for their "killed." Mosby was sitting with Polanyi, trying to console him, but Polanyi was still shaken by his early hit.

"I figured I was better than that, Sarge," he said as they waited for transport. "I can't believe I'm dead."

"Hey, you'll be alive again as soon as we get back to base."

"Yeah, but I'm dead *now*, Darryl. You don't know what it's like!"

The chopper drowned out the rest of their conversation, but it stayed with Crane for a long time, all the way through the rest of the fight for the North Valley, which was considered a tremendous success and got the colonel a rave review at that evening's after-action session.

Polanyi was right. And although he was raised from the dead later that afternoon, he never forgot the feeling of being picked off, and he and Mosby had a different relationship for about a week, until Mosby got "killed" in a strafing run—caught in the open while on a latrine trip by an OpFor Hind—at which point they became good friends again, because they had both been dead and they both agreed they hadn't liked it at all.

Crane always remembered that moment, when Polanyi had first realized he'd been hit, that he was dead, that there was no negotiation about it. He'd seen it happen a long time before the NTC, had watched the terrible understanding develop in a boy's pale blue face. The difference was, at the NTC, these kids didn't have to pay for the understanding with their hearts' blood. Maybe one day, if they got into a real war, it would save their lives, and the lives of the men they were leading.

For once, the Army had gotten something exactly right.

Well, thought Crane, the odds were with them. Not even the Army could screw up *all* the time.

CHAPTER TEN

HAMMERHEADS

FEBRUARY 24, 1991

It was midnight, the dead heart of a long damp night. In a haze of rain and fog and tension, Crane and DerHorst and the platoon LTs were bunched up in the doorway of Wolochek's hootch.

They were in full combat gear, Crane with a SAW and several grenades and DerHorst with an M16 and *two* 9-mm Berettas, Petrie with—God help us—a Stoner M63 that he'd wangled from a Ranger in King Khalid Military City, Seafferman and Rossberg with M16s. They were watching the company LT, Ackisson, who was watching Captain Wolochek, who was talking on the scrambled phone that connected Baker to the 16th HQ down the line. He was talking to the battalion XO, Crane knew, because Wolochek's voice was muted and slightly distorted by a fearful awe.

Outside the captain's hootch, the men of Baker Company were arranged in parade formation, four platoons of forty men plus the HQ platoon sergeants and the squad leaders. They were at parade rest and had been for about three hours. Now they were sitting or standing around in a ragged formation, smoking, talking softly, listening to the artillery parks cranking up, listening to the tankers rev their engines and the ordnance people check the fire-readiness tags and magazines. Now and then a couple of Apaches from the 4th Cavalry—their air-support choppers—would hammer through the wet night air a few hundred feet overhead.

It was cold and wet and the air reeked of diesel and JP5 and the stink of the burning downrange. Visibility was less than a hundred yards and the whole company was pretty much agreed that Saudi Arabia was where they'd put the hose if the world needed an enema. Inside the hootch, Wolochek nodded three times reverentially, put the scramble phone down into the clamps, and looked up at them all, his face pale and his eyes wide.

"He wants me to say something to the guys."

DerHorst and Crane grinned through their face paint, and DerHorst said, "Tell them we canked the war, sir, it was all a mistake. Homer just got lost on his way home from work."

Wolochek smiled back at him. "No, let's get out there, say something stirring. I hope I can think of something."

The platoon LTs backed up in a tangle and went to their positions and DerHorst brought Baker Company to attention. As Wolochek struggled with his MOPP bag and his pack and his side arm, Crane thought about last night, what he had said to Mosby and the other fire-team leaders in Baker Company.

They'd come to his tent after the word had come down from HQ that they were definitely going in. Twenty or twenty-five young kids, a deputation from the whole company, each one of them a kind of leader, the standout kids in the unit. Crane had been expecting a few, but twenty-five was a surprise.

They'd knocked on the door of his hootch while he was cleaning his SAW. "Jeez, troops, what's this? A choir?"

Mosby had laughed and there was a scattering of smiles.

"No, sir. We come from the guys back on the line."

"Don't call me sir, Mosby. Don't hurt me like that."

More weak smiles. "Okay. Let's hear it."

There was no hesitation. Mosby was clearly the spokesman, although there were three corporals in the crowd behind him.

"Sergeant, we've seen the briefing maps and the aerials and . . .

well, it doesn't look to us like there's a lot of damage out there. I mean, things look pretty solid, the berms and shit.''

This Crane did not like.

"Mosby, I got no time for—"

"Sergeant, we're not—nobody's wimping out or anything. It's just that some of the guys, we were hoping maybe you could tell us what the brass is gonna do. Nobody's telling us anything and that leaves us all thinking."

"Too much, Mosby."

"Yes, sir—"

"Don't sir me, kid . . . look . . . I've been under a Buff strike. It has a pucker factor of ten outta ten. And you guys have all seen the PsyOps leaflets, you've been briefed on how to process prisoners. These guys out there, I guarantee you, they're colder and sicker and a damn sight hungrier than you, they got fleas and ticks and dysentery and a lot of them haven't eaten anything but fingernails for weeks. I don't want you to underestimate them, but don't make them bigger than they are."

"We're not, Sergeant. All we're looking for is some tactical info, we can take it to the guys, just so they'll know."

Crane, torn and irritated, considered them. They weren't kids anymore. They were soldiers. He ought to tell them to shut up and go away, take their problems to Mom or their wives and girlfriends. Here's a quarter, kid. Call someone who cares. But he didn't.

"Look, I'll tell you what I honestly believe. . . . I believe, in my heart, that we are going to blow their doors off and roll over them like they were speed bumps. We have total air superiority so we can bring in the snakes and the Warthogs, shoot the shit outta them. This is classic AirLand War, it's doctrine all the way. We are the best the world has ever seen. You are the best grunts this Army has ever fielded. If you keep your heads, do what you've been trained to do, those ragheads out there are knocking on heaven's door right now. You cannot lose. That's what I believe. You cannot lose. Is that good enough?"

"About casualties, Sergeant Crane—"

Oh, Christ.

"Yes, son? What about them?"

"You think there'll be a lot?"

"Not on your end of the barrel."

"But . . . there'll be some . . . there have to be."

"Yes. Yes, that's true. There'll be some, and some will catch a round or maybe step on something. There's no way around that. I don't know how to talk that away for you. I wouldn't try if I could. I have more respect for you than that. But we all die sooner or later, and I believe in my heart that it is better to die trying to do something . . . that sounds like bullshit, but . . . what we have to do, that's important. Maybe it didn't have to happen, this war, like I told you back in November when we deployed. But what it is, it goes back a thousand years, and the First goes back a hundred years, and if it happens to you—and it probably won't—then you'll be a part of that, and no one in the First will ever forget you. Your name will be up there on the wall at Danger Forward for as long as there *is* a First Infantry. If that doesn't help you guys, I don't know what else to say."

Christ, what a speech. Where the hell did this come from?

They were grinning now and Crane felt a rush of strange emotion, and his throat hurt and his face was hot.

"Thanks for talking to us, Sergeant Crane."

"Mosby, the honor was mine."

And they left, a straggling pack of little kids with guns, shuffling, pushing each other, laughing, walking away into the misty darkening air under a sky that looked like the lid of a crypt. Crane watched them go with his throat tight and a burning in his eyes.

It was true. The honor was his.

A few hours later, near dawn, the barrage began.

The artillery of the 3rd Air Defense Brigade and the 5th Arty—the multiple rocket launchers capable of firing twelve missiles over sixty miles, the M109 and 110 self-propelled howitzers, and the smaller towed M102 105s—opened up in a ragged, rolling, gathering blast of fire that became a sky-wide sheet of white flame crossed by thousands of red tracers and rocket trails, all of it heading north into the berms where the Iraqi 26th Infantry was dug in behind a complex of kill zones.

For weeks now the air war had pounded Iraqi positions. One of the goals of the air campaign had been the elimination of Iraqi minefield defenses. Every kind of ordnance was dropped on the AO, including at least seven BLU-82s, fifteen-thousand-pound Daisy Cutter bombs that detonated at three feet off the ground, designed to literally crush and explode antitank and antipersonnel mines in a thousand-yard radius. The concussive force of one BLU—called Blues Brothers by the 1st Special Ops Wing—can cause massive internal bleeding anywhere in a radius of one mile. BLU-82s, beehive bombs, and fléchette rounds had all been used in an all-out attempt to clear a path for the ground assault. Now the final stage, the artillery barrage, had begun.

Each time the guns fired, the flare and the blowback would light up the buttoned-down turrets of M1 Abrams tanks spread out in skirmish formation along a six-mile-wide line. Behind them came the armored personnel carriers, the Bradley fighting vehicles, and the weapons-configured humvees of the scouts and the HQ battalions, and behind that the trucks and the armored tankers and the communications vans. The formation was Traveling Overwatch, as it had been at the NTC, a Movement to Contact with the certainty of a full-line attack at the phase line.

It was about an hour before dawn. The terrain in front of them was filled with drifting black smoke, with fog and rain and the haze of ten thousand vapor trails, the gathering fog of battle.

The entire division was up and armed and in formation. During the last week, they had been restricted to hardwire communications, absolute radio silence. Entire battalions of armor and mechanized infantry had moved out of their bases and deployed along their jump-off sectors. Crane and Wolochek had briefed the Baker Company sergeants a few hours before, but their basic assignment had been obvious for weeks. They had about ten miles of flat desert terrain to cover at speed. They were taking on an entire Iraqi regiment of infantry supported by tanks and artillery, dug in and fortified along a line about eleven miles wide.

The Iraqis had burrowed in and bermed up, and every stretch

of open ground would be assigned to some interlocking source of fire—machine guns, tank fire, rifle fire. The forward sections of the lines would be covered in mines. Then the tanks and the heavy armor would have to breach the ten-foot-high walls of sand, only to come down into a kill zone covered in razor wire and more mines, backed by antitank ditches twelve feet wide and ten feet deep, filled with metal spikes, burned-out vehicles, concrete blocks, and command-detonated fifty-gallon oil drums filled with fougasse and napalm. And while the forward tanks and IFVs were trying to negotiate this maze, they'd be taking heavy fire from tanks and zero-cranked antiaircraft guns hidden behind hardened fire-point berms, flanked by infantry troops with RPGs and machine guns and grenade launchers.

And the whole ugly array would be backed up by another squadron of heavy T-55 tanks inside triangular fortifications—sand berms piled up to ten feet high, two thousand meters to a side, with entire infantry companies of two hundred men dug in at each of the three corners of the triangle.

It was a classic killing zone, designed to tangle up, stall, and finally destroy the assaulting forces in a carefully calculated terrain where every weapon had its specific yardage to cover, where all the fields of fire were interlocking and overlapping, where the only cover would certainly be a mined command-detonated trap designed to lure the ground trooper looking for a place to dig in. From the air, the Iraqi positions looked like a long line of saw-toothed iron and sand berms, even after the weeks of aerial bombardment. Even after the B-52 raids.

The order of battle was classic tank warfare, the tactics very similar to the way infantry maneuvered. During an assault, the Abramses were deployed in platoons of four tanks each, moving at a spacing of about fifty feet, with the platoon leader slightly in the lead and second from the left, and the platoon sergeant's tank to the right of the platoon leader and slightly rearward. Two tank was on the far left, and four tank on the flank right. Called a Combat Wedge, the inner tanks (the platoon leader and platoon sergeant) would engage targets to their front, and the flank tanks would take on targets to the right and left.

In the Combat Column formation—similar to fighter-jet combat formations called "finger-fours," the platoon leader moves with the two tank on his left, four tank to his rear, and the platoon sergeant tank to the rear and the left of the four tank. In this diamond-shaped pattern, the two lead tanks would move forward to engage an enemy while the two following tanks would get hull-down and provide covering fire, in the same manner that infantry squads carry out Bounding Overwatch assaults.

Tankers would maneuver in leapfrog formations, at sixty miles an hour, acquiring targets in their infrared laser range finders, firing at will, killing enemy tanks and heavy-weapons emplacements, leading the assault.

In between the tank echelons, the infantry IFVs would maneuver in skirmish formation, each IFV armed with a TOW II antitank rocket launcher and a 25-mm chain gun. The IFVs were tread vehicles with a top speed of sixty-six miles an hour and they were capable of taking light to medium fire and surviving. Each IFV carried seven troopers, a fire team of riflemen, grenade men, and the squad auto man.

Even under the best circumstances, traveling in a buttoned-up Bradley was an ugly business, seven men jammed onto two narrow benches, gear and munitions underfoot, hanging on to belts and handholds as the machine jolted and pounded over the terrain, seeing nothing, listening to gunfire and the chatter of the radioman, waiting for that HESH round to come arcing in through the steel walls and turn the inside of the IFV into a Cuisinart. To the infantry grunt, the IFVs were quite literally hell on wheels.

As long as the tank advance was moving well, the men would fire and fight from the open hatches of their IFVs, but once they hit the Iraqi lines, it could turn into a dismounted and hand-to-hand fight, on foot in the smoke and fog of battle, each trooper in a way on his own, each fire team trying to accomplish its objectives and stay in touch with the other teams.

Overhead, Apache and Cobra gunships would see the "painted" targets picked out by ground troops with lasers, take them out with chain guns, Hellfires, TOWs, and bursts of 70-mm folding-fin rockets from circular pods under their stabilizers. And above that, the Warthogs, at five hundred feet and three hundred miles an hour. It was a blitzkrieg war, and for the one hundred and seventy men remaining operational in Baker Company, the time had come to get the answer to the only real firefight questions.

Will I fight?

Will I die?

And for some of the men and women of the 1st Infantry Division, there was a special significance to that last question, since the last time the Big Red One had fought in a foreign desert, it had been in Tunisia, in northern Africa. The name of the place was burned into the skin of the 1st Infantry.

The Kasserine Pass.

CHAPTER ELEVEN

SOME GREAT THING

THE WESTERN MEDITERRANEAN, NOVEMBER 1942

They had cleared Gibraltar at dawn and steamed eastward into the Mediterranean all day and into the night, but now, at a little past midnight—November 8, 1942—a couple of miles off the coast, one of General Terry Allen's officers called up to his cabin and told him how it was for the men in the holds, that it was like a Turkish bath down there. Could he let some of the troops go on deck, get some air?

Allen said, Yes, get them ready, we'll be going in soon.

First Sergeant Drew Spotwood brought his squad up in a straggle, sweating like miners climbing out of an iron ground, Spotwood fighting his seasickness, hungry for a look at a place he had never seen, a place out of Conrad, or Melville. That was when they all got their first look at Africa.

It filled the southern horizon, a low rolling landmass dusted with starlight, immense and velvety-looking under the gliding moon. Chains of yellow and pale blue lights lay scattered along the coastline, gathering into constellations like a bowl of jewels at Algiers and the port of Oran. The huge lighthouse in Oran harbor sent a dense blue-white tube of light out across the bay, the glare sweeping over the dark rusted hulls of the troopships. Shore lights lay on the deep blue of the Mediterranean, a scintillation of liquid fire all the way to the beaches, and the night sky full of stars was in the water too, so that when the men looked down from the rusted hulls of the troopship into the water it was dizzying, as if the sky was beneath them and the deep blue sea above.

Soon all the men were on the deck, leaning out over the water, breathing in the strangeness of Africa, breathing in the scent of oranges and cedars and rotting fruit, of salt marsh and seaweed and drying fish on the docks down in the harbor, the acrid reek of cooking oil and ghee and spilled arrack, and kerosene from the heaters, and diesel oil from the French ships, the smell of hashish and roasting meat, and underneath it all that ancient eternal sweetly rotten fragrance of the Mediterranean.

For Drew Spotwood, it was Youth, it was the breath of the East, the walking ghost of the ancient world, the heart of darkness itself, and he believed that every man on the ship with room for anything other than his own fear must feel a kind of silent rushing exhilaration, must feel that for once in his short life he was at the edge of some great thing, that forever afterward he would come back to this hour, turn it in his hands and hold it up to the light of memory, see himself inside that moment—unchanging and perfect in his youth—see down the spiraling nautilus of time and hear once more the lost voices of his friends, hear the wind from Africa and the booming of the surf on that glittering distant shore.

Spotwood felt the cold iron railing in his hands, and the crush of men around him, their voices high and brittle with tension, and through the iron he could feel the steady rumor of the engines as the troopship churned at half speed through the cold water. He looked at his watch—the Hamilton that Penny had given him when they left Fort Riley; it was midnight and someone remembered to get the radio.

One of the Abel Company kids, a fisherman from Carolina named Peak, set it on a pile of landing nets and fiddled with the knobs while everyone gathered around, Frewer and Turwhitt and Boone, Steiner and Occhionegro, Callan, Dent, and Gruenwald, and behind them, in the rigging or lying on armored vehicles and crated supplies, in full combat gear, holding their Garands and Thompsons, their faces stiff with tension, the rest of the men of the 16th Infantry.

Peak slapped the radio once—the set hissed and crackled like bacon in a skillet—someone laughed, and then they heard his voice, the voice of the President, that old familiar slightly nasal patrician drawl.

"Hello, Morocco . . . to all the people of North Africa who are this night suffering under the crushing Nazi yoke . . . all my life I have held a deep friendship for the people of France. I know your farms, your villages—"

"Your sisters," said someone, and they laughed.

"—we arrive among you with the sole objective of crushing your enemies . . . we assure you that once the menace of Germany and Italy has been removed we shall quit your territories—"

"Vichy bastards," said Peak, who had been talking to the Free French sailors and had learned to hate Pétain.

"—appeal to your realism, to your self-interest, to French national ideals. Do not, I pray you, oppose this great design. Lend us your help wherever you can . . . and we shall see again that glorious day when liberty and peace once more reign. . . . *Vive la France éternelle!*"

Spotwood watched the faces of his men, half-trained kids who had been holding up malt-shop counters or running harvesters for Dad less than six months ago, civilians in uniform with no combat training and damn little unit cohesion.

Turwhitt had been a shoe salesman, Boone a museum guard, Steiner a postman, Occhionegro worked in his father's lumber mill in Portland, Gruenwald had been something minor in a Woolworth store in Columbus, Dent a draftsman with a planning council in Kansas City, Peak and Frewer runaways from a fishing village in the Carolinas. . . .

Spotwood and the other sergeants, they'd done what they could with them at Riley and later in Scotland, but they'd been too busy chasing the pub girls in the town, spending all that Yankee scrip—Christ, a PFC in the 1st was making *five times* what a Tommy made; it was no wonder the Brits were cranky with the Americans. Well, payback was coming up. The party was definitely over and Spotwood had a feeling it was going to take more than sweet talk from FDR to get the Vichy French to put their guns down.

He was looking back out over the water when one of the other ships fired three flares up—they arced and floated down, trailing white smoke, three of them—red—white—blue—the colors of the U.S. and the colors of France.

They fluttered down over the water, gliding down to meet their rising reflections as the boys on the decks cheered and some seamen sounded a blast on the whistle—so much for surprise, thought Spotwood, feeling another wave of seasickness come over him—and at that point the mammoth lighthouse in Oran harbor flicked off.

Now that, thought Spotwood, is not a good sign.

———

And on the shore of Africa, no more than two miles from Spotwood, Admiral Darlan, commander of the French forces in North Africa, stared back out at the ships lying in the roads of Oran harbor and swore softly to himself, remembering how the British had seized his ships in Portsmouth two years ago, killing three of his sailors, and later, at Alexandria, the same thing, and then, right here in Oran and at Mers el Kebir, the British fleet shelled them and planes from the *Ark Royal* bombed them all through a hot July afternoon, and by the end of that day, one thousand men were dead and three ships of the French Navy were hull-down in deep water and well afire, a battleship and two destroyers—and that fat Anglo pig Churchill with his pious lies about the war effort and the Nazis and the judgment of history—the little fat sailor in his tight blue uniform was literally hissing with anger—and now they are back—and *les amis* with them—and they want to come ashore. . . . Well, let them come on, Lafayette or no, and we will see how it goes for them.

———————

On the troopship a siren sounded and Spotwood's belly jumped. He leaned over the side and returned his dinner to the elements, getting a slap on the back from Peak, and a cheer from his men, and a curse from a sailor in a landing craft below him. An officer yelled. More sirens.

And then the nets rolled down the hulls and they were climbing down toward the rolling waves, the men all around him, no talking now, just the business of getting into the landing craft, and the officers yelling orders. Spotwood jumped to the deck of the craft, stumbled, and was caught by an English sailor, who grinned at him, holding Spotwood's arm in a fist as hard and gnarled as a briarroot. And all the way in they sat in silence, feeling the engine vibrating in the hull, bobbing and tossing in the little plywood shells, listening to the waves slap and burble, listening to each other's shallow, ragged breathing, waiting for the shore batteries—the mammoth French 75s that could throw a shell out nineteen thousand yards—waiting for the first air-splitting boom and the rushing runaway shriek of incoming shells . . .

. . . that never came.

They made the beaches south of Oran, clambering up out of the water, soaked and heavy in their woolen uniforms, sand in their collars and in their mouths, hundreds of men gathering in knots and clusters on the rocks and sand of Africa, some uneven and panicky fire came in, rifle rounds—the effect was electric, jolting, and all down the beachhead they dropped to the ground and fired into the darkness beyond the sand, and they could see little blue-white flickers, returning fire, and more rounds came hissing and zipping in like little hornets.

But it was still ragged and careless, the French, whoever, and after they fired back for a time, the resistance stopped and the beach was theirs. The 1st Infantry was back in a war, after twenty-eight years, and it seemed to Spotwood and his men that so far this was okay, it wasn't as bad as they had thought.

They hooked up with the men and vehicles of the 1st Armored Division and started up the road toward the city itself, ready to take Oran away from the French, who didn't seem to have a real good grip on reality and would have to be shown whose side they were on.

Out in Oran harbor, the *Walney* and the *Harland*—a couple of U.S. Coast Guard cutters, manned by English sailors—tried to land some Rangers in the port area, and at that point, things started to get a little wilder. Spotwood could hear firing—big guns—as they worked their way along a beach road, and when they came up a long rise, suddenly the entire port was laid out in front of them.

They got there just in time to see a long, white-hulled French sloop—it was called *La Surprise*—make a ramming run at the *Walney*. Even from shore Spotwood could hear someone on the *Walney* using a loud-hailer, telling the French to stop, to pull away, but the French could only see the British ensign on the mast of the *Walney* and it blinded them with anger.

Now tracer fire began to flicker and arc across the water. To Spotwood and the troops of Abel Company it looked like a fireworks display, the lights of Oran shining across the water, the chatter and crackle of small-arms fire and the sudden barking report of ship guns, spouts of water jetting up, smoke blanketing, and the white wake curling out behind the ships like lace torn from a gown. The fighting was getting hotter and the smell of the cordite drifted down the sea breeze toward Spotwood, like the visible spirit of combat. It was as if someone was slowly turning up the dial, accelerating the fight into a real war, the French at first halfhearted but now the guns were banging away and men had begun to die, now the blood was up and Spotwood felt heat rising into his face.

Peak, who had been a fisherman and knew about boats and sailing, yelled something about raking fire, and sure enough, the

sloop *La Surprise,* sails fluttering and ragged now, turned to port
and came about, running parallel to the *Walney,* sliding past it in
the opposite direction.

They could see it coming. Suddenly the entire starboard rail of
the French sloop flashed into fire, a shattering enfilade of rifle
and cannon fire, and they raked the *Walney* from bridge to fantail.

"That ship's full of Rangers," said Frewer, Peak's buddy, and
someone at the rear of the column said, "Not anymore."

Cannon fire began to come in from French batteries on shore.
The shells straddled the *Walney,* zeroing in on it, and the next one
blew it apart. They could see men flying up from her deck in crazy
doll-like contortions, borne on a pillar of fire, coming apart, and
more Rangers trying to get into their landing craft, ducking down
as spouts of water blossomed around them, and the rumble of the
fighting grew into a sustained deafening, rolling explosion that
Spotwood and his men could feel on their cheeks and against
their chests and bellies, a soft insistent push.

They watched the *Walney* burn and sink, men struggling in the
burning water. French guns now found the other Coast Guard
cutter, the *Harlan,* which was also full of Yanks, Rangers, and some
men from the 9th Infantry—old friends of the Big Red One—and
in a moment the *Harland* took six shells and she seemed to lift
up—to rise up out of the water, as if taken from beneath by a
white whale, and as she rose up she broke apart in a billow of
yellow and red fire and another concussive wave rolled over the
water and up the headland and slapped their faces, and it came
to Spotwood at that moment that FDR had his answer from the
Vichy French, and Oran would have to be taken away from them
the hard way.

It was the same down at Casablanca and Rabat, where Patton
was getting his nose bloodied for the first time since Mexico, and
for General Ryder, who was east of them, landing at Algiers, and
all along the North African coast.

The British and the Americans had to take Morocco and negotiate around neutral Spanish Morocco and grab as much as they
could of Algiers, and every one of the fourteen French divisions
in the territory fought them hard and long, until Admiral Darlan,

his honor satisfied, allowed a cease-fire after two days and Spotwood and his men were now free to go east with the 1st Armored and fight a different army—Rommel's Afrika Korps, waiting for them in the desert. Waiting for them on the downhill slope of the Kasserine Pass.

––––––––––

Spotwood came awake under a soft rainfall, the droplets making a ticking sound on his helmet like a tin clock working, at four in the morning by his Hamilton. Looking down at it in the darkness, seeing the glowing numbers, he thought about Penny, what was she doing right now, what time would it be in Kansas now, and it hit him with a jolt that this was Valentine's Day, the fourteenth of February in 1943.

He struggled out from under his poncho and stumbled, stiff legged and chilled to the core, across the stony little wadi toward the latrines. The rain came down harder as he walked, and someone on the hillside above him coughed and stirred, sending a stream of pebbles down the cliff face. A picket. Who was on watch?

Frewer, maybe. He had turned into a loner since Peak was bayoneted to death by an infiltrator, alone and with his goddam pants down, killed while taking a shit, for chrissake—Frewer had hunted for that infiltrator for a day and a night. So Frewer could be depended on to stay awake on a night watch because he liked to kill Germans and was getting pretty good at it.

The rest of Abel Company—what was left of it and some replacements—were scattered all up and down this wadi, holding a position beneath a hill called Djebel Lessouda, where the 1st Armored Division had an observation post.

They'd come two thousand miles from Oran in the last two months, trying to bring the Afrika Korps to a conclusion, with damned little success, dying in stupid accidental firefights and ambushes—learning by dying, Spotwood called it—finding out some ugly things about their Honey tanks—that the antiaircraft guns would jam if you fired them full auto because the links on the ammo chains were faulty and every fifth or sixth round would rattle loose at the worst possible moment.

Also they learned about blitzkrieg, about the sudden whirlwind of guns and steel and Stukas that would rise up out of nowhere and roll over you like a landslide. Did you know, for example, that Stukas had sirens on their wingtips? And the sound of a Stuka coming in was like a gut-shot horse screaming in a well and could frighten a man quite literally to death. Occhionegro, the lumber-man from Portland, had died of a heart attack during their first meeting with a Stuka the week before Christmas.

They learned as well that the Germans were very, very good and even if you drove them out of a position, they immediately re-grouped and came right back at you, or if you drove them off a hill and down a valley slope and figured you had them on the run, you'd find out they had hidden a machine-gun nest in the down-slope and now they were behind you and you were in the open and had your back turned so that the first clue you had they were there was when the front of your chest blew out and you saw your lungs hit the rocky ground just before you did.

And then there were the Panzers—Christ, the Panzers were sixty tons of moving iron. They were the war gods of battle here in North Africa. Spotwood, who was educated, always heard Wagner when he saw a Mark IV Tiger coming up the wadi. It was Götter-dämmerung and the *Ring* cycle, and he remembered that Julius Caesar never beat the German tribes, that the Tenth Legion had lost their Eagles, and Varus, before he died under an ax in a forest near the Rhine, liked to say that the Germans were either at your feet or at your throat.

Well, here in North Africa, it was all throats and axes and iron crosses painted on pale yellow steel, and Wagner would have been in heaven.

But for the Yanks it was not heaven, not at all, unless you got there the way Peak did, wrapped around a German bayonet, alone in a ditch with his pants around his ankles and a piece of Army form blank clutched in his bloody fingers. It was a kind of pale ocher hell where the deaths were as sudden as they were obscene.

Now and then, in a long watch, staring out across the silver and gray of the Medjerda valley under a night sky full of alien ice-cold stars he would remember how he had felt back at Oran, about

Conrad and the mysterious East, and it was hard to balance that with Peak's death, or Occhionegro, struck to the ground by sheer animal terror.

Or consider Gruenwald with his legs blown off by a British mine, killed by a burning Sherman full of cooking corpses that was still rolling, still churning forward, and Gruenwald unable to get out of the way.

Spotwood, seeing it too late, had tried to shoot Gruenwald and missed, and the Germans were shooting at him as well—maybe even out of compassion—because no one could go out into the beaten zone to get him, and Frewer was up the line, so Spotwood tried again and missed, and then the Sherman had ground across him, traveled another ten yards, and blown up.

It was a nasty thing, this war, and if there was some greater purpose to it, it was not clear to Spotwood, not clear at all.

It was a hard war for the Americans. The 18th got mauled at Longstop Hill, Djebel Almera, during the Christmas fighting, and the 26th after that, along with the Brits—the Lothian Horse and the 17th Death's-head Lancers too—although the British were damn good and knew what they were doing here in Africa. They had kicked Jerry in the nuts at El Alamein last year.

If it hadn't been for the Brits, they wouldn't have gotten as far as they did, pushing the Afrika Korps back—rock by rock and death by death, two thousand miles, all the way to this long ugly valley, the Medjerda valley, with Tunisia and the sea in the far blue distance, and the entire Afrika Korps on the flat plains and rocky hills in between.

Spotwood hated the entire country, had come to hate anything remotely Arabian, and above all he had come to hate the Medjerda valley itself, and all that it contained, living and dead, British and Yankee, stone or bone.

At Djebel Lessouda—*djebel* meant "hill" in the hideous gargle talk of the Arab tribesmen who infested the place—you could see twenty-five miles down the valley and across the flat plains toward the Kasserine Pass, the end of their advance so far, and beyond that to Tunis, see the shimmer of the salt lakes around Tunis, and see the road they would one day have to fight along, because all of that valley and the city of Tunis belonged to the 10th Panzer Division, to Rommel and von Arnim and the Afrika Korps. They could have it.

Really it was not a valley at all, Spotwood thought, looking at it. It was a wasteland of alkali flats and dry washes, divided in a haphazard way by chains of rocky mountains about a thousand feet high, the Dorsales, yellow as an old man's teeth, worn by sand and wind for thousands of years.

They had shoved Jerry backward out of Algeria and on into Tunisia and now the front had stalled into a long curving chain of ruined armor and dead men that ran down the center of Tunisia, from the north coast near Bizerte and Bone, and southward all the way to Gafsa, about halfway through the country, where it ran west again in a sharp hook, ending in a great salt flat called Shatt al Jerid.

Everything east of that line, and everything south of Shatt al Jerid, belonged to the Tigers and the Panzers. The Brits held the top of Tunisia, around Le Kef, and then the French—the turncoat bastards nobody trusted and never would, not after Oran and Algiers and Fedala—and dead in the middle of the worst of it were the Americans, holding the valley and the mountains.

And in the very center, shaped like a huge ragged stone X, the Kasserine Pass, which led down into the plains and the coastal regions of Tunisia.

If they were going to go after the Germans, they'd have to come down through the Kasserine to do it, and no one was under any delusions about that job. They'd had a bellyful of the Afrika Korps.

And it was also clear to every line trooper in the theater that when, not *if, when* Jerry decided to come out of eastern Tunisia after them—because Jerry's back was to the sea and Rommel was the best there ever was—then the door that Jerry would kick in first would be the road leading from Faid across the Sbeitla Highway, and that road led, like an electric wire, directly into the Kasserine Pass; when Rommel came, it would be the Americans who would have to stop him.

Right there, on the map. X marks the spot.

The 1st Infantry, the 1st Armored, and the British tankers, the 17th and 21st Lancers—their badge was a silver skull and crossed bones and the motto "Or Glory"—were stalled at Djebel Lessouda on the fourteenth, dug in and stalled, and as far as Spotwood and the rest of the men of the 16th Infantry were concerned, the Germans could fucking well *have* Tunis and the rest of North Africa as well, including every Arab tribesman from Rabat to Tripoli.

Spotwood and his platoon and the tankers of the 1st Armored were getting extremely tired of digging in at a position, camouflaging it, setting up an ambush—because an ambush was the only way you were going to take out a squadron of Panzers—and then looking down the valley and seeing some Arab tribesman squatting in the dust beside a German scout car, chattering away in the blue hazy distance with the Germans all around, and then he'd point up the slope toward the American position and everybody would groan and swear because another little raghead bastard had just sold them out. Again.

The men of Spotwood's unit, especially Frewer, had taken to simply shooting them out of hand. When Frewer was a fisherman he used to shoot sharks with an old Springfield rifle his father had brought back from the Great War, and he was a very good shot then, but now, hardened by Peak's ugly ending, he had become very strange and was now a flawless rock-steady sniper.

Two days ago, on the hellish road to Djebel Lessouda, Spotwood and Frewer were scouting up a wadi when they cleared a hilltop and got a long look down a valley and out into the plains.

Way off in the distance, hazy and shimmering in the wind, Spotwood had seen a small cluster of vehicles. He tapped Frewer on the shoulder and Frewer had taken a look through the binoculars, his mouth opening in a sideways kind of grin that resembled someone peeling leather off bone.

Frewer carried a bolt-action Remington .308 with a heavy barrel and a Bushnell hunting scope. He pulled it around on the sling while Spotwood took his jacket off and bunched it up on a rock so that Frewer could rest his elbow on it as he braced.

Spotwood watched the vehicles through his binoculars, saw the

Arab tribesman squatting by the *kugelwagen,* and the two Germans
in their dusty pale Afrika Korps uniforms—why did Arabs always
squat when they were making a trade? By the range marks in his
field glasses, it was almost eight hundred yards. He sat very still
while Frewer steadied, saying nothing, doing nothing to break
Frewer's concentration. Frewer was becoming stone, and had a
way of getting so still that it was hard to tell he was still alive and
was not just an outgrowth of the wooden stock on the rifle.

A soft wind was sighing in Spotwood's ears, and he felt the cold
in the stones under his knees. Clouds moved across the pale sky
and a huge blue-gray shadow was floating across the distant valley.
It looked like a manta ray gliding over the ocean floor.

There was a short, sharp click, then the big percussive crack of
the Remington—Frewer's body jerked a bit and dust lifted off the
rocks in front of the muzzle—and in his glasses Spotwood could
see the little blue cloth tangle of the Arab as he tumbled forward.
Now the echo of Frewer's shot was rolling away down the rock
face and fading, and Frewer worked the bolt—the Germans were
scrambling into the *kugelwagen*—Frewer fired again—the German
behind the wheel snapped backward, his head jerking, the other
German was pulling at something in the back—a rifle—and he
got his hands on it, it was hard to see because dust from Frewer's
firing was drifting across his vision. He heard Frewer's bolt clack-
ing and snapping and the tiny metallic *ping* of the spent cartridge
as it hit the ground—*boom*—another deep sharp crack and the
kugelwagen jerked forward. The soldier must have started it from
under the dash and it was in gear now although no one was at
the wheel and the German was trying to get his rifle free of the
baggage in the rear. Spotwood grinned and imagined the man
crying and cursing, struggling with the weapon, his hands trembling, the bolt snapping again, another delicate crystalline *ping* as
the cartridge bounced on stone—*boom*—and suddenly the
German pitched sideways and was gone, and they watched for a
while as the *kugelwagen,* its wheel cranked right, began to run in
a slowly widening circle, around and around the pile of tiny blue
cloth in the middle of the valley.

It was still running in that circle when one of the 1st Armored Shermans reached it a half hour later. And that night they took up their positions along the slopes of the Djebel Lessouda and thirty-six hours later, on Valentine's Day, the Tigers came out of the east.

———

It was the first day of the battle that would later be known as the Kasserine Pass, because that was where it all was decided, and throughout the next days and nights it was fire and run and pull back in the face of the oncoming German assault—pull back out of the ruined bases—out of Sidi Bou Zid and Bir el Ali and Feriana—the Germans had broken through all along the Dorsales and were inside the rear areas now—pull out of Gafsa where the 168th Infantry had been decimated, its hundred eighty-nine officers and thirty-eight hundred men reduced to fifty officers and less than a thousand men.

They were herded, in a way, although the terrain dictated the rules, but it seemed that there was nothing to do but withdraw all along that front.

Some of them walked, some of them rode, and many of them ran, an ugly thing to see. Whatever the cause, whether you walked or ran, you could see very clearly what was going on, and what was going on was a major German breakthrough all along the front. There was fear and ruin in the wind, and all the way back from the Faid Pass toward Kasserine you could see burning American tanks and at the crossroads where the Sbeitla Highway met the Kasserine road, and everywhere in between, there were tanks killed, and sixty half-track carriers, and twenty guns and twenty trucks in smoking ruin. It was the worst defeat the American Army had met so far and would not be repeated until the Ardennes offensive at the Battle of the Bulge in 1944.

———

Now, by the evening of February 18, 1943, it had come down to the Kasserine Pass. They had mined the valley floor in front of the pass, amazingly. They had the mines because Terry Allen had gotten, finally, extremely angry and goddam-well *forced* Fredendall to hand them over.

The sad truth was that the Americans were brave and hardened but they were not well led, and although Terry Allen, the CO of the 1st, had done what he could, there was no way to balance the sheer stupidity and arrogance and drunken carelessness of Major General Lloyd Fredendall, the II Corps Commander in Chief, who was holed up in a bizarre HQ eighty miles back from the front, in a narrow ravine that ran up a pinewood ridge near the town of Tébessa, a place that every field officer who had to go there considered more of a hideout than a military encampment.

Fredendall sat there in comfort, nursing very fine scotch, and issued vague and contradictory commands to whoever wandered in. It was a sorry sight, and Terry Allen stayed away as much as he could, finally going there during the hard fight from Djebel Lessouda to Kasserine, asking for—*demanding*—mines.

For once Fredendall, the commander of II Corps, had gotten off his patrician butt and seen to it that every available mine in the North African theater was sent to the valley of the Kasserine. There was a pinch in the center of the pass, where it closed in to less than a thousand feet, with the Hatab River on one side and the rocky heights on the other reaching up to nine hundred feet. So if you mined the flats and forced the Germans to stay on the road that ran through the center of the X-shaped pass, then maybe the Ronsons—the Shermans—and the dug-in infantry, all two thousand of them, could jam a stick in the German wheels.

Spotwood and his platoon were holding a sidewinder-shaped position about five hundred yards past the narrows, with a broad belt of antitank and antipersonnel mines in front of them. It was a good position and he felt some confidence returning now that they had stopped running and were turning to fight.

Making a stand was something that appealed to him, something to set against the gathering fear he could smell in the men around him, fear that came from running, and the running came from fear, a reciprocal and accelerating loop that could break an army wide-open if the leadership let it.

The story had come down that Fredendall had called up Colonel Stark, who was commanding the 26th Infantry, that Fredendall had told Stark to "get up to the Kasserine right now, pull a Stonewall Jackson."

Stark, a grim-faced old-line soldier, had said nothing and gone forward to see to his positions, and they all settled in for a long night watch, knowing that the Germans were coming, not knowing they were already there.

———————

Now it was eight in the morning on the nineteenth of February, a bitter rain was falling on the men in the shadow of the Kasserine hills, and a rolling mist was coming up the lowlands in front of their positions, driven by a fitful wind. The American troops were tired, cold, wet, and weary, sick of the campaign and sick to death of North Africa, afraid of the Panzers, afraid of dying under them, with their backs against the stony canyons and rocky passages of the Kasserine Pass.

On the wind there came the sound of firing, a distant brittle crackle and then under it a rolling boom and a growling muttering that faded and came back again and faded away.

Down on the road between Faid and Lessouda the infantry watched as something vague and shapeless developed into something massive and moving and coming forward out of the mist and the cold wind.

Then they went for their weapons.

Tigers, someone shouted, the Tigers are coming.

What was left of the 1st Armored scrambled into their tanks—the Honeys—fifteen of them came out on the flats to try to slow down the oncoming Panzers and the Panzers opened up on them. The math was the terrible thing, because it was all math for the tankers—the Panzers had a range of three thousand yards and fired a 75-mm shot or an 88-mm shot straight and level and insanely fast.

The Honeys fired a 37-mm shot that was effective out to twelve hundred yards. That meant that when the Honeys closed with the Panzers, and they had to because the Honeys were the only things standing between the 10th Panzer Division and the infantry, then they were going to be exposed to incoming German tank rounds for eighteen hundred yards before they could hope to get off a single telling shot.

So, math being math, all fifteen of the 1st Armored Honeys were blown up and the few tankers who did get off a shot watched the round bounce—literally *bounce*—off the steel hulls of the Tiger tanks, and what began to spread at that moment was a terrible slithering emotion, horribly contagious, and that emotion was panic.

Now Messerschmitts boomed out of the early dawn light, coming in at fifty feet off the ground, cannons hammering at them and the flicker of fire sparkled all along their wings as the machine guns opened up. The Messerschmitts got into rear areas and shot up everything and everybody, got into staging areas and rear-echelon storage units, into the cookhouses and latrines and hospitals—men were running and shouting, trying to get into field gear, snatching up rifles and running toward machine-gun posts, many not making it.

Below the heights, as the light grew, Spotwood and his men could see over eighty Tiger tanks churning up the valley, weaving in and around the burning shells of ruined Honey tanks—the 1st Armored was getting chewed up and cut to pieces. Now the Shermans were getting into it, coming suddenly in at the flanks, firing shot at two thousand yards.

The Germans fired back, maneuvering right and left, traversing their big main guns, and Spotwood knew what it would be like inside the Shermans, the gunner and the driver trying to coordinate, trying to get the optical sights lined up on a Tiger even as the rounds came howling in and the earth was blowing up around them, trying to guess the range off the ranging marks in the telescope sights, working to traverse the gun and elevate it and get it on the target. The loader grabs the shot from the racks behind him. If the Tiger moves, the gunner has to *lead* it—also a guess—and if his own tank is on uneven ground, and moving besides, trying to stay alive, then the gunner has to figure the lead range and allow for the cant or the tilt of the tank, because that changes everything. Cant means that when he raises the gun it also elevates sideways in the direction of the tilt, so *that* has to be guessed as well—and the Tiger's getting closer, another round slams in. No, they're not dead yet, although the steel hull of the Sherman is ringing like an iron bell, so he figures the cant and swivels the turret to compensate for that, and out on the flats there's a crosswind, and the Tiger, still moving and cutting back again, is out there a long way so the crosswind will change the trajectory. And all the while he has to remember that a *hot* main gun fires differently from a cold one because the barrel changes, drops a degree as it heats up. And if the Sherman is old or has been in a lot of action then the barrel is also *worn* so his first rounds may fall *short,* and he fires—checks the fall of the shot—*long*—fires again—traverses—a *miss*—and he yells for another shot from the loader and then there's a *huge* clanging bang and—he looks up and *sees* a German shot. It has penetrated the Sherman turret and now it's *spinning* around inside the turret, clattering like a tin cup on prison bars—insanely *fast*—and if it catches on anything it will shatter into a thousand flying steel splinters and they'll all turn to meat. Oil is spilling now and the turret is glowing red—the heat boils his face—the tank commander is gone from his knees up, the loader is scrambling downward to the escape port. He gets up from the chair and dives as the gasoline begins to burble out of a broken line—and suddenly his world is full of fire. . . .

Spotwood, watching the Sherman burn, cursed and slid back into a stony ditch. The Ronsons were all burning . . . the Tigers were grinding up the slope . . . and Fredendall, hiding out in his Boy Scout camp eighty miles back, had ordered the 1st Infantry Division—the 26th in the front and the 16th as support—to make a last stand, to stop the German advance.

And the pass had to be held because if the Tigers got through and into the plains west of the Kasserine there would be nothing to stop them. They could roll all the way to the port of Bone in the north, cut off the British and the French, slice the entire Allied force in three pieces, and retake Algeria—*if* they got through the Kasserine Pass.

There was more fighting in the north, on the Sbiba Pass road. Tigers were hitting the British Guards regiment, and the 18th were getting it as well, but in front of their position the Tigers were holding back, trying to work a way around the minefields and get at the infantry. Spotwood was having a hell of a time holding his own men in place, because they could see other units—truckloads of engineers and even some other units of the 1st Infantry—and they were . . . running was the word. Running away.

Spotwood watched this happening and felt a terrible loneliness.

He was overwhelmed with a desire to get up and start walking away, start walking into the west where, sooner or later, he'd reach the sea, maybe at Oran, and he could go down to the dock there, untie a small boat, push off and drift out beyond the Oran light and into the Mediterranean. One of his men, Dent, was shouting at him, and he looked up to see units of the British armor in between the Tigers and their positions, and the dark brown masses of American infantry—it was the 18th—pulling back slowly in front of the Tigers, trying to bring the Tigers into the minefields. Spotwood watched as a squadron of Valentine tanks from the Death's-head troop—the Lancers—came out to engage the Tigers. One by one, like rooks on a fence, they went down; the Germans shot them into ruin, into molten scars and craters on the dead-bone yellow ground.

By midday the Germans had halted in front of the Kasserine Pass, halted because their Arab spies had told them exactly where the minefields were and the Germans were trying to work out a path through them. It was a chance, and the U.S. artillery in the hills made the best of it. A battery of the 151st opened up on the scattered Panzers down in the valley—the shells racing down from the cloud cover and slamming into the flats, bursting up out of the yellow dirt like a gas main blowing up, a short, sharp fire fountain, and the Panzers began to scramble, grinding right and left, guns traversing, like cockroaches caught on a kitchen floor was how it looked to the gunners on the height. They kept at it, and smoke began to fill the long valley.

When it cleared, the Panzers were in flames and twelve of them were on the run, pulling back out of the range of the guns until the Germans could bring up field howitzers to shell the hills.

Spotwood saw German Pioneere sappers working at the forward edge of the minefields, on their knees in the dirt, digging away with bayonets. Too far away for a rifle shot, even for Frewer. He rolled over and looked up at the sky, Dent beside him, Frewer a little way away, staring down the barrel of his Remington, motionless and silent, in his separate place.

Spotwood pulled out his canteen and offered some of what was in it to Dent. Dent took it, swallowed, grimaced, and smiled as he handed it back. Spotwood took it with his eyes on the clouds.

Dent asked him what he was looking for.

Stukas, said Spotwood.

Oh, yeah, said Dent. Well, they'll be along.

———

An hour later the eastern reaches of the Kasserine valley exploded in smoke and thunder along a line about five hundred yards wide. Spotwood and his platoon scrambled back to their firing positions in time to see the last of the roiling smoke rise up and out of the flames and a steel curtain of rising shells, dense and fast. The fire arced up into the sky and curved down, and now they heard a terrible sky-shaking racheting vibration unlike anything they had ever heard before, and suddenly—*instantly*—the sky came down on top of them like an avalanche of iron.

The Germans had brought up something new, a battery of eight-barreled electric mortars they called the Nebelwerfer— "storm maker"—and they were throwing eighty-pound rounds four miles across the valley into the American positions. The intensity of the incoming rounds—the size and the frequency and the accuracy—was literally shattering.

At Spotwood's position, it was as if they were all little lead soldiers on a tabletop and someone was slamming the tabletop with a twenty-pound sledge. Rocks were tumbling down the slopes in growing slides, entire clusters of men would disappear in a terrible burst of fire and steel. Awful things would strike the stones and stick for a moment before beginning a sickening red-stained slide down to the ground, and the ground itself was turning into water, shivering and trembling and shifting under the incoming rounds. And there was nothing—nothing—that Spotwood or Dent or Frewer or anyone in the little wadi could do about it.

Across the valley the battery of Nebelwerfers were churning out rounds in a brutal mechanical rhythm. It was Wagner again, thought Spotwood, his heart a cold stone in his chest and his bones rattling in his flesh as the shells came in and he pressed his face into the dirt and dug his hands into the barrel of his rifle.

Down in the valley, the German Panzers had regrouped and now that the American guns in the heights had been silenced and the infantry were all cowering in their holes, the moment had come for von Broich and his 10th Panzers. He was giving orders when a scout car pulled up and Rommel himself jumped out. He pointed to the heights and to the road leading into the Kasserine Pass and said only one word. He said, "Go!"

Colonel Moore's command post was the first to go, and then the tankers started to get the range of the Engineer's positions and then it was the turn of the 26th—now more shells were howling in—the Nebelwerfers' firing accelerated—and the Panzers came in, main guns firing, and it all rolled into one continuous thundering wall of noise where single shots and the screams of wounded men and the bursting of earth itself could not be separated, as if there were no single incidents but only a kind of seamless inexorable red flow coming up the valley floor and drowning everything in the way in a sea of fire.

Spotwood managed to lift his head and look out over the berm. Panzers were less than five hundred yards away, grinding over Shermans and British Valentines, grinding over the positions of the 26th down below him. And everywhere there were Americans running back toward his position, and machine-gun fire spattering over the rocks around them, taking whole chains of men down— Spotwood saw the tiny blue sparkling fire in the hull of the Panzers as the German machine-gunners traversed the field—and the main guns fired again. He looked to his left and Dent was dead— erased was the word—and he looked over at Frewer, who was firing his Remington, his face empty of emotion, working the bolt, coming into stillness before every shot.

Frewer was quietly and surgically picking off the German infantry that was now coming up the valley, the men of the Afrika Korps firing and dropping and running from stone to stone. He watched as Frewer aimed and fired and a German dropped a hundred and fifty yards away. Frewer rolled backward down the slope, tugging at the magazine, flipping it out, and in that moment Frewer looked over at Spotwood—there was no one else alive—and all the blankness left his face and he was smiling at Spotwood.

Frewer opened his mouth and said something that was lost in the thunder of the shells and the firing of the guns, slammed the magazine into the Remington again, slapped the butt, and crawled back up toward the edge of their berm. Spotwood watched him moving and looked around at the dead men.

This wadi belonged to the dead now, and they were in the world of the dead. Spotwood turned and crawled up beside Frewer, for some reason no longer afraid, but somehow *inside* Frewer's silence, in a kind of dream landscape where he felt a wonderful serenity come over him and the sound of the guns and the shells receded and Spotwood no longer cared if he was alive or dead. He felt a sudden overwhelming love for Frewer, and for the men who lay dead all around him, or killed on the road from Algiers, for Turwhitt and Boone and Callan, for Dent and Steiner and Gruenwald, for Peak in his glory, and Occhionegro, betrayed by a crack in his heart.

And Spotwood came at last to a new place where he felt only a spreading calm and a rising rush of warm blood in his beating heart, and even as he squeezed the trigger of his rifle and the Panzers came forward out of the smoke and the bursting earth was all around him, he felt himself at the edge of some great thing.

CHAPTER TWELVE

THE BEATEN ZONE

The overall command of VII Corps belonged to General Fred Franks, but the commander of the 1st Infantry Division was Major General Thomas G. Rhame, a young infantry commander who had seen action in Panama and Grenada and who had taken over the leadership of the 1st on July 7, 1989. Rhame had learned some hard lessons in Grenada and he intended to apply them here in Saudi.

His orders read simply: "On order, 1st Infantry Division (M) attacks as the VII Corps main effort to penetrate Iraqi defensive positions and conduct the forward passage of VII Corps forces. On order, follow main attack in zone to destroy the Republican Guard."

The principles under which he was expected to achieve this objective are described in the TRADOC manuals as AirLand Battle, and they bear many similarities to the German blitzkrieg tactics of the Second World War. You cannot win a war without attacking. A defensive success is a postponement of the final conflict. You win offensive wars by maneuvering your forces so as to concentrate overwhelming strength at the weakest point of the enemy's lines. The purpose of this assault is to break through the enemy lines and race out into open territory so as to bring your strength against the flanks and rear of the enemy troops concentrations. In this war, the ultimate fighting power of the Iraqi forces was the Republican Guard and it was the main purpose of the coalition forces to cut off and kill those units. The key phrase of the Air-Land Doctrine is "getting inside your enemy's decision cycle," in other words, to move so fast and strike so hard that by the time the opposing commanders get word of your movements, the information is obsolete. The Iraqi Army was solidly committed to "positional warfare," which is primarily a defensive stance. Therefore, the advantage in the field went to the army that could maneuver aggressively against those positions, get behind them, surround them, and wipe them out. AirLand Doctrine calls for a coordinated combined-forces assault using air superiority and tactical surprise. For hours now, units of the Marine Expeditionary Force, accompanied by Saudi and Kuwaiti armor and Egyptian mechanized infantry had been assaulting Iraqi concentrations around Khafji and up the coastal AOs. But the action was diversionary, intended to anchor the Iraqi armor in place while the VII Corps—with VIII Corps for cover from the north—broke through the Iraqi flanks and raced into the KTO. Schwarzkopf called it his Hail Mary plan—go deep and pray: cut off the Republican Guard and trap the Iraqis in a kill zone.

For Rhame and his superiors, the way the 1st was going to achieve its goals under the principles of AirLand War was to use "target acquisition" superiority and air power to punch through the Iraqi berms and blow the shit out of the defenders with everything they had.

What they had was, among other things, Crane and DerHorst and the rest of the officers and men of Baker Company. When commanders use terms like "penetrate," what they mean is that

combined-forces ground troops, in this case armor and mechanized infantry, will advance in coordination with available air cover
and artillery support, in line-abreast formation with scouts and
skirmishers out, until they get near enough to close with and kill
the enemy with tank fire, rifle fire, their bare hands and bayonets,
with any means necessary.

This is what is meant by the word combat.

———————

They were at the lock-and-load line, waiting for the word, an entire
infantry division set to go under a ragged winter sky, a wall of
military machines, tanks, IFVs and humvees spread out in a long
clean line, facing north, staring out at a vast and empty plain ob-
scured by fog and smoke and trailing veils of soft rain.

The artillery barrage had been going on for an hour now. The
night reeked of cordite and superheated air and the ammonia
stink of rocket trails. As soon as the barrage stopped, the division
would start to move. By the time they reached the distant Iraqi
berms, the entire assault force would be moving at sixty miles an
hour.

Crane was in a scout humvee equipped with a .50-caliber machine gun. He had enough pull to pick his own driver and he'd
asked for Mitchell, the black kid from Chicago. The rest of Mosby's fire team was assigned to Baker 19, a Bradley IFV equipped
with a chain gun and a TOW antitank system. All of Baker's IFVs
were spread out in Traveling Overwatch behind the lead tanks of
the 2nd Battalion, 34th Armor, all of them M1 Abrams main battle
tanks.

Each of the tanks was carrying a load of fascines on its rear deck.
Tanks could cross traps by dumping in the plastic piping and then
driving across it into the kill zones. But Rhame wasn't leaving it
up to the fascines to get his tanks across the traps.

From Crane's position, he could see several M60 tanks equipped
with scissors bridges, hydraulically operated extension bridges that
could be deployed in three minutes. Each bridge had a span of
sixty-three feet and could be retracted and used again in less than
ten minutes.

And idling there under the low gray clouds, lit by the headlights of the Bradleys and the humvees, there was a line of six M9 combat earthmovers with hardened Chobham Armor and a nine-foot-high bulldozer blade. The M9s were as fast as the Abramses and completely armored, some of them armed with chain guns and antitank TOWs.

To the rear of the assault columns were the comunications trucks and the armored vehicles with the forward observers, Range Data specialists who call in the artillery fire from the massed batteries in the rear, and behind these vehicles, separated by about a mile of desert terrain, were the armored columns of the rest of VII Corps, two brigades of the 1st Cavalry Armored, two brigades of the British First Armoured Division, and brigades of field artillery, an aviation brigade of Hueys and Cobras and Kiowas, and even—somewhere back there—the 14th Military Police Brigade, ready to control POWs and handle traffic control in the kill zones.

From the air, they would have looked like a steel city six miles wide and twenty miles deep, with choppers circling overhead and outriders in humvees cruising on the flanks. Crane looked around the troop lines and saw Huckaby waving from the hatch of an IFV, and Polanyi beside him.

Down the line of IFVs, Shabazz raised his fist in the air and shouted something but it died out in the rising roar of engines and the hammering beat of the choppers moving overhead.

Mitchell looked over at Crane and tried for a grin. At that moment, the artillery barrage stopped suddenly. The last of the tracer rounds arced up and out into the desert, and a vast shroud of silence descended on the massed columns.

And out of the dark, from somewhere off to the right, carrying over the gathering crescendo of diesel engines and the reek and fog of exhausts and the drifting smoke of the oil well fires, Crane heard music.

Music. Somebody had had the lunatic idea of bringing up the band. They couldn't see it from their position inside a puzzle of tanks and IFVs, but from over on the right the sound came floating, tinny and insane, as thin as Saudi beer, and under it the sound of drums.

"What the hell is that, sir?" asked Mitchell.

Crane listened hard, and it came to him. He laughed, partly at the absurdity of it, partly to keep from choking up, partly out of a sense of sudden exhilaration.

"That, kid, is the 'Garryowen.' It's a cavalry song."

It faded away forward as the unseen band marched slowly up the ranks of vehicles and guns, far away to the right, until it was lost in the hammer of engines and the whine of turrets swiveling. The headset radio buzzed in his left ear.

"Baker Blue, this is Six Actual, you read?"

"Five by five, Six Actual." Wolochek was off to the right, in an HQ Bradley with his radiomen.

"Column formed, Baker Blue?"

"They are, sir."

"Then let's go. You're next!"

And it began. He nodded his head to Mitchell, and Mitchell put the humvee in gear. Up ahead, the first of the Abramses was pulling out just as the pale gray light of the morning tinted the cloud cover. The inside of the humvee filled with the fumes from the Abrams.

In three minutes, the whole column was in motion, spreading out across the terrain, tankers moving into delta formation, the IFVs trailing, choppers beating overhead. Their speed climbed. Forty. Fifty. The ground was rushing up and racing underneath them. Mitchell was singing something to himself but Crane couldn't make it out under the accelerating roar of the advancing columns. He looked around at all the IFVs, the tanks racing now, feeling the mass of men and machinery all around him like a river at full race, carrying them all away to war, and he began to feel what all men feel at a time like that, and it was sheer joy, a crazy, wild rush of power and confidence.

" 'I love the smell of napalm in the morning,' " said Crane, grinning at Mitchell, and Mitchell shouted something, but at that moment the lead tanks started firing.

The concussion blast hit Crane's ears like a blow of a fist. The humvee lurched and Mitchell corrected, taking them to the right and accelerating. Orders and cross talk were crackling in the headset, and he could hear the tank commanders talking.

"Delta Green Three! Check one. Take him out!"

"Roger, Delta Green One. Two right. Wait one!" And then there'd be another hammering blast up ahead, the tank would lurch and a cloud of dust and dirt would blow up around it, a jet of fire coming from the main gun, the red tracer round streaking out flat and straight, something blowing up out of Crane's vision. They were killing Iraqis, right now!

Up ahead they could see a low line of black, and explosions behind the line. Off to the right, a plow-configured tank had the blade down. Far to the front of the tanks, about a half a klick from the first berm, a sudden magnesium flower lit up the sky.

"Daisy Cutter! They're taking out the mines!"

More distant explosions. The Engineers were firing line charges, flexible hoses filled with explosives, attached to a rocket. The rocket carries the line charge over the minefield and lays the hose down on it. When it's down, the engineers detonate the charge and it clears a path for tanks. The line charges went off like horizontal Roman candles, like a string of firecrackers, and the mines burst up out of the terrain, blue-white puffs of fire and sand.

Beside the rocking humvee an IFV from Baker was careening and drifting at sixty miles an hour. Crane could see the driver's face. The kid was laughing and pounding the turret hatch. Behind him in the hatch, three grunts were crowded together, watching the big sand berm come closer, their eyes wild and their faces raw from the wind and the dust, weapons at the ready. One of them was holding on to the butt of the chain gun, his fists tight and white.

Now they were in the minefield, speeding across it, part of a charging line of tanks and IFVs. The Abramses were firing at will, cranking out rounds at sixty miles an hour, the shells arcing up in a line of red fire and dropping beyond the berm.

Two Thunderbolts hurtled overhead at less than a hundred feet, and then three more. Puffs of red fire came from their wings. A series of Maverick rockets streaked down behind the berm line, followed by a huge white glow and a spray of molten metal. Mitchell was coming up too fast.

"Christ, kid, slow down. Let them break this open."

The battlefield was in a haze but here and there Crane could make out a racing tank. The fog was split and shredded by fire and tracer rounds. Some Iraqi fire was coming up from behind the berm, trying for the Apaches and the A-10s. And their artillery was trying to get the range, firing blindly into the advance, unable to see the approaching ground forces. Although some rounds had come in to the front of the lead tanks, huge red blossoms ripping up the yellow dirt, there had been no hits. Behind the berm wall, a thin wavering necklace of golden BBs was crossing the horizon line.

Crane had Mitchell brake the humvee on a small rise about five hundred yards from the berm. The Baker IFVs were slowing now, waiting for the berm to be breached, the Abramses taking fire positions about two hundred yards from the berm, cranking out rounds as they rolled forward. At what, Crane couldn't tell.

A tank equipped with a pavement roller was clearing a path through part of the minefield, explosions marking its passage. Three M9 armored bulldozers were behind it, and now they were taking fire from Iraqi artillery, the shells slamming in randomly, many of them hundreds of yards off the target. Three more A-10s came in from the south and six lines of green fire streaked out from under their wings. More white-hot explosions from behind the berm now, and the counterfire stopped just as the first of the M9s hit the sand berm.

The M9 dug in, settled, pushed forward. Its treads were churning up dust and clumps of earth. The berm gave way, ocher sand sliding down the sides and spilling backward down the berm. Another M9 bit at the berm fifty yards down, and cut through the wall as if it were butter.

"Jesus," said Crane. "They're through!"

The berms were collapsing backward, folding away as the M9s plowed through. One M9 took a round in the plow, Crane couldn't see what kind, but it slammed into the steel blade and detonated in a spray of blue fire and sparks. The M9 shuddered and accelerated and suddenly one was through, and then another, and one was backing up to let an Abrams in, and another Abrams was racing for the breach, firing through the slot as it hit the wall, and Crane said, "Okay, kid, let's get in there!"

As the humvee accelerated down the slope, the Abrams tankers were grinding through the breaches, firing and swiveling and firing again. On the radio, Crane heard excited young voices, cross talk and curses, and shouts and cheers as the shells slammed into targets beyond the berm.

By the time Crane and the IFVs reached the breaches, the tanks were almost all through. Crane waved a Bradley down and cut in front of him. The berm was filling his side window, the humvee straining in the deep sand, slowing, grinding, and then it let go of them and they seemed to spring out into the flat terrain. It was like kicking in the front door of hell.

Crane saw a wide panorama of bursting sand dunes, bombs and shells coming in, and white flickering flame, tiny points of fire along thin black lines a hundred and fifty yards away on the left and the right, and now something was slamming into the panels of the humvee. The tiny blue-white twinkles seemed to brighten and flicker faster. Dirt and stones flew into the air in front of them and then the humvee rocked and trembled as something like a chain saw ripped across the armored grille. They were taking rounds.

Crane clambered back to the .50 and cranked the bolt, swiveled the iron sights to cover the trench line. Mitchell was moving the humvee fast to the right and the fire was still coming in, rocks and earth blowing up around them, climbing up the little ridge. Crane slapped the bolt cover and thumbed the half-moon triggers. The .50 felt like a jackhammer in his arms and shoulders. Bright brass cases churned out of the breech and a red ribbon of heavy tracers soared across the plain toward the distant Iraqi trenches.

Crane traversed the .50 slowly, watching the tracer line, looking for the beaten zone. The red fire arced over the trenches, high.

Now the armor on the humvee was shuddering and chattering. Crane's headset was filled with excited American voices, shouts, orders, counterorders, incoherent yells and cries. Crane saw a chain of green sparks wavering and crossing in front of him and he slammed the .50 butt with his hand, lowering the muzzle. He saw the rounds slicing into the thin black trenches, saw dust and clods of earth fly up. Then someone in an Abrams off to his left got the range and fired into the same trench.

Twenty yards of it rose into the air in a billow of fire and earth, small black fragments twisting and flying inside it. Mitchell was slapping Crane's right leg and screaming something at him, fighting the wheel. Something massive and dark passed overhead, no more than fifty feet above him. An Apache, so close he could see the huge round missile pods under the stabilizers, see the white stencil markings for the safety tug and fire hatch, see the red markings on the noses of the missiles.

The Apache hovered, steadied, and fired two Hellfires at the Iraqi tank line in between the two infantry trenches. The Hellfires flew a flat sloping trajectory and slammed into the tank line. Secondary explosions sent a cloud of molten metal and white fire into the smoking air. More rounds from the tanks to the right and more Warthog fire from somewhere overhead.

The whole interior of the Iraqi berm was full of fire and smoke and the battle narrowed down to the few square yards that Crane could see around him, a hallucinatory bubble of slowed time filled with pounding shells and the racheting clamor of chain guns, the drumbeat of choppers above, and the screech and clanking of tanks maneuvering.

The humvee was taking no rounds at all, and it seemed to Crane that the level of incoming fire from the Iraqi lines was slowing, becoming ragged and intermittent. Out of the smoke and fog on his far left, an Abrams materialized, moving at speed, treads churning. Crane slapped his hands over his helmet as the tank steadied, canted, and braced. Inside, a gunner would be locked into his site, reading range data and windage, and now the round slammed home and the gunner hit the red Fire button and suddenly Crane's world was a crystal glass full of *silence* and then the blow came, slamming the roof and the walls of the humvee. The tank rocked and disappeared in blowback and the shell arced up and rocketed into an Iraqi target lost in the rising dust and debris. Crane looked up at the tank commander, an impossibly young kid whose face was smeared with sweat and grime, grinning hugely down at Crane, shouting something beyond hearing. Crane waved him on and Mitchell accelerated to come in behind the Abrams as it flanked left and raced out across the fire zone toward the Iraqi trenches.

On the far right, Crane could see Iraqi troops now, out in the open, arms up, waving white cloth, running and stumbling beside the tanks. From the open turrets, tanker commanders were yelling at them—Get to the rear, get out of the way—but on the left there was still a lot of machine-gun and rocket fire coming from that long slit trench.

Behind the trench there was ruin. The Iraqi artillery was shattered, all of their tanks now red hot and in flames, the men inside roasting like beef. The entire tank and IFV advance was closing in on a pair of Iraqi trenches, and the Iraqis were pouring small-arms fire, RPG rounds, and machine-gun fire into the forward tanks.

In a rapid right-and-left flanking movement, the Abramses and the M9s swept through the razor wire and across the tank trenches, the M9s with their blades down. Mitchell brought the humvee to a stop beside three IFVs. Huckaby was sitting on the turret of the first one, his face bright and wet, holding a SAW on his knees.

"Hey, Sergeant! What's up?"

Crane leaned out the window.

"Hold here. Now we find out if Colonel Hawkins was right."

So far there'd been no need to dismount from the IFVs, so most of the infantry troopers were crowded into the hatches, trying to see what was going on. The IFVs were in a defiladed or covered position, the gunners putting out chain-gun rounds sporadically at whatever Iraqi helmet showed itself. The range was around three hundred yards. Forward of their position, the Abramses and the M9s had reached the eastern flank of the Iraqi trenches and come to a full stop, their barrels depressed, the M9s with their plow blades lowered to the ground. The sound of amplified voices speaking Iraqi reached across the battlefield. Mitchell was standing beside the humvee now and he could hear it too.

"What's that, Sergeant?"

"They're telling the Iraqis in that slit trench to surrender."

Overhead a flight of Kiowas and Apache choppers blew by at a hundred feet. Away to the west, a pair of Warthogs circled and rose into the gray sky.

Shabazz and his squad pulled up in a scorched IFV. Mosby and Polanyi and Orso called out to Mitchell but Crane waved them down.

The loudspeakers were silent now, the guns lowered. An M9 earthmover had taken up a position at the end of the trench line. Even where they were, three hundred yards away, they could see the little black forms milling and moving around in the trench lines.

Shabazz stepped up beside Crane. "How many men you figure in that position, Sergeant Crane?"

"Fifteen hundred, two thousand. More to the west there, and more in the rear. We've taken a lot of prisoners but there's easy five thousand down in those trenches and back in the artillery parks."

"Christ . . . what're we waiting for?"

"Watch. Learn."

A moment passed, and another. From the far edge of the trench line some Iraqi launched a Sagger. It impacted on the lowered blade of the M9, blossomed into a spray of white fire and smoke.

"Holy fuck," said someone in the rear, but his voice was drowned out in the sound of guns and tanker fire. Four Abrams tanks opened up on the trenches with .50-caliber fire, and the M9 earthmover started to grind forward. In front of the broad blade a wall of red and yellow earth rose up and rolled away. It filled the trench line and crashed down like a brown wave of dirt and rocks and sand. They could see men running, other men firing, little white sparks and popping sounds, but the blade kept coming and the Abrams tankers poured more small-arms fire into the trench line.

Dust and smoke rose up over the trenches. Through it they saw the M9 grind down the entire length of the entrenchment, pushing before it a wall of sand and dirt ten feet high, covering everything in front of it, burying it and crushing it down, rolling over the whole position. The whole incident had lasted no more than five minutes.

"Jesus Christ." Shabazz's young voice was reverential, full of awe.

Someone else was struggling with a camera, snapping away at the wall of dust and smoke, inside which huge shapes were moving. The sound of heavy-weapons fire seemed to die away.

Crane looked down the slope at the trench line. It was gone.

In its place was a mound of tread-scarred earth two thousand yards long. The M9 driver and the tankers down there had just buried over twenty-five hundred men. Buried them alive.

They stood there, in a brief silence, each man alone, as the wind and the smoke of the battlefield whirled around them and the muttering roar of the distant tanks came to them across the plain.

Finally, Crane shook himself. His headset was crackling.

"Baker Blue, this is Six Actual. Come in."

"Six Actual, this is Baker Blue."

"Crane, I can see your position from here. What the hell are you guys doing? There's a goddam war on. When you finish your picnic, how about getting into it!"

They broke and climbed back into their vehicles. As Shabazz turned away to his IFV, Crane heard him say something.

"Shabazz, what'd you say?"

He looked back at Crane.

"A prayer, Sergeant Crane."

"Who for?"

"Man," said Shabazz, "I don't know."

Crane climbed back into the humvee and buttoned it up. He smiled at Mitchell, who was looking very beige, and re-engaged the hydraulics for the .50-caliber. At that point, a Command humvee went snarling past, something fluttering on its antenna. Crane braced himself as Mitchell hit the pedal and the humvee churned up the dirt. The radio was full of cross talk and the entire front was moving forward, tanks and IFVs in line formation, humvees flanking, scouts out. Mitchell was dogging the Command humvee and as they came up on its right flank, Crane got a clear look at the cloth strip that was fluttering on the humvee's aerial.

It was a banner. The colors of the 1st Infantry Division, its battle streamers, the Victory insignia. Through the smoke and the dust of the armored advance, Crane saw the words "St.-Mihiel" and "Montdidier-Noyon" and "Meuse-Argonne," and there was "Tunisia," "Sicily," "Normandy," and "Kasserine," and for a moment he felt himself a part of something old and fine. It didn't last. The forward humvee plunged downslope and into a roiling cloud of fire and smoke. A second later—Mitchell shouting, Crane with his hands clenched around the .50 controls—the cloud had swallowed them up too. Blinded, they could hear heavy weapons, and something hammered across their flank. The humvee rang like an iron bell.

CHAPTER THIRTEEN

MIRAGE

All that day and into the early evening, into the rain and fog and the salt-marsh wasteland that made one solid gray sheet out of earth and sky, the IFVs of Baker Company had played a long maddening game of follow-the-tankers.

On the way, they had encountered virtually nothing. It was as if the Iraqis had drifted away into the desert on a soft wind, or shivered into air like a mirage. The fight at the breach had been short and nasty, but the breakthrough afterward was a headlong charge into southwestern Iraq, with everyone tensed for incoming, everybody straining to see enemy formations, ready for an ambush that never came.

Nevertheless, Crane was shocked when the orders came down to bivouac in formation that first night. Everybody knew that the plan called for Franks to engage the Guards, but Franks was playing it safe. Rhame was probably boiling about it, but what could he do?

So they huddled in their IFVs or in shelter halves strung from

219

vehicle to vehicle, digging morosely into their MREs and staring out into the rainy night. The bivouac lasted a few hours, time enough for some fitful sleep and on-the-fly maintenance, but little else. The chopper scouts were up and out, and the word from Corps Command was that the download from the J-STARS showed distant Iraqi formations—probably the Tawakalna and Medina Divisions of the Republican Guard—but no one in the immediate AO.

It was, militarily, all wrong.

Not even the Iraqis could be *this* stupid.

They weren't. By 1900 hours of that first day, only fifty percent of VII Corps was actually through the Iraqi berms and into the rear areas. General Franks was looking at his troop dispersions in the J-STARS download—the God's-eye view provided by reconfigured Boeing 707s loaded with radar and heat sensors, flying high above the battlefield—and he was not a happy man. As far as he was concerned, last-minute troop redeployments coming out of CINC, or Commander in Chief, back in Riyadh had screwed up his logistics. It looked to him that he had half his corps strung out in a long wide-open line running sixty miles into hostile territory with zero protection on their flanks. He was also getting Intelligence reports that some of the toughest Iraqi Guard units were right in his path, and he wanted to engage them in strength. So Franks did the cautious thing, and pulled the 1st Division up short and lagered them for the night while he hammered at the rest of his corps commanders to get their asses up into the AO on the double. Of course, no one was telling any of this to the grunts, or the sergeants.

Crane himself was feeling the beginnings of a weird imbalance, a kind of vertigo, a sense of falling forward into chaos. They had leaned the full force of all their armor and guns up against a solid wall of Iraqi demons, and the demons had turned to water. They had steeled themselves to kill and to die, they had gone forward to do it as well as they could, with all the weight of their beliefs and their professionalism, and they had encountered . . . nothing.

Yet all the Intel reports—at least those with CIA backing—had stressed, to the point of paranoia, the awesome combat firepower the Iraqis had in the field: entire divisions of T-72s backed up by BMPs and support units, whole parks of artillery. And they were battle-hardened from ten years of war with Iran.

Schwarzkopf and dozens of analysts had been on the tube warning America about the ferocious, fanatical force that they were going up against. Back in the States, the families of all the troopers were sick with fear, expecting the worst, waiting for the hall phone to ring or for that tan cruiser to pull up in the driveway with two base officers on board.

CNN was everybody's amphetamine every night of the week. And Crane knew that the drill was to impose a complete press blackout as soon as the ground war started, which would send all the home folks straight into cardiac arrest. Yet out here in the field . . . nothing.

Nothing. It was making him crazy.

It was also making him suspicious, but he wasn't sure what it was he was suspicious about. All of these emotions slammed around inside his chest for a long time until they settled down into a deeply felt unease and a hair-trigger hypervigilance.

Then he realized with a jolt that he hadn't felt this kind of intense hypervigilance since that last night back in August, when they'd first gotten the news of the Iraqi invasion. That made him grin. At least, this time, he had a damn good reason for it. Maybe he ought to find a pay phone and call Carla, tell her how he'd cured himself. He just took his paranoia overseas until he found a place he could really use it.

The kids saw it all very differently, of course, because this was their first look at the tiger, and as far as they were concerned, things were going just fine, thanks very much. There had been injuries, though, and not just the Iraqis back in the trench lines.

It was strange the way the modern war was like an electric web— they were so interconnected that right now the thermal and radar image of their company parked in a delta formation along the east bank of this little wadi was showing up on the radar screens of the J-STARS five miles up. There were two J-STARS in the KTO, reconfigured Boeing 707s, loaded with Norden multimode side-looking radar linked to seventeen onboard screens and twenty data techs.

The twenty-four-foot radar boom along the underside of the J-STARS could pick out any vehicle—stationary or in transit—within a one-hundred-and-fifty-mile radius. The entire Department of Defense Internet communications web was globally interlaced and instantly accessible to any commander—or so the manuals promised—from Schwarzkopf to a Spec 5 looking for fire coordinates, and the web was so delicate that when one of the Kilo Company IFVs had driven over a mine, they had all heard that brief electronic *snap* when Abel Three had blown up. Seven men badly injured. And all they knew about it was that short sharp snap, like a nerve firing, a little tremble of the big web and they were all rolling by it, rolling on into the big Iraqi dark. The kids had been quiet for a time, and they had chased the M1s a little more carefully, barely keeping them in visual contact, staring hard into the dense black night just to see the red slit lights on the rear of the vehicle ahead, relying on the Kiowas and the GPS to keep them all in formation.

Their part in the battle had been like a slingshot, with the British 1st Armoured Division as the stone. The 1st was charged—*tasked*—with the job of breaking through the Iraqi lines along an eleven-mile front, and they had done that. Farther to the east, there were two more massive divisions committed to the breakthrough, the U.S. 1st Armored Division on their left flank about twenty miles off, and beyond that, aiming at an Iraqi town called Makfhar al Busayyah, the U.S. 3rd Armored Division.

And far beyond *that* advance, deep inside Iraq and only a hundred miles south of Baghdad, the XVIII Airborne Corps had driven all the way to the Euphrates to block any reinforcements from the east and to slam the lid on every Iraqi unit inside the AO.

This entire operation—this wide sweep under cover of air superiority—was the main-force strike in the Gulf War. The Iraqis had been deliberately conned into believing that the main assault would come on the beaches of Kuwait City and along the Khafji road. The first day of the ground war had added to that impression, as two Marine divisions and coalition forces breached Iraqi lines along the Kuwait-Saudi border. Hussein and his generals had taken the bait and all of their attention was focused on Kuwait City.

So, in a massive main-force assault, VII Corps had taken his flanks and cut them wide open. It had taken about two hours of tank and Kiowa and Warthog fire, and of course the thing was done at the trenches, those big dozers just rolling down the trench line, like a kid pushing sand into an anthill, but after the word went down the Iraqi lines, the resistance had, basically, stopped.

Crane and Baker had come in through a gap behind a delta of tanks from the 1st Battalion 34th Armor—behind Boomer Riebold's Abrams, as a matter of fact; you could always tell Boomer's M1—he had an old cavalry guidon on a whip antenna and was always the first one into a breach. It had been like slamming into a prisoner-of-war camp.

When the smoke had cleared and the battle ended—a space of time that felt like an hour or a year depending on how close the enemy fire was coming to your personal AO—Crane and the men of Baker Company got a view of the entire fortification: a set of four triangle-shaped emplacements with the broad bases forward, running maybe two thousand yards wide for each triangle, a total of about twelve thousand yards wide, and the entire position was now a smoking wasteland, littered with the flaming hulks of Iraqi armor and the blackened craters where enemy artillery had once been. Pillars of blue and red fire rose up all around them, and their M1s and M9s and their IFVs were running all over the Iraqi positions.

Trench lines had been plowed over or filled with plastic fascines, tank traps crossed with bridging vehicles, fougasse trenches ignited and bypassed, razor wire shredded and scattered around the landscape like Christmas tinsel.

And the dead.

It took a minute to make the leap, to *get* the gestalt, to see suddenly that the shape inside that armored car was not the stuffing from the bench, or that this blackened heap over here, at the center of a cratered smoking pit, had hands stretched outward from the center of the burning, or that across the line of tracks

there, that huge stain in the sand had once been a running soldier. But they got it. It could not be missed.

The dead were everywhere, thrown in tangled heaps by incoming missiles or main gun rounds, burned into skeletal cinders or
shredded by minigun and chain-gun fire, weapons scattered, helmets upturned, limbs and torsos torn apart, jaws gaping in cooked
faces, bodies crushed into a kind of jelly out of which bright pink
bone chips rose, sections of rib or spine or thigh bone, little arcs
of skull fragments, red as taillight glass, heads without faces, ropes
of fat purple entrails fifteen feet long, great pools of blood like
freshly spilled lacquer, or shiny and wet on scraps of uniform, on
pale bellies. . . . Driving over the site was an unspeakable experience and it would take hours for the rain and the sand to clean
the tank treads.

They were glad, finally, for the reek of cordite and fire, because
every now and then a wet wind would blow the stench of some
soldier's opened bowels into the vent of an IFV or a tank intake
and the men inside would stop talking and gag.

Welcome to the war. Take a deep breath. Never forget this.

Driving through it, Crane was not surprised. It was something
he had seen before, a long time back, and the only good thing
about it this time was that no one on the ground in front of his
humvee had been a friend. He could see what was reflected on
the faces of the cherry troops—sick shock, sudden silence, and
underneath it a kind of heart-racing, hammering pulse, your own
blood in your own body, and death all around.

But not *you*.

And from every possible direction, there had been Iraqis.

They were coming out of bolt-holes all over the battered terrain,
scraggly guys in shit-brindle uniforms, unshaven, soaked in urine
many of them, or reeking of their own shit, lousy with fleas and
lice, dehydrated, covered with white silica sand, eyes red rimmed
and wild, shaking in mortal fear, dropping rifles and RPGs, and
every goddam one of them was waving one of those safe-conduct
passes the PsyOps guys had dropped all over the AO.

They'd come up with the idea back at Fort Bragg, a creation of
the Green Berets of the 4th Psychological Operations Group. Each

safe-conduct pass was printed on a photocopy of an Iraqi dinar—
there was an engraving of Saddam on every one—and on the back
of the copy, there was a set of Arabic instructions for surviving a
surrender:

SAFE-CONDUCT PASS. YOU DO NOT HAVE TO DIE. YOU CAN BE SAFE
AND RETURN TO YOUR FAMILY AND LOVED ONES IF YOU CEASE RE-
SISTANCE. YOU MUST FOLLOW THESE STEPS: REMOVE MAGAZINE
FROM WEAPON. SLING YOUR WEAPON OVER YOUR SHOULDER MUZ-
ZLE DOWN. APPROACH SLOWLY. HOLD THIS PASS IN YOUR HAND
ABOVE YOUR HEAD. IF YOU DO THIS YOU WILL NOT DIE. YOU WILL
BE TREATED WELL AND SOMEDAY YOU WILL RETURN TO YOUR FAM-
ILY.

Crane had seen truckloads of these leaflets stuffed into plastic
water bottles. The Air Force and the Navy had floated or dropped
them all over the KTO. More rear-echelon patty-cake as far as he
was concerned, but here they were, well and truly into the war,
and there were long lines of Iraqi troops, and each trooper was
waving one of these things in the air and saying *Salaam* and *In-
shallah* and Please don't blow my balls off, Mr. Grunt, and, well,
it was just plain weird.

Mosby and his boys had climbed out of their IFV to shake down
a file of Iraqis at the far side of the first berm. Crane pulled up
with Mitchell to cover them with the .50. For Mosby and his fire
team, it was a dreamlike interval, Crane could see it on their windburned and dusted faces as they pulled their scarves away from
their chapped lips and bailed out of the rear gate, M16s at port
arms, safeties off, selectors on full auto.

They were aching to rock and roll, pumped up and primed by
two years of training and six months of listening to Saddam
bullshit the planet, and here they were, on the ground in Saudi,
with about a hundred goddam Iraqi troopers scrambling around
the IFVs, gabbling like turkeys.

That was when Crane had begun to feel that slight sense of
vertigo, of something surreal and false about the whole breakthrough. But for Mosby and the guys, it was a moment, and Crane

saw them ready to fire, thought for one mad moment that one of them *might* do it, might open up on the crowd of prisoners.

Things like that happened all the time. Surrendering was one of the most dangerous maneuvers a fighting man could ever undertake. There were unwritten rules and you could never be sure that everyone was on the same page. Sitting there behind the .50, Crane traversed the muzzle along the crowd of Iraqis, watching each face and every pair of hands, looking for a sign, a twisted expression, someone racing to a stupid conclusion with his eyes fixed on a martyr's dimwit death.

Mosby was out now and running down the line, his SAW on guard, and he was waving for the Iraqis to drop their rifles and hit the sand, which they did, a sudden clattering tumble of guns and belts, all the prisoners talking at once, falling down wherever they stood, and Mosby's men spreading out to cover them, and more IFVs and tanks grinding up to bring their chain guns and .50s onto the Iraqi troops.

Hearing the rifles hit the dirt reminded Crane of that old joke about the Arvins in Vietnam: Wanna buy an Arvin rifle?

Never been fired. And only dropped once.

They'd been drilled on prisoner processing back at Riley, by noncoms from the Military Police section, who would ultimately be taking charge of the POWs the ground attack would generate.

Mosby and his squad were running the show, and the crowd of beaten Iraqis was growing rapidly as clusters of men saw the activity and came forward, waving their passes. Polanyi—his face thinned by stress and adrenaline—was prodding them into a line with the muzzle of his M16, while Orso and Mosby and the rest of his team stood back and provided cover. Polanyi, who had a talent for languages, was saying something to them and the Iraqis were nodding, still trembling, eyes *huge*, and dropping to the ground. Other troopers were coming in and frisking them.

Frisking them meant stripping them down to their shorts, and in the cold and rain, it was a miserable sight to see. Crane felt something like embarrassment and shame for the soldiers—a feeling he crushed as soon as he became aware of it.

If they were so goddam upset about being soldiers, then one of them should have found the sand to take Hussein out. Instead, the whole country had jammed itself into the streets of Baghdad, waving their fists in the air and screaming about the Great Satan.

Fuck them all. As far as Crane was concerned, this was a long-overdue payback for all those years of impotent rage, sitting in the base PX with a can of warm beer and watching a crowd of rag-heads in Tehran shove a hostage around, listening to Khomeini gargle away in that rasping drone, looking for all the world like Charles Manson in a toga, or crying for two hundred and forty-one poor son-of-a-bitch Marines in Beirut, and for Colonel Higgins, twisting in the wind, and the fliers Hussein had humiliated and beaten in the early days of the war.

Fuck them all; sorry *now* doesn't cut it.

It was sweet to sit there in the rain and feel his thumbs on the .50 triggers, see a whole gaggle of piss-stained Iraqis crying in the dirt at the far end of the barrel. Sweet, and long, long overdue.

There was a burst of angry chatter at the end of the line, where a Spec 4 from Charlie Company was shouting at an Iraqi and the Iraqi was shouting back. The outburst sent a shock wave down the line. Mosby and his men were bringing up their rifles. Mosby ran down the line, shouting at the Spec 4.

"What the fuck's the problem?"

The Spec 4—a massive black soldier—never took his eyes off the Iraqi in front of him. The Iraqi was on his knees, his hands locked behind his neck, but he was white faced and shaking his head back and forth.

"This raghead won't shuck!"

Mosby turned to look down at the man. The Iraqi's eyes were red and his windburned skin was dusted with white sand. His uniform was worn and torn. He looked like something that had been run through a shredder.

"Polanyi, get down here! Tell this dumb fuck to get his pants off!"

Polanyi, enjoying the sudden rise in status, ran down and began to shout at the Iraqi. Now there were three troopers standing around the man, all of them shouting at him, and finally he bowed his head and—incredibly—the man began to cry. The tears made brown lines down his dusty cheeks, and the man's mouth was twisted in a terrible way. Crane could see this from the deck of the humvee and suddenly he *knew*—dumb bastard.

"Hey, Mosby!"

Mosby swiveled and sent Crane a hard look, and Crane saw for the first time what he had been hoping to see in the kid. He saw iron. Mosby had finally shown up for his life, he was here and fully engaged.

"Come here, would you?"

He made it soft, so Mosby wouldn't lose face. Mosby jogged over, his rifle at port, his face wary.

"Yes, Sergeant?"

Crane leaned down and spoke softly to Mosby, whose face closed up, set, and then broke open again. He looked up at Crane, his eyes wider.

"Happens a lot," said Crane.

Mosby walked back to Polanyi.

"Take him to a latrine, let him clean up, will you?"

Polanyi looked puzzled, and then it hit him.

"Oh . . . Jesus. Of course."

He said something to the soldier, and the man, his head still lowered, got to his feet and shuffled away in front of Polanyi, and as he went they could see how he had fouled himself.

Mosby told the rest of the squad to get back to it, and walked over to Crane's vehicle.

"Jesus, why'nt he say something?"

"You're gonna see a lot of that."

"What's with them? The trots?"

Crane looked at Mosby, thinking, Mosby, you're gonna be a good soldier, and it's time you found out a couple of things they didn't put on the recruitment posters.

"Darryl, you're gonna find, in this pack alone, a whole bunch of them will have done that. They can't help it. It happens to everybody if it gets bad enough. You never been shelled, or got your berm pounded by a Buff. It's an automatic response, you can't help it. Only way to get around it, hit the latrines every chance you get, so when it gets hairy, you're empty. Getting shelled, it's the worst. It's like, you lie there, you're more scared than you ever been, only you can't *do* anything about it. That's worse than a firefight, because in a fight, you can change the situation, but when you're on the wrong end of Arty, each round comes in, it goes through you like a jolt of electricity, or like you were lying under a subway train. It is *huge*. These guys, they've been to a place I hope you never go."

Mosby looked up at Crane for a time, processing the image. His face lost a little bit more of its youthfulness.

"Christ . . ."

"Yeah. Well, it's reality. Don't tell the folks at home, though. That kinda thing, it don't play on Regis and Kathie Lee."

"Man. I won't."

"Anyway, bag these and saddle up. We still got a war on."

It had been a big moment for Mosby and the rest of the 1st Infantry Division. Taking a surrender is an exhilarating experience, if you're not too far into the war.

Back in the Triangle, they had taken a lot of prisoners during the first few months. And they'd gotten a chance to see what happened to some of them. Every platoon had a couple of Arvin G2s along, interpreters and Intelligence guys. They were not nice guys.

After Crane watched what happened to maybe ten VC over six months in the bush, he and the others had pretty much given up on taking surrenders. And when the VC found what the Arvins were doing to their prisoners, they started doing the same thing—and sometimes much worse—to any GI they caught alive.

Crane had come across two guys from the 16th, left in the treeline by a cherry LT after a VC ambush near the Courtenay Plantations up by Xa Cam My—Shock-Me was what Crane's unit called the place—and what the VC had done to those guys, it was something a Comanche would have admired, one professional to another, something one of the old cavalry sergeants would've talked about, stuff he'd've seen when Kansas was a territory, not a state. Come to think of it, everybody in the 1st used to call the Iron Triangle Indian country—after a while every grunt in Vietnam called the bush Indian country. Some things never changed.

Anyway, after that, the whole question of taking VC prisoners was pretty much set aside, and they usually capped off any live dink they got their hands on. *Shin loi,* VC.

Crane watched Mosby and Polanyi and Orso go through the routine, telling the Iraqis they were gonna be okay, they were gonna be fine, and not to worry. Crane got some more of that off-balance vertigo feeling.

So far, Baker Company hadn't lost anybody, just a few burns and scrapes and one guy rotated for dysentery. But if the Iraqis had fought harder, maybe killed a few people? When the blood was up, all a guy wanted to do was kill something. At Iwo Jima, there'd been, what, twenty thousand Japanese on the island. Maybe one hundred were taken alive.

It was one of those rules. If the enemy fought all-out, did terrible things, killed a bunch of your friends, then he had no right to surrender. And even these clean young high schoolers, these farm kids and football jocks, Mosby and every last one of them, they'd light up the whole crowd, turn them into road kill, if they'd lost a few friends. Call it the My Lai factor: leave a grunt out in the bush long enough, especially in some rat's-ass counterinsurgency meat grinder where he can't tell the VC from a friendly—let him see some of his buddies cut up like a Christmas turkey or step on one too many shit-caked pungi traps, and the time will come, he'll get his payback, even if he has to light up a choir to do it.

You don't like it, then don't start wars.

Looking at the guys right now, Crane could see they were still cherry, still untouched by the thing, and he didn't know what he really thought about that. Maybe it was a good thing.

But probably not.

Well, right now it was all high fives and big grins and Iraqis begging for mercy, and all around them that big iron and smiling tankers and . . . well . . . by Christ, it was very, very sweet, and they were all Jolly Green Giants in ten-league boots, and the U.S. Army was the meanest son of a bitch in the whole goddam valley. It made him nervous.

Crane tried to enjoy it too, but something was all wrong. It made him nervous.

The surrender, though, that had been very fine.

As soon as the 1st had broken through the Iraqi forward positions, the armor and the mechanized infantry units had pulled off to the right and left flanks of the breakthrough, herringboned, with muzzles out into the desert and thermal imagers on.

Someone had painted a sign and planted it in the middle of a plowed-up berm. It had the insignia of the 1st, a large red numeral 1 on an olive-drab patch. The sign read:

WELCOME TO IRAQ

COURTESY

OF THE

BIG RED ONE

Once they'd cleared the breach, the second echelon of armor in VII Corps had hammered through, the Warrior IFVs and the Scorpions and Scimitars, the Striker AFVs, and of course the Challenger tanks of the British 1st Armoured Division—Crane watched the Challengers go by and shook his head for the poor sons of bitches who had to go to war in them. Firing the main gun was like trying to program a VCR upside down in an iron lung. Blindfolded. God bless them.

The entire action was essentially a slingshot maneuver, with the 1st doing the initial pull and providing the momentum that would take the British tankers on into the Iraqi rear echelons, where they'd seek out and destroy whatever Iraqi armor they found in flank attacks. The idea was to cause so much unexpected havoc that the Iraqis would break and run for it, or wet themselves and faint.

And all through those first hours, it was a headlong charge into thin air. After they'd punched through the initial Iraqi defenses, all three divisions had advanced miles into Iraq and the only hard contact had come at Al Ubayid, where the 101st Airmobile and elements of the 82nd Airborne literally dropped in out of the sky and surprised the hell out of an entire Iraqi division, the 26th. They'd taken five hundred prisoners and lit up an unknown number of others, men who would never see daylight again, men who died in an eye-blink flash of white phosphor or HEAT rounds, or got chopped into bits by chain-gun fire and missiles.

This branch of the frontal assault consisted of two thousand soldiers, fifty IFVs and humvees, towed artillery and supplies, all of it lifted by three hundred Chinooks and Sea Kings, supported by Kiowa and Apache assault choppers, their mission the creation of a sixty-square-mile cleared area deep inside Iraq, called Cobra Base. For the Iraqis who found themselves underneath the assault as it came down, it must have looked like a coffin lid closing.

To the west and south of this position, the 1st Infantry Division was pushing ahead, but not as fast as they would have liked. The terrain sucked, the salt marshes and the rotten weather slowing them.

Crane, in his humvee, kept in radio contact with DerHorst and Wolochek, and with the fire teams and IFVs in their echelon. Everyone was painfully alert, expecting to run into a strong enemy position at any moment, expecting mines or arty, expecting a battalion of Iraqis to rise up out of the wet sand like plumes of pale fire. They had one hard contact when a burst of heavy-caliber fire sprayed the flanks of Mosby's IFV, making a neat row of bright polished-steel dents in the dull ocher paintwork, but they never established where the rounds had come from, and Crane privately put it down as friendly fire from some overwired boot down the line, a sloppy traverse, or just plain asshole behavior from one of the other platoons.

And so it had gone, until Franks pulled them up at the wadi and told them to wait for backup. Their entire division was spread out along the Wadi al Batin, right on the Kuwait-Iraq border. Now that they had reached their first objective and all they could do was wait for the 2nd Armored Cavalry on their left to come up and cross in front of their lines, they had time to consider.

These kids were going through a sea change, turning from well-trained civilians in uniform to combat soldiers, and the thing that made that change was the act of killing another human being. Back at the trench line, as the M9s plowed down the line and the Iraqis died in their position, all the men had watched in shock.

Now no one seemed particularly upset about it, although Crane could hear the difference in their voices, and see it in their eyes. They had practiced the maneuver over and over again, but seeing those plows go down the lines, seeing that wall of sand falling forward like a big brown ocean wave, and the arms and legs and shapes struggling under the surface . . . well, it was ugly. He noticed Mitchell was silent too, and Crane let him get out and walk over to his unit.

He slid out and slammed the door and Crane got in behind the wheel and took his helmet off. The Motorola radio was buzzing quietly and now and then he'd hear Wolochek or some query from the colonel, but mainly there was silence all down the line, except for the muted growling of the engines, and the whine as the M1 tankers swiveled their main-gun turrets and established fire zones.

Turrets clanged and doors grated open, choked with sand and dust, and hundreds of guys all down the line were walking out into the desert to piss while their buddies sat behind the chain guns and covered them, staring out into the night. Now and then a Kiowa would hammer by overhead, its Midnight Sun searchlight flickering over the underbrush and down the rocky canyons of the Wadi al Batin.

There was nothing around them. They had driven so far into the AO that none of the Iraqis even knew they were there. As a military maneuver, it had been an unqualified success, and it seemed to Crane that the Iraqis had better get their shit together in a hurry or they were going to get mauled.

Crane was parked beside the wadi, facing west into Kuwait, looking out over the sodden expanse of the valley, into the darkness of Kuwait itself. The troops were sitting all over their IFVs, under ponchos or canvas, eating MREs and talking things over. Crane could hear their voices, rapid chatter and sudden barking laughter, as they stitched their worldview back together in a slightly different pattern. He was proud of them. They'd done their jobs well, and no one had screwed up badly enough to attract an officer's attention.

But then the ground war was only twelve hours old.

That business of the trenches, they'd hear about *that* later. Let the press get wind of that, they'd be howling like wolves. Maybe that was what came of letting the public wander around with deeply vague ideas about combat, all those John Wayne fantasies about guys only getting shot in polite places, dying neatly in an artful pose against a bamboo plant, looking up with Bambi eyes at their high school buddy—Christ, was there a polite way to kill somebody?

The idea was to kill the enemy. Why was it okay to shoot the shit out of him, or smash him flat as road kill under a Buff strike, or nuke a couple hundred thousand, but for chrissakes don't *bury* them! Civilians.

The only real feeling Crane had taken away from that experience was the main and most important one; thanks to Colonel Stephen Hawkins over at the Engineers HQ, the 1st Infantry Division hadn't lost one man on that assault. Not one. Hawkins deserved a medal and a handshake from every living grunt in the KTO.

Crane dug an MRE—Mainly Rat Entrails—out of the food locker in the humvee and walked around to the engine hood release, the MRE in one hand and his Beretta in the other. Although he was in the middle of an entire infantry division, he could still feel the weight of all that empty desert off to the west, and the threat of hidden Iraqi armor beyond the horizon line.

He tugged the outside lever and lifted the hood, placing the MRE on the engine block to heat up. He was staring out over the wadi, leaning on the humvee grille, his mind at Harry's Uptown Bar, when he heard someone calling his name.

Sergeant DerHorst was walking across from his IFV. Rimed with white dust, sweat stained from the overheated IFV interior, his eyes were red and his lips were blackened from the windburn.

"Hey, Dee—what's for dinner?"

Crane grinned back at him. "Paws and tails. What're you having?"

"Dog lips in a snot sauce. It's superb! Boomer's a goddam cordon blue. Gimme some room here."

He settled back against the humvee beside Crane, tugging at

his neck scarf. Miserable rain was pattering down on them, making little tear tracks in the white grit on DerHorst's face. He looked back at the MRE on the block.

"You really gonna eat that?"

"Somebody has to. We leave them lying around, some kangaroo rat will eat one and die, we'll get sued by the Sierra Club. Where's Wolochek?"

"Over at Baker Tango Oscar with Boomer, waiting for a fax."

"How're the looies?"

"Ackisson's wrapped too tight. Not that he doesn't have balls. But he's afraid to make a mistake, so he waits too long. Back at the breach, he was through in his IFV and then he stops—*stops* dead—and I pull up, he's got his driver doing a GPS verification. Fucking *rounds* are coming in, his boys are stuck in the hold, pissing themselves, tankers are hitting their sirens behind us, here's Ackisson doing a sit-rep update for the log!"

"What'd you say?"

"I sucked up nice, suggested he should redeploy out of this AO on account of there seemed to be an overload of incoming ordnance."

"Bullshit you did. I heard you on the 'net. What's a tanglefoot?"

"It's a horse, can't walk without tripping."

"How'd he take it?"

"He's okay. Bugged his eyes out, then swallowed it and moved out. Came up to me a while back, thanked me for the pointer. He'll be okay. Petrie I like; he gives you the idea he's having *fun*. His boys like him, and he knows his stuff. By the way, ask him about that Stoner he's got. Anyway, he listens to his noncoms and doesn't trip on his dick. Seafferman . . . man, he got it from Wolochek, I don't know why, he's sitting over there in a humvee, staring at his crotch. He might be crying. Rossberg . . . I don't know. I mean, he *looks* busy, but his platoon was always just getting there, always a few seconds late. I think he might be holding back a bit, maybe afraid to lose a man."

"That's the best way to lose one. It's the timid ones get lit up first. They have no forward motion, easy to nail. You want me to talk to him?"

DerHorst considered it while he ripped the top off a pack of something that claimed to be pork and rice in a barbecue sauce. He dipped his fingertip into it and tasted it, made a face, and began to eat, talking around his mouthful of mystery meat.

"My job, supposed to be. But you're the pro around here, it'd be easier, coming from you."

"What do you want me to say?"

"Tell him that story, about the pencils."

Crane stared at DerHorst.

"Hey, Dee . . . it was a *joke!*"

Crane had nothing to say.

"I know, let's get him some grenade rings, he can stick them on that boonie hat of his."

"What will that do for him? That was a Nam thing."

"He needs to connect, get *into* the war."

"He's in it, all right. He just doesn't know it yet. I'll say something to him. He probably just needs an ear. He thinks he's the only one worrying."

"Then he's not watching Wolochek."

"How's he doing?"

"Good. Like I say, you can see him worrying. He worries about everything. I like a captain who worries about his men. But he gets it done. He's got his shit together. Loves the Internet toys, though. One of the tankers had a wiring glitch and Wolochek got the Internet to download a schematic of the wiring buss from the factory in Michigan, pulled it off the fax, and walked it over to the tank and unrolled it like it was a Dead Sea scroll. Very neat."

"Christ. This isn't war, it's a computer game."

"Yeah. It's virtual reality. I think your meal's ready. It stopped screaming just now. It *is* a weird war. I look up, try to see a J-STAR, I know it's up there looking down at us. They could pick up the heat from all the grunts pissing into the gully over there."

"They probably can. They're sure getting returns from all this hot metal. They can see right through the cloud cover."

"Thank Christ. *Damn,* this is a miserable country."

"That it is."

"Figure the Bear is watching us?"

"No. I guess the CINC would stay back in the rear echelon. That's doctrine. I hear they have something like thirty mobile satellite uplink stations in the KTO. I mean, the goddam *tanks* have fax machines and video monitors. Look at this—" Crane dug his hand-held GPS receiver out of his ALICE gear and punched the keys. The little LCD screen lit up and flickered through some numbers. "See—lats and longs. By the numbers. This is where we are, and if I walk away fifty yards, the numbers change. We have three geosynchronous satellites above the horizon line right now. In Vietnam, we had maps and compasses and we guessed a lot. Orders were ticker-tape rip strips. There was a reason they called the radios Prick-Two-Fives. Even with a Two-Niner-Two extender, the goddam things might as well have been tin cans and waxed string. Wolochek over there has his own laptop computer, a modem, we can auto-encrypt at the flick of a switch and talk to your mom in Buttwad—"

"Benewah."

"—Idaho . . . get a download of Iraqi positions, assign fire missions and deploy elements. Today I heard one of our Kiowas doing a rapid-burst encrypted upload of fire data. It went from the Kiowa to a J-STAR and from the J-STAR back down to a battery of arty six miles in the rear, went straight into the Range Data computer, didn't even have to be keyed or encoded. It was like the pilot was the gunner, setting aim points by computer from miles away, while he's looking right at the target. . . . It feels very strange. I never thought this shit would work, but so far . . . it's been okay. Not perfect, but better than the last war."

"You're a dinosaur, Dee. When this is over, you oughtta take an Early and sit by the river, tell your grandkids lies about the war."

"I don't have grandkids . . . anyway, I thought I was supposed to put in for TRADOC and climb the stairway to heaven."

"An obsessive consistency is . . . is . . . shit. Something about little minds, would have been a very neat quote. Some guy with three names said it."

"James Earl Jones? Frank Lloyd Wright? Lee Harvey Oswald?"

"Whatever . . . So, waddya think so far?"

"About what?"

"This *war*, goddamnit!"

Crane smiled at DerHorst. "Remember what Tonto said to the Lone Ranger?"

"Tonto said a lot to the Lone Ranger. All they had was each other and the horses. You get lonely out there on the range, and Tonto had wonderful soft brown eyes. But then, so did Silver. What was the question?"

"Tonto and the Lone Ranger are sneaking up on this Indian village, and the Lone Ranger says to Tonto, Say, it's kinda *quiet*, isn't it, Tonto? And Tonto says, Yes, Kemo Sabe. Almost . . . *too* quiet."

"You think we're gonna get something slammed on our fingers?"

Crane shrugged, took in a long breath, feeling the stiffness in his back and legs, and the bruises from being bounced around in the humvee. The morning seemed a century in the past. "That breakthrough . . . what the fuck are the Iraqis *doing*? They're supposed to be soldiers, fought a big war for ten years. Why the hell fall apart like that? It's just too easy. It worries me. Remember the Fetterman massacre?"

"Not offhand, but I'm sure you'll bring me up to date."

"This was in '66, Red Cloud's War—"

"This would be *1866*?"

"Yeah. Fetterman was a lieutenant, he was stationed at Fort Phil Kearny, that's in—"

"I know where it was! I'm from Idaho, not Pluto! It's in Wyoming, up near the Montana border. Wyoming is right next to Idaho, Dee. Hasn't moved an inch for years. Try to keep up, will ya?"

"Yeah, and Fetterman, he was a real badass, itching to get out there, kick some redskin butt. So this time, Crazy Horse and a bunch of braves, they come in real close to the fort, up into these low hills all around it, and Crazy Horse, he pretends that his pony is blown, he draws Fetterman out. Now, Fetterman has orders, don't go flying off into the distance chasing the Sioux, but now his blood is up, he sees Crazy Horse and his braves just out of reach, so he goes charging up over the hill and down into the valley beyond it—gets all stretched out, cavalry in front, all his infantry lagging behind, out of breath—''

"And of course, all the Indians in the world ride down on him. I know the story. Red Cloud called it the Hundred in the Hands. They butchered them all, Fetterman included. I've seen the cairn, it's just off I-90 south of Sheridan. You can see it from the interstate."

"Yeah."

"So what you're saying is, Hussein's doing a Crazy Horse on us, drawing us in and letting us get all strung out, get ahead of our supplies, then he whacks us?"

"I can't think of another reason why he'd leave his flanks so weak. He can't be that stupid!"

"Why not?"

"This is a tricky part of the world. Fools don't last long. Hussein managed to run a ten-year war with Iran, fought them to a standstill."

"Yeah, and that's his problem, Dee."

"What?"

"He stands still. They all do around here. They play positional warfare, they sit and wait for someone to come ahead, take them head-on. They can't maneuver without stepping on their turbans. They're not real soldiers, anyway, they're fucking fanatics."

"It still worries me. It feels wrong."

"Fuck 'em. They wanna be martyrs, here's the Third Army, come to help them get to paradise. Hussein's not eleven bravo, you said that yourself, back in Riley. I heard you telling the grunts."

"Maybe, but it seems too—"

They heard some low talk and laughter, getting closer, and boots on the stony ground. Shabazz and Fanand's replacement, another black kid named Duvall, were picking their way across the rocks, Shabazz listening hard to some story that Duvall was telling him, his face set and a big grin showing.

"Hey, Shabazz," said DerHorst, "go down to the PX, get me a six-pack and some Twizzlers, will ya?"

Shabazz and Duvall came up just as another Kiowa slammed through their airspace, kicking up twigs and stones. Duvall looked up, gaping, as it flew overhead. Crane was peeling his MRE and watching Duvall.

"You like the choppers, Duvall?"

Duvall ducked his head, looked for a second like a twelve-year-old, then smiled at Crane.

"Yes, Sergeant Crane. I put in for Scouts when I signed."

"What happened?"

Shabazz shook his head. "Homey don't play that. They dissed the nigger good."

Crane hated the word "nigger." And "dissed," and "word," and a lot of other black slang. It grated on him, but the blacks used it like salt, spiced up every conversation with it, and anyway he was getting to the age where it was easier to list the things that *didn't* irritate him.

"That's not true, Sergeant. Shabazz turns it all around."

"It's word, nigger!"

"No, it isn't. I can't take heights."

DerHorst laughed. "Well, that's a problem."

Shabazz was smiling too. "Nigger can't drive either. This brother, he belongs in the infantry."

"Not you, though," said DerHorst, who liked Shabazz in spite of all that black attitude.

"Not me. I get out of this, I'm transferring to the one-oh-one."

"Intel? You?"

"Military Intelligence, that's *it*. I get out of the shit, I'm going to work *uptown*, get rank. We need more niggers in the upper echelon."

Duvall was looking nervous. "We already got General Powell."

"Powell's not a nigger. Powell's an African-American, homey! We need a brother up there in the sky, give all the white boys conniptions."

"You tell Powell that, Shabazz," said DerHorst. "He'll fry your black ass. He's been to the mountain already."

"I know that! I ain't dissin' the man. But he ain't been where I been, either. The corporation still got a thumb up its butt, and that ain't gonna change until enough wild niggers get to the Palace."

Crane was interested. "How'd you change the corporation, kid? What would you do first?"

Shabazz looked at Crane, trying to read him, see if Crane was angry. "Well, Sergeant Crane, I don't mean no disrespect."

"I know that, kid. I'm just asking."

"Okay . . . don't take this wrong, but we oughtta bring back segregation, stop trying to mix the races."

DerHorst started to say something, but Shabazz hurried into it.

"You see, homey, he don't *wanna* assimilate! You guys, you're Irish-American, or Italian-American, or Swedish-American, but the black man, if he ain't *black*, what is he?"

"What about African-American?"

"Man, what about it? What's Africa to me? I was born in Chicago, Sergeant. I don't know *shit* about Africa. How'd it be, I go back to Africa now, say to some homey sitting on his butt in, wherever, Zambia, and I say, Hey, bro, it's *me*. I'm *home*. He's gonna look at me, say Who the fuck are you? I got no other thing to be than black. I assimilate—which ain't gonna happen anyway—what have I got left? I'm a Twinkie, got white on the inside. The black man, he has to stay away from all that Africa shit, because that's just like, you're a Jew from Wichita, you go back to the homeland, to Israel, land on some Palestinian, he's been there a thousand years, you walk into his house, say June, I'm home! I got no more rights to a piece of Zambia than a Jew has to a chunk of Palestine. That country, it belongs to whoever *stayed* there. Black man, he has to *accept* that he's got no place to go home to. It's either the United States or start swimming."

DerHorst looked angry now. "So be an American. That's what I am."

"Look, I don't mean to . . . you asked me, Sergeant."

Crane was looking at Shabazz and thinking about Vietnam. "He's not leaning on you . . . I don't think you're right, though."

Shabazz looked down and up again. "All due respect, Sergeant, but you . . . you're not black. You can't know this stuff without you been there. No offense."

DerHorst looked at Crane, waiting.

"We had this kind of thing in Vietnam," said Crane, looking past them out at the wadi, still nervous about all the possibilities out there. "The bloods kept to themselves, had their own hootches, places like the Can Hoi Tan Town in Saigon, where you couldn't go, that 'dap' thing, set themselves apart a thousand little ways. But all of that, that was a fire-base thing: In the bush, it was different. It was very different."

Shabazz started to say something but Duvall raised a hand.

"I know about that, Sergeant. My dad was in the Eleventh Infantry, the Americal. He said one of his best buddies was a white guy, he still has the guy's picture in his wallet."

Shabazz looked at the ground. "Yeah? And *after*? After Vietnam? They have barbecues? Go to Disneyland together? You dating the guy's daughter? Shit!"

Duvall shook his head. "No. Guy was killed, at a place called Quang Ngai."

"That's a province, not a place," said Crane. "But Shabazz gets the point."

"Well, I do, but the war—"

Crane finished off his MRE and used some crackers to scoop up his applesauce. It was pretty good, actually.

"The war *is* the point, Sergeant Shabazz," he said, dropping the MRE kit at his feet. "I get what you're saying, about the Irish and the Swedes all having a homeland, not that I could go back to my folks in England and expect anything different from your guy in Zambia. But you go look back there, look in the mirror of that humvee, see how much of you is black and how much is desert camo, chocolate chips. Maybe you got a point, about being black in the States. But years from now, you'll remember one thing. You were Army. You were eleven bravo, and all these men, they are your brothers, they will die for you. You go ask some homey in Chicago to do *that* for you."

"It's more complicated than that. There's a life after the Army. We get back to Fort Riley, I'm still a nigger. Same shit, different day."

"Yeah—it is. But not right now. While we're out here, we're

brothers, and anyone who tries you on, he takes us all on. You get back to Chicago, you'll never know anything like that ever again, and the day will come, there'll be a reunion, and you'll squeeze back into your Class As and you'll come in the door, your head on a swivel, looking for Duvall, for Mosby even, and Polanyi, for me and DerHorst, all of us, because we were all your brothers. You know why?"

Shabazz was silent, staring at Crane, intent on his words.

"Because we all of us *left*. We joined the Army."

"But we're the American Army, Sergeant."

"And if this war goes sour, how many civilians are gonna die in it? How many American civilians?"

"None, I guess . . . unless you count the Spooks from Langley."

"That's right. Everybody who's gonna die is a soldier. When they put it on the wall at Danger Forward, it's not gonna say 'a civilian of the First Infantry Division.' You get out of this war alive, Shabazz, I promise you, when you think about who you really are, from now on, you'll think, well, whatever else, I was a soldier."

There was a silence.

Finally, DerHorst slapped his gloves down the side of his BDUs. A spatter of white grit fell off him into the headlight glow in the front of the humvee. "Damn, I think I've teared up. Anybody got a Kleenex?"

Shabazz and Duvall tried for a smile. DerHorst looked at them and raised his eyebrows.

"Okay . . . show's over. Go see to your flock, kids."

They started to salute, stopped themselves, and turned away.

Crane was looking off into the wadi, feeling stupid.

DerHorst slapped him on the back. "Hey, Dee—you okay?"

"Shit, I'm fine."

"Well, I gotta go. We're gonna saddle up in five."

"I know. See you."

"Tell you what."

"What?"

"You doing anything with that humvee, has anything to do with the war effort?"

"Not really."

"I been riding with Boomer Riebold, in Blue Four. I'll take your humvee, get Mitchell off your hands. You can go along with Boomer, see what the war looks like from a tank. So far, this ain't been an infantry show anyway. All we're doing is a ride-along. How about it?"

"Wolochek wants me with the IFVs."

"And the IFVs'll all be with Boomer and his tanks. For chrissake, Dee, I already cleared it with Wolochek. This war isn't gonna last forever. Get it while it's hot!"

Crane stood up and stretched. "Where the hell's Boomer put you? There's not a lot of extra space there. What're you doing, standing behind the loader?"

"Yeah. Don't need air-conditioning. They got the hatch open, I get the seven-six-two, wind in my hair, blow off smoke grenades. I look like Lawrence of Arabia. Gonna get the cover of *People,* anybody sees me. You'll look *marvelous,* Dee."

"Well, I am sorely sick of that humvee."

"Done, then," said DerHorst, grinning. "Tell you one thing ..."

Crane waited.

"I think I get it now, why you stay eleven bravo."

Crane gave him a sideways look, waiting for a punch line.

"No punch line, Dee. I mean it just that way. What you said to Shabazz, that was pure iron bravo."

"Iron bravo? What's iron bravo?"

DerHorst grinned and walked away a bit. "Iron bravo. Haven't you ever heard them say it, on the 'net, in the field?"

"No, I haven't. What's it mean?"

DerHorst spread his arms wide, palms up, and pulled his shoulders in, a very Italian gesture for a guy from Idaho. "Fucked if I know, Dee. Take it as a compliment."

He was gone, leaving Crane alone by the humvee grille, staring out across the wadi into Kuwait. It seemed to him that he could see a far-off flicker of yellow fire, as if the land itself was burning.

Which it was.

CHAPTER FOURTEEN

GODZILLA

Crane did a slow walkabout at the Wadi al Batin, seeing to the junior sergeants, making sure that everybody in the company had eaten. The AO was littered with MRE wrappers and plastic trays; so what? Let the Iraqis clean up.

All over the AO, troopers were walking out with pieces of Army form blank in one hand and their side arms in the other, taking the chance to ease the pain in their bellies. Dysentery or just a local version of the two-step, whatever it was, it was running through the division like Sherman through Georgia. Crane had a supply of Lomotil, but that was just a delaying tactic and would have to be paid for. Suddenly.

Stretching out, legs shaking, he lengthened his stride, feeling the fatigue in his muscles. Behind his eyes there seemed to be sand grating against bone. He looked up at the sky, a low feature-less black like a bolt of cloth, with rips here and there and bright cold stars showing through the rents. He was thinking about the bosses.

Now, *that* was a miserable job, and Crane didn't envy the brass in the slightest. Sure, if it all worked out, there'd be glory for a

while, and lots of press, and maybe a parade. But let things go
wrong, and things going wrong was what wars were all about, then
the brass might as well eat their 9-mms, because for the rest of
their lives all they'd ever have would be this burning coal in their
hearts, the souls of all the dead men under their command . . .
like . . . what the hell was Crane trying to remember? It was something about this advance . . . no, it was gone again.

Well . . . whatever . . . so far so good. Slow. But good.

Crane came across Mosby and Polanyi and Mitchell and the rest
of the guys a few meters down the wadi, slouching around the
base of their IFV, talking about football, cleaning their rifles and
filling magazines from ammo boxes. Mosby was looking at his GPS
set and checking the reading against a fold-out map, intent and
oblivious to Crane as he walked by, head-to-head with Orso and
Polanyi.

Polanyi saw Crane going past, started to get up, but Crane raised
a hand and waved him down again. He was pleased with them,
with all of the kids in Baker Company. They were doing it all right,
just like at the NTC, and Crane remembered the old military slo-
gan: easy training, hard combat. Hard training, easy combat.

It wasn't precisely true, but it was in there somewhere.

He passed through the rest of the Baker AO, through clusters
of troops doing fast maintenance on the IFVs and humvees, checking and rechecking gear, or standing at water blivets, filling bottles
for the next leg of the advance.

The talk was low and cheerful. Morale was high, although there
seemed to be a general feeling of suspended belief, as if it was all
too easy, like there had to be a catch somewhere. And everyone
was having that adrenaline backlash, that underwater slow-motion
feeling that came over you after a hard advance.

Crane was grateful for the cold and the rain, in a way, because
it woke you up, kept your edge. He needed that.

Underneath everything else that Crane was feeling—relief that
no one had been killed in the breach, the concern he always felt
for the command, his developing realization that no matter how
many push-ups he did in his room, he was getting old—underneath all of that, Crane was carrying a strange nameless anxiety.

The whole advance—it was too easy. It didn't add up. They *had* to be running into something. This was a war, not a field trip. The Iraqis had just come out of a ten-year war. Surely they had learned *something* about tank warfare in all that time? For God's sake, didn't they lose a half a million men? No, this was all wrong.

Crane tried to find a recognizable hook to hang his worries on, but all he could get was an image of tanks blowing up and men running across sand, and rain coming down over it all, and out there in the great desert night, something *huge* moving, something *massive.*

Christ, he thought, get a grip. The kids are watching.

As he walked through the AO, Crane answered whatever greetings and questions were put to him, but all in all it looked like his junior sergeants were doing very well, and there wasn't very much for him to add. All the IFVs were hull-down and herringboned. Every platoon had a squad out in forward positions, providing flank cover and observation posts. The perimeter was covered, secure. Nobody had gotten loose or careless. No one had forgotten that they were in Indian country, open to an assault without warning, extended and exposed and well inside enemy territory.

Most important, everybody seemed to have a good idea of where everybody else was, about the only real protection there was against friendly-fire accidents. The people back home would forgive a lot, but friendly fire was not one of them. And in this kind of battlefield, there was no doubt they were going to have some. Maybe a lot.

A squadron of Apaches and Kiowas boomed through at five hundred feet, pods full of Hellfires, chain guns swiveling. Crane got a momentary POV shift and saw the armored column as it looked to the Kiowa pilots—a mass of dull ocher iron shapes dimly visible in the damp blue night, no lights showing, engines idling and muttering, all the sounds rolling together into that unique growling ironbound thunder that armor makes.

But that was wrong, he realized. To the Kiowa and Apache gunners, the column would look like a long string of bright green glowing metal, as if it was on fire, truck-shaped blobs of green light, smaller shapes that looked manlike, green light rippling around the exhaust vents of the M1s, and at the hatches and turret gates, wherever there was a heat differential. For the pilots wearing NVGs or looking at their thermal imagers, the whole western bank of the Wadi al Batin would look like a bright green brush fire in the shape of machines and men.

The fast movers and Warthog pilots would call this a major TRE—a Target-Rich Environment.

They were strung out for miles along the Wadi al Batin, stinking of JP5 and kerosene fumes, heat haze shimmering over it all, with the big M1s echeloned on the flanks and forward, main guns trained on their assigned fire sectors, the infantry IFVs interspersed down through the tanks, ready to support them in a defensive reaction.

Mist and slow rain drifted downward through the smoke and the heat rising from the exhaust vents of the armor, onto men walking with rifles at port arms. The night was filled with low voices, sudden barking coughs, muttered commands and curses, cigarettes flaring like tiny red sparks in the blackness, the clanking of iron and steel as hatches slammed down and turrets swiveled, the sudden explosive roar as idling tanks fired up and blew clouds of dust and fumes outward, and treads started to churn.

Like a python stirring, a visible wave of accelerated movement rippled down the line as the 1st Infantry Division started to move out again, this time straight across the Wadi al Batin and eastward at speed into Kuwait, heading straight for the two divisions of the Republican Guards that had been located by the J-STARS a few hours before.

He found Boomer Riebold's Blue Four Abrams a few hundred yards down the column, parked off to the east of the line, part of a tank platoon attached to 3rd Platoon of the 34th Armor.

Crane could see Wolochek's humvee parked alongside the tank, and a group of men gathered around the humvee. The tank was idling slowly and the engine hatch was up, a grunt halfway inside the engine compartment, his legs sticking up, held there by a huge black man in a flak jacket. As Crane came up, the group around the humvee broke up—the Baker Company LTs, Seafferman and

Ackisson, Petrie, Rossberg. They waved a variety of careless salutes as Crane snapped to, and Petrie, grinning hugely, stopped in front of Crane, a cigarette hanging from his mouth, his GPS set in his left hand, and something slung on his back, some kind of assault weapon.

Crane remembered it, that bloody M63, the Stoner! Petrie had wangled it out of somebody back at King Khalid. Petrie had his fitted with the plastic one-hundred-and-fifty-round box magazine, SEAL style. It looked like a fat black barracuda hanging off Petrie's shoulder. DerHorst had said something about it.

"Tell me, Dee, are we having fun yet? Are we not the very strackest pack of fucking strackers you have ever fucking laid your optical sensors upon? Blow me if I lie!"

"Sir, we are radically strack and that's a fack, jack."

Crane had to grin; you saw this a lot, in the early days of an LT's career. They had it rough, the cherry LTs, not just young and green, but carrying command, responsible for forty men and a mission. Being a platoon LT was where the rubber hit the road. Few of them had a good time, and in hardcore combat, the life expectancy of an LT JG was about three weeks. So far, Petrie was looking very good, and he knew it.

"Sir, may I ask you a question?"

Petrie bowed like a cavalier, making a sweeping gesture with his left hand, and the Stoner slipped off his shoulder and dropped down to his elbow, where the sling snagged on his flak strap. Petrie swore and tugged it back up in place.

"That was my question . . . you fired that thing yet?"

"Yes, I have. I fired it a great deal, Sergeant, and we have reached an understanding, this Stoner and I."

"Which is . . ."

"That this weapon is a holy weapon, and I will cleave unto it, and have carnal knowledge of no other weapon before her, nor suffer the other weapons to look upon this Stoner askance, for she is mine alone."

"You like it, huh?"

"Dee, this Stoner is—it's Thunder in the Hand. I have named

her Maria, and Maria makes me feel like fucking Thor. When the war's over, I'm taking this home with me, gonna put it in a shrine in my rec room, light a candle to it.''

"You actually *hit* anything with it?''

Petrie's face hardened, chilled, thawed, and the grin came back.

"Yeah, Dee. I hit four anythings with it. It saved my ass and the ass of my own beloved driver, who is like a son unto me. Why you asking?''

"I wondered what Wolochek was saying to you.''

"Captain Wolochek was watching. He was about fifty yards away. We come in through the berm and I guess some of the ragheads had gotten past the tankers because when we cut left, there's a goddam BMP with a Sagger rocket, we're looking right up the flute, and before I can think of anything, I drag this thing around and empty it at the BMP. It was like watching a hamster get fed into a document shredder. It was very messy. I believe the phrase is 'rock and roll.' ''

"Full auto? How many rounds?''

"You'll forgive me if I did not keep an accurate count. Know what I was screaming?''

"No—what?''

"Ramirez says I was screaming 'Resistance is useless' at the BMP. I think I got it out of that series, *The Hitchhiker's Guide to the Galaxy.* I think it was the Vogon war cry. Funny thing, huh? So Wolochek was impressed and he has approved our relationship.''

Crane was impressed as well. Petrie saw Crane's reassessment and was pleased by it.

"You gonna ride with Boomer, so I hear?''

"If there's room, sir.''

Petrie looked back at the massive tank. The crew were closing up the engine hatch, and the big black man in the flak jacket was stretching a piece of fabric out, holding it up into the cone of red light from a work lamp and nodding his head slowly.

"Panty hose, that's what they're replacing. Who'd have thought you'd need panty hose to run a war?''

Panty hose had turned out to be a perfect solution to some of the filter problems with the M1 Abrams. It was something the press people hadn't found out yet. They would.

"In the bush, we used condoms on the M Sixteens, cornstarch for jungle rot, C Four to cook with, dried our BDUs on air-conditioning vents outside the mess when we were in the rear. . . . You make it up as you go along, sir."

"True. How're the kids doing?"

Petrie was the LT in charge of 2nd Platoon, Shabazz's immediate boss.

"I was just talking to Shabazz. He's doing fine, I think. You having any problems with them, sir?"

"None so far. Anything you want to let me know? Any advice?"

"Well, sir, nothing beyond . . . this breakthrough. It worries me."

Petrie's lean unshaven face changed. "It's a runaway, Dee! And stop with the 'sir' stuff for a second."

Crane smiled at him, thinking how *young* the guy was, maybe twenty-eight, less. . . . "It's no more than a feeling, sir. We're a long way in, and all strung out. We got flanks longer than the New York State Thruway, our ribs are all showing. We got all our faith in those J-STARS and the Kiowas, and the cavalry scouts, but what if they miss something?"

Petrie looked at Crane for a while, his grin slowly fading away. He capped his silver flask and tucked it away, probably thinking about General Franks, thinking what he could say to a noncom and what he could not. Finally, he slapped him on the shoulder.

"Dee, I hear you. I hear you five by five."

"That's all I meant, Doug."

"I know it. I'll see we don't go all limp out here. Hell, so far it's been a tanker show anyway."

Wolochek stuck his head out of the humvee window.

"Sergeant Crane, can I see you? Petrie, you hustle back there, we're moving out."

Petrie's grin came back and he saluted as he turned away again and kicked into a slow jog back along the column, his boots crunching and his gear jingling and bouncing, that big Stoner thumping on his flak jacket. Wolochek was looking at a GPS set and making marks on a grid map when Crane stuck his head in the window.

"Hey, Dee—how they hanging?"

"One in back of the other, for speed, sir."

Wolochek grinned at him, a brief contraction of the jaw and cheeks, not reaching his eyes. He looked tired and tense, but he was steady.

"DerHorst says you're gonna ride with Boomer."

"If that's okay, sir?"

"It's okay. How'd Mitchell do with your humvee?"

"He's a good kid. He did well."

"They all did. You know what's coming up?"

"I do."

"The Brits have encountered some resistance up the wadi, we think the Forty-seventh Infantry, and now the Brits are going wide, on a sweep to our north and east of us, so we're gonna go on down this line—" He traced a route through the grid map, his finger following a series of way points marked off in ballpoint. Crane, looking down at the map, saw nothing in the way of landmarks. It was wadi and salt marsh and open desert, a vast expanse of low hills and immense plains, with nothing to go by but the division GPS and the reports of the 4th Cavalry scout vehicles. It made Crane's flesh cold and his mouth felt dry. "—to about *here,* where, if Command is right, these forward elements of our armor are gonna engage the Republican Guard, the Tawakalna, and probably elements of the Twelfth Tank Division."

"Where's the Second Cav?"

Wolochek flipped the grid map over, holding it under the red map light set into the humvee fire wall.

"We've crossed over their lines—here—and they're gonna provide cover on our left flank as we go east—they're coming out of Makfhar al Busayyah, that's up here, about forty miles—and past them, way to the west there, we're told the Twenty-fourth Mech has made big headway, and they're all the way to the Euphrates, they crossed the Tigris yesterday—so, that's all she wrote. The lid is on tight and now we go in the box and kill everything we can find. Everything. And the vehicles. We don't leave one gasket on another, one bolt still screwed. If it moves, we kill it, if it don't move, we torch it. That's orders."

"Prisoners?"

"Wave them to the rear. We got support battalions, they'll control that. They don't drop their weapons, you light them up. That's straight from the Emerald City. Okay?"

"Yes, sir. How far are we gonna go that way?"

"Until we hit beaches. Until we find ourselves among Marines."

"And then? We gonna turn around, go to Baghdad?"

Wolochek was looking down at the map again, his mind spinning through the logistics. It took a second for the question to register.

"Baghdad? Christ . . . it would be sweet. Don't hold your breath. Let's just take care of this part. You got the picture?"

Crane could see it tactically. The entire armored breakthrough along the Iraq border with Saudi had turned into a race—block all the roads out, control the bridges, own the air—Jesus. . . .

"Man . . . it's a killing ground."

Wolochek looked up at Crane, his face unreal and wolfish in the red glow of the map light.

"Yes. That's the general idea. Baker's gonna travel in Overwatch, we'll keep the IFVs inside and put the M Ones out and forward along with the ITVs, and the IFVs will support the tanks with TOW Twos and engage directly any BMPs, Erks, BTR Sixties, any infantry concentrations. The M Ones'll lead. The visibility sucks and we figure the Guard has no NVG capability, just laser range finders, so the tankers can just ease on in there, get their targets painted for the Apaches or do it themselves. Blow their doors off. You can stay on Tac Kilo One, I already told Boomer, so if I need to coordinate Baker IFVs and TOW launchers I can work it through you and you can keep an eye on the forward units, see if we got infantry concentrations. You got the eye for terrain, you'll know if we're running into an ambush or getting suckered. See I get the news *first*, okay?"

"Yes, sir." Wolochek was all business, and under the control Crane could see a suppressed excitement. War was like the little girl with the curl. When it was good it was very, very good. He smiled at Wolochek, who grinned back, and this time it was a full one, and his eyes were hard red pinpricks in the darkened humvee. His teeth looked red, as if his mouth was full of blood. It was an unsettling image.

Crane saluted and slapped the hood of the humvee and walked away toward Boomer's M1. It was like walking up to a medieval castle and banging on the gate.

There was a dark shape filling the commander's hatch, lit from beneath by the glow of the tank interior. Hatless, bulky inside a full flak jacket, the figure pulled itself up and clambered across the hull, dropping down onto the ground beside Crane.

"Boomer," said Crane, recognizing the man as he straightened up.

"Sergeant Crane! Welcome to my nightmare!"

He swiveled in place and slapped the side of the hull rhythmically. It made a dull thudding sound, like a slow heartbeat inside something very old and very large. Boomer stood back, made a gesture.

"Dee, I want you to meet my tank."

"Meet your tank? I've met your tank. What's it . . . Elvira something?"

"Oh, God, no . . . they took Elvira from me. I got an upgrade in December, a whole new monster."

Boomer looked at Crane, up from under and sidelong.

"Waddya think I named her?"

Crane thought.

"Godzilla?"

Boomer's smile flicked off and he frowned.

"Somebody told you."

CHAPTER FIFTEEN

RONSONS

FEBRUARY 25, 1991

Boomer Riebold was a small man, no taller than five seven, with a pit-bull body, very heavy in the chest and shoulders, but narrow in the hips and slightly bandy-legged. His face was pitted with acne scars, he wore his hair in a boot cut, high and tight, with a razored zigzag pattern down the right side of his temple. His hair was bright white blond and he was deeply tanned, with deep-set pale blue eyes. When he talked his voice seemed to be coming up from the bottom of a well, a three-in-the-morning FM DJ voice. It was the voice, deep, carrying, powerful, that gave him the name Boomer. He was in his late thirties and held the rank of master sergeant.

Boomer Riebold was a career tanker, a lifer, who had been with the 34th Armor ever since he'd graduated out of noncom school at Leavenworth. His father had been a tanker with the 1st Battalion of the 1st Armored Division during the Second World War. Boomer had grown up with tankers and had never once dreamed of being anything else.

That was the way it went with tankers. It was as close as the Army ever came to a hereditary tradition. Crane shook Boomer's hand, feeling the power in it. Boomer slapped him on the shoulder, took his M16 and his ALICE pack and clambered back up onto the M1.

"Come on, we'll get you stowed. We're moving out in five. You eat?"

"Yeah. Had an MRE," said Crane, coming up onto the hull.

It was always the same for Crane, climbing up onto armor. It was like saddling up a dinosaur. Boomer was leaning into the commander's hatch, dropping Crane's gear into someone else's hands, laughing as he did it. Crane stopped and looked around him.

He was eight feet off the ground, on top of sixty-five tons of iron, thirty-two feet long and twelve feet wide, arguably the best tank in the world. Right now.

But then, now was all that counted, wasn't it?

Slab sided and Chobham plated, the M1 was painted desert ocher from muzzle to blast plates. There were two hatches in the turret, the commander's hatch on the right side of the turret, complete with a swivel-mounted .50-caliber, and a secondary hatch to the left of the command hatch, supplied with a 7.62-mm machine gun, also swivel mounted. Just forward of the commander's hatch was the metal shroud covering the laser range finder and thermal imaging sensors. On each side of the turret there were smoke grenade launchers.

Past the turret, Crane could see the head of the tank driver, just level with the open hatch on the forward slope of the tank hull. Under way, the driver was separate from the three other crewmen, who shared a cramped but electronically loaded compartment inside the turret. Normally the Abrams had a crew of four: the tank driver, who had night-vision screens and a video screen that could be switched from a forward camera to one mounted in the tail, and in the turret itself, the commander, the gunner, and the loader.

The commander and the gunner both had their own laser range-finder screens, NVG thermal imagers, and passive optical sights. The commander's chair was just behind the gunner, but most commanders liked to run the tank from a standing position, head and shoulders through the hatch. The fire system in front of the gunner included the thermal imagers and laser range finders, as well as the screen of his ballistic computer. The loader was seated sideways, facing the gunner, at the breach of the main gun. His job was to manually insert whatever round the gunner had called up on the fire system, solid shot or HEAT shell. The main gun, twelve feet long, 120-mm smoothbore, fired a round nearly five inches in diameter, accurate out to three thousand yards.

Even in the dark, Crane could make out the small cylinder at the muzzle, part of the muzzle reference system, a laser-beam sensor that kept track of the barrel warp caused by overheating during rapid-fire engagements and fed the changes into the tank's ballistics computer. Looking behind him, off the rear of the turret, he could see the blast plates over the engine and ammunition-storage compartments. They were breakaway covers, designed to blow up and out if the tank took a shell in the ammunition-storage section, dispersing the explosive force away from the main body and the crew. And idling away under the hatch was the fifteen-hundred-horsepower gas-turbine engine capable of delivering speeds up to seventy miles an hour on pavement and forty miles an hour in the field. Carrying forty rounds, the M1 could fire at a rate of twelve rounds a minute, either High-Explosive Antitank shells, called HEAT, or armor-piercing fin-stabilized discarding sabot ordnance, which were, in simple terms, plain ordinary "shot," in many ways similar to a rifle round, a streamlined dart of depleted uranium encased in a breakaway "sabot" or aluminum casing that falls off as soon as the round clears the muzzle. Each dart has fins to stabilize it in flight.

Crane had seen them come in, a silvery flicker of light, shrieking, just suddenly there, an eye-blink explosion, so that the interior of the target vehicle became a kind of meat grinder, a steel jar filled with flying shrapnel that sounded like a hive of bees, metal splinters hissing and clanging off everything and into everyone. And then there was the HEAT round. They were even worse.

A HEAT round—really a "shell" as opposed to a "shot"—was a more complicated device and had become, in Desert Storm, the main kind of tank-killing weapon because it could be fired at lower velocities with undiminished effect, even delivered as missile warheads or from optically guided infantry weapons like the TOW and the God-cursed and thoroughly loathed Dragon.

HEAT rounds were essentially shaped charges, "shaped" in the sense that it was a peculiarity of high explosives that they tended to reproduce a "negative" of their shape in the target material. If you were using plastic explosive, you applied it to a wall in a cup shape, with the hollow side down against the wall. When it was exploded, the force of the blast was shaped and directed by the hollow space, generating a phenomenal level of force. So each HEAT round carried an explosive charge that was hollowed out at the impact point. It exploded on contact, which was why the speed of delivery didn't really matter, and because of the shaping effect on explosive material drove a stream of molten metal, usually tungsten, in a highly directed way against the enemy armor. The liquid powered through the armor in a nanosecond and literally *sprayed* itself, at supersonic speeds, all over the interior of the tank.

Crane had seen the results back at the Iraqi entrenchments. HEAT rounds hit whatever was soft and organic inside the tank and *vaporized* it. All that was left was a kind of thick red paste, sticking to all the surfaces, drying and blackening in minutes, reeking of copper and couscous and shit. Tankers were calling that paste "raghead puree," which, for Crane, had pretty well summed up tankers and Iraqis and this goddam war all in one striking phrase. Boomer popped up through his hatch, lit from below, crew-cut, with that hard bony face. Crane had to laugh at him.

"*Christ,* Boomer, you look like a goddam *Nazi!*"

Boomer gave him a solemn look. "Heinz Guderian was the finest tanker that ever walked on this planet. It would have been an honor for Patton to hold his gloves."

Crane had heard this before. Boomer was a repository of tanker history. "I wasn't putting Heinz Guderian down, Boomer. I got a picture of him in my wallet, right next to my mom."

Boomer leaned down, yelled something to the driver, and the

huge iron mountain began to grind to port. There was a burst of dirty thunder from the exhaust and a cloud of smoke rolled up to envelop Crane. Boomer popped up again and threw Crane a crew helmet. Crane took his boonie hat off, tucked it into his BDUs, and slid down into the loader's hatch. It was like dropping into the control room of a submarine, a tight little compartment packed with electronics and glowing screens, ventilation ports, communications gear—even a download modem for the ballistics computer—what looked like, and turned out to be, a small microwave, a food locker, a water blivet and coffee maker, the delivery port of the tank magazine, and in the center of the small cabin, the breech of the main gun, polished steel and dark green paint, a huge construction of breech plate and hydraulics, the soul of this new machine. Crane fought off a sudden attack of claustrophobia and took it all in—he had seen it before but never in combat conditions—and then he smiled at the loader, the massive black soldier he had seen working on the filter. The man was way too big for tanks, but Crane wasn't going to tell him. He had the name Lymons on his BDU shirt. He smiled up at Crane and said something, tapping his helmet.

Crane, realizing, pulled the mike boom around.

"Welcome to Godzilla, Sergeant!"

"Thank you. I'll stay out of your way. You want me to get out of the hatchway, just point."

"If I need to get out that hatch, Sergeant, I'll carry you out with me." Lymons leaned forward and tapped the gunner on the shoulder. The man turned around and Crane saw a very young face, pale skinned and with large green eyes—the kid looked about fourteen. He put out a hand and Crane took it.

"Spec Three Meyer Rix, Sergeant Crane. Welcome aboard."

Crane resisted the temptation to ask Rix how old he was.

Boomer slapped Rix on the helmet. "Bigrig's the best goddam gunner in the universe. If he lives through this war, we're gonna buy him some pubic hair. Bigrig, this here's First Sergeant Dee Crane who has been to see the elephant and has graciously decided to come along as antiballistic material upgrade. In the event of incoming, he will throw himself in front of the ordnance and save your pert little butt so you can one day grow up and have actual body hair just like us real men.''

Boomer sat down in the command chair and punched in some numbers on his GPS screen, still talking. "You on the 'net there, Jimmy?"

Crane's headset crackled as the driver answered.

"Aye, aye, Captain."

"We have a visitor, Jimmy, say hello to Sergeant Crane of the Poor Bloody Infantry."

"Hello, Sergeant Crane."

"Jimmy."

Boomer slapped Bigrig's helmet again. Crane figured he did that a lot and wondered how long it would take Bigrig to turn around and hit him with a breech iron. Crane hated having his helmet slapped yet it was something almost everybody in the Army did.

The tank jumped forward and Crane was thrown back into the magazine port. The interior of the turret dimmed down and brightened up. Bigrig was flicking switches and buttons on the computer screen in front of him. Boomer got involved in cross talk with the section leader, Blue One.

Crane stood up and braced himself in the hatch, watching the tankers form up and move out. He hit the swivel release on the 7.62 and flipped open the breech to make sure the rounds were feeding. All around him there was the rising elemental roar of moving armor and he felt some of his lingering uneasiness start to flow away, vibrated out of him by the deep murmuring rumble of the tank engine.

All along the wadi the division was coming into line. The rain had stopped and there was a cold wind blowing fitfully from out of the east, carrying a scent of burning oil and wet wool. Boomer called for a right wheel and Godzilla pitched suddenly forward and down into the Wadi al Batin, churning up brush and stones, picking up speed. Three more M1s pulled alongside, keeping about twenty yards separation. Boomer's Blue Four accelerated up the far slope of the wadi and ground out onto the level. Crane could hear Boomer talking on the headset, short level-toned communications with the LT of armor in Blue One.

The LT would be in touch with the cavalry scouts as well as the squadron leader, but they'd keep it brief. Although the cross talk was encrypted, it was still noise, a telltale, something that could be triangulated. And too much radio chatter was dangerous and distracting. You could always tell a green unit because they were on the 'net all the time, chattering like finches on a wire.

In a few minutes, the tank section had pulled away from the main body of the column, and Godzilla had moved into a forward position, taking the point about fifty yards out and to the right of the delta-shaped unit of five tanks. Crane looked back behind him, saw a long sweep of dull iron shapes lumbering along behind them, looking like a tidal wave of yellow iron that filled the horizon. He checked his watch. A chill wind burned his cheeks and he tugged a scarf up, tucking the edge in under his goggles. It was 0400 hours, early in the morning of February twenty-fifth, a Monday. They'd been camped down by Wadi al Batin for the whole night, waiting for Franks to get the rest of the corps across the berms and into the first of their phase line commitments. Most of the officers had by now figured out that there had been some screw-ups, and everybody wanted to get out there, make up for the lost time, achieve their Task Force objectives.

They were the Big Red One, goddamnit. Where the hell *was* everybody? Why wasn't Franks taking them right into the fight? Where the hell were all these Iraqis?

———

They ran all day Monday and through Monday night, stopping now and then for refit and refuel, or for a head count, spread out in assault formation, running with their cavalry scouts out and their chopper cover—what they could get, anyway—up and out, depending on visual contact to keep their column together. The GPS sets started to screw up a lot, and the Internet was shutting down without warning, making the officers crazy. For the tankers, it was a tense and tiring push, everybody straining to get the first sight of the enemy. *Any* enemy. There were reports of brief con-

tacts, always followed by immediate surrender of any surviving
Iraqis, but for Crane and Boomer, virtually nothing. They got reports of firefights to the east, and they heard distant thunder from
out of Kuwait, where the Marines and the coalition forces were
supposed to be taking Kuwait City. There was fire and black smoke
just visible on the distant eastern horizon line. But out here, it was
like traveling on the moon. Desolation, rain, patches of grassland
and rocky defiles, and then they'd clear a low crest and what they
would see was more of the same wall-to-wall fuck-all. Tuesday the
twenty-sixth was more of the same.

By Tuesday evening, around 1930 hours, after sixty solid hours
of reconnaissance and maneuver in enemy territory, Crane was
bone weary, as if his body weight had increased a couple of hundred pounds. He leaned forward against the hatch rim and rested
his head against it. Somebody slapped the back of his helmet.

"Hey, Dee, want some coffee?"

Boomer was up in his hatch, holding out a canteen. He was
smoking a short cigar. Crane took the canteen, feeling the heat
through the plastic, even through the leather of his gloves.

"Boomer. You look like a bomb with the fuse lit."

Boomer grinned around his cigar and tugged one out for
Crane. They smoked awhile in silence, staring out at the terrain
they were grinding over, braced against the jolting motion, their
ears full of engine roar and wind rush. The cloud cover was ripping open and they could see a few pale stars gliding above them.
Crane sipped some coffee, hot, black, and thick, felt it burn down
into him. He was looking so hard into the far distance that his
eyes were watering. Off to their left, Blue Three was jouncing and
jolting over a rocky defile. To their rear, a TOW-equipped M901
was closing up in column, and an IFV with the Baker Company
guidon was running alongside it, troopers in the open hatch. Behind those vehicles, the main force was spreading out into a front
about a half mile wide. In the cold damp air the sound of the
oncoming division was immense, a grinding, churning sound like
continental drift, a sound you felt more than you heard.

"So where the fuck *is* everybody, Boomer?"

Boomer was silent for a moment, calculating.

"They gotta be out here. If they haven't scatted."

"Scatted *where?* We were told they were all over the place."

"Have some faith. They're here. You watch, we'll be into them in about an hour. If they have forward elements, gonna try an ambush, maybe sooner."

"You think they know we're coming?"

Boomer smiled around his cigar.

"They'll be deployed behind every rat-hole and djebel in the AO, hull-down, fields of fire—probably mines. Just like the NTC drills. Only difference, the OpFor *knew* we were coming, knew *when.* Bob's out there, in the dark, finger on the trigger, piss stains in his BDUs, he's been waiting for *days.* But they won't know we're around until their hulls start to melt. You just wait."

"They're supposed to be pretty hot."

"Fuck 'em. They got those Dolly Partons—up-armored Seventy-twos, if they're lucky, most of them'll have Sixty-twos with laser sights retrofitted. Seventy-twos got laser, gun is stabilized, but can't hit out beyond two thousand yards. Godzilla can kill at three thousand yards. We got Chobham armor, they got plate. We can fire on the fly, Bob has to slow down, or *stop,* just to get a round off. Toast, my brother. Raghead puree. Godzilla ain't no Ronson."

Crane had to shout to be heard above the wind rush and the snarl of the engine, the clatter of the treads on stone.

"Ronson?"

"What my daddy called his Sherman. Those Panzer Mark Fours, they used to put an eighty-eight-millimeter shot into the rear drive sprocket. Right next to the engine? Thin plate, plus the engine was gasoline, so *poof!* Thirty-one tons of Sherman in flames. Called them Ronsons because they lit up so easy."

"Where was this?"

Boomer looked at him, offended and disappointed.

"I'm disgusted. And you a lifer, oughtta know better."

Crane shook his head, held up a hand. It was coming.

"Come on, Dee . . . what's the date?"

"February twenty-six . . . oh, shit!"

"Forgot, huh?"

And then it hit Crane. All through the advance, something had been nagging him, a sense of wrongness, of something massive waiting to happen to them. They were all stretched out in the desert, firing along in echelon through a raghead wadi—he got a quick flash of that yuppie doctor leaning on the bar at Harry's, talking through his beard—

"February nineteenth, 1943," said Boomer, his scarf flying in the wind, his face raw. "My daddy was there. First Armor."

"Yeah," said Crane. "So were we."

They both fell into long silence. Crane was stunned. How the hell could he have missed it? All this last week, he had felt . . . something.

The 16th Infantry. And Panzers, out of the dark, in the desert, in the mist and rain, coming out of nowhere and the men dying.

At Kasserine.

Crane wiped his goggles off with a piece of his scarf and set his Fritz back on tight.

Well, one good thing.

Now he knew what the hell he was worried about.

For some strange reason, that made him feel a little better. He felt a slow kind of calm slipping down from his shoulders and easing up the tension in his belly.

Ten miles up the wadi, they found the Hoo-Yah.

CHAPTER SIXTEEN

COMBAT

FEBRUARY 26

The wind had come around and was now blowing out of the east, out of the burning oil flats of Kuwait, and their eyes began to sting. Boomer took to wiping his goggles again and again, or ducking down into the turret for prolonged periods. There was some room for Crane behind the loader's station, but it was cramped and the uneven jolting motion made him sick. Inside the turret chamber, Lymons and Bigrig and Jimmy—unseen, but a presence on the crew 'net—were intensely involved with the thermal-imager screen in front of Bigrig.

Beside the imager screen was the gas-plasma screen of Godzilla's ballistic computer, which was constantly updating wind speed and fire-vector coordinates, as well as the duplicate GPS display, the same one that Jimmy, the driver, had up front.

Boomer's headset was patched into Blue One and the tank platoon commander, who was in his turn connected with a forward fire observer—probably in one of the cavalry IFVs way out in front—and with the choppers of the 4th Battalion, 1st Aviation, who were flying air cover missions.

The choppers were having refueling problems, largely because of the unexpected speed of the breakthrough, so chopper cover was not up to operational standards. Putting it more plainly, there wasn't any they could count on.

That left the armored column pretty dependent on the scouts. Thinking about the cavalry way out there on point made Crane feel a little better, but it also brought home the idea that they were definitely in Indian country. Sometimes he found himself *looking* so hard that his eyes burned, and the oil reek wasn't helping. Still, it was better than being reduced to supercargo below-decks, so Crane wrapped a kerchief around his face and stayed up in the hatch.

Overhead the clouds were scattering but the stars were dim and wavering, as if seen through muddy water. All around the tankers the desert stretched away into a wide flatland of salt marshes and gravel fields and random rutted wadis bermed with flood-driven stones and scrub pines. The back of Crane's throat was beginning to burn and he felt as if he had smoked too many cigarettes. Coughing didn't help. As they went east it got worse and worse.

"That's the wells," said Boomer, topside again. "Can you imagine what it must be like for the Marines? They're right down there in the heart of it. They're all gonna have cancer when they get back."

Crane coughed again and watched Blue Three as it ground its way through a thicket of wait-a-bit thorn.

"What the hell was in their minds?" said Boomer, more or less into the chilly night air, but Crane knew what he was thinking about.

"Oil has done more to fuck up this part of the world than religion. Seventy years ago, these people were tribesmen, lived out in the desert with goats and horses and camels. You see that big expanse back there, when we were on the line at Hafar?"

"What, all that wall-to-wall fuck-all? Yeah, I drove Godzilla over some of it and flew over the rest."

"That was the Nafud. You remember Lawrence of Arabia?"

"Yeah. Made me thirsty."

"Remember when he talks Anthony Quinn into taking his whole damn tribe across the desert, so they can take that port?"

"Aqaba. Yeah, I remember."

"That desert, it was the Nafud. That's where we were, just a while ago. Here we are, back fighting in the same damn territory they all fought over, eighty years ago. Only now, we're back because of oil."

"I can do better than that. You know where we're going? Where Basra is? It's on the Euphrates, right. And beyond the Euphrates, that's the Tigris. You religious, Dee?"

"I believe He's out there. I don't believe He's watching CNN."

"In Bible class, they used to tell us that the original Garden of Eden was right there in between the Tigris and the Euphrates. In Mesopotamia—that means 'between the rivers.' Waddya think of that?"

"Makes my point. Once it was the Garden of Eden, now it's a war zone. Or a prison, if you look at it that way. And all because of oil."

Boomer grinned at him, his cheeks blackened by oil smoke and his teeth very white. "You don't think we're here for God and Country? DerHorst was saying you been giving all the grunts a pep talk, how we're here because we're soldiers, and some war's gotta be fought. God and Country."

"No. I said we're here because we're eleven bravo—at least, I am—and that's what we do. We fight."

"Right or wrong?"

"You tell me what's right or wrong, Boomer. They say we were wrong to fight in Vietnam, and what happens as soon as the VC get control? They start killing everyone and set up a communist state and now it's twenty-five years later and their economy's in the dumper and *boom*, they want to be capitalists and get aid from the U.S. Here, we got the Kuwaitis, a country full of fat-assed sheiks and spoiled playboy greaseballs who never spend more than three weeks in-country if they can help it, but they have oil and if Hussein gets the oil, then who knows what he's gonna do with it? So no, we're not going in to free Kuwait, because Kuwait isn't free and never has been, but we don't want Iraq to get the oil and then come in and take Saudi, so there you go. And who's gonna fix it?''

"Godzilla will.''

"Yeah, so my point is—''

Boomer held up a gloved hand. "I get your point. I'm here, ain't I? But don't it ever get you pissed? You know, Bush backing Hussein and then all of a sudden, Hussein's a bad guy and we gotta go in, slap his wrists? How come they didn't see that coming? Save us all a world of shit.''

"Shit, it's *Washington,* for chrissake. You ever wonder why Reagan was supposed to be such a strong president, a *military* president, and the only war he ever saw was two Italian hairdressers fighting over a bottle of henna rinse? And Bush, supposed to be fighting the 'wimp factor,' the guy was a goddam combat pilot, flew thirty-some-odd missions, actually got shot at, got blown out of the sky, went back to do it again, but *he's* the wimp? You looking for good ideas out of Washington, you need to take a nap. Anyway, like Robin Williams said, reality is just a group hunch.''

"Yeah . . . still, I can't see why the ragheads blew off all those wells, and dumped all that oil into the Gulf. Who's that gonna hurt? How's that help their goddam jihad?''

"Waddya think a war is? A war is . . . gimme a minute . . . a sustained exercise in state-sanctioned crime—I forget who said that—and once you start one, you can expect it to go nowhere but nasty. People are basically nasty and if you leave them at war long enough, they'll do some stuff, it'd break a hyena's heart.''

"Even us?''

Crane was silent for a long time, looking out over the desert, listening to the sound of the tanks and the IFVs all around them, breathing in the gathering reek of oil and the cold wet wind off the salt marshes, thinking about pencils.

"Yeah, Boomer. Even us.''

———

The strange calm dragged on, hour after hour and mile after mile with no significant contact. Crane was chafing at their rate of progress. They had an objective—Collins—that was still miles ahead of them. There were rumors that the 24th Mech west of them was sixty miles in and red-lining all the way, over uglier terrain than this salt marsh and desert scrubland. The rumor was that Jack the Bear was even more pissed at General Franks, and was telling him to get VII Corps out there and *engage*. But Franks was a careful man and he was on the ground here, not Schwarzkopf. But it was getting to all of them now, not just Crane, and everyone was hungry for some contact.

They got it.

They had come some miles east through a rising slope of loose stone and salt flat and the clouds were thickening overhead. The rain was as steady and monotonous as a confession. C-65 was powering up a kind of broken wadi on their left, grunting and chuffing like an iron bull in a pen, when Crane heard a sharp *click* from away to the left and he was just turning, traversing with the 7.62, when Boomer started to shout and a squad of infantry in a Bradley opened up, tracers almost a stream of liquid fire, rounds snapping and jolting off crazily as they hit the rocks at the top of the wadi they were crossing.

"What the *fuck?*" said Crane, thumbing the triggers, the machine gun rocking in its swivel, a burst of white fire blinding him as he stared out into the darkness, and at that point a blue streak skimmed across their bow and struck Blue Three on the forward slope of the hull, just below the driver's hatch. It *bounced* and flew off spinning, a white-hot match-head into the dark, and the Commo 'net was full of chattering voices.

"Red right—"

"Are you damaged?"

"Contact contact bearing zero-five-three—"

"Deploy, goddamnit!"

"Negative, Blue One, we're operational."

"Six Actual, this is Kilo Four Scouts, we have contact at—"

"Kilo Four, what's your twenty?"

"Say again, Six—"

"Who's got forward fire? Get us a Kiowa!"

Boomer's voice was on the crew 'net saying, "Jimmy, go right—

Bigrig, you got it,'' and then the whole turret was whining and moving right, coming in on the top of the little rocky defile. Crane, riding with it, felt the tank settle and the right treads digging in and then his whole landscape lit up and his ears were slammed with concussion as Godzilla fired a 120-mm HEAT shell up the arroyo. The arroyo erupted, disappeared inside a white flower of molten metal.

"Secondary," said Crane, his heart hammering in his chest. More little explosions popped and blossomed as whatever they had hit started to burn and the ammunition cooked off.

The Bradley on their right churned up toward the burning, Baker Company troopers in the hatch firing their M16s and working the chain gun. Crane saw something small flickering at the edge of his vision.

Iraqi soldiers—it had to be—had somehow gotten in behind the forward tanks and were now running between the rocks on their flanks. Suddenly Crane heard rounds thumping against the Chobham plate—they went skittering and zipping off—and Crane opened up on the gray flitting shapes, seeing the ground in front of him lit up by the muzzle flash, seeing his tracers streaming outward in a kind of wavering, pulsing chain.

Godzilla was slowing and the turret moved again—that solid hydraulic whine—and the main gun was traversing. Crane braced himself again as down in the turret Bigrig stared into his thermal imager, seeing moving ghostlike green glowing shapes surrounded by a kind of grainy green mist.

Boomer popped up through his hatch again, reaching for the .50-caliber as Bigrig fired at something only he could see about a thousand yards out in the night.

The shot went flat and impossibly fast—it hit in the space between one heartbeat and the next—*blam*—and something huge and iron rose up out of the desert floor, rolled, and started to glow. Secondary explosions blipped and popped off as the Iraqi BMP's ammunition cooked off. And another three in rapid succession, as the Saggers in the magazine blew up.

Blue Three and Blue Four were spinning outward, getting a field of fire, and Boomer was yelling something into his mike and then he looked up at something past Crane and pointed urgently. Crane heard his voice inside his helmet: "Sagger—Bigrig, what the fuck's with your infrared?"

Crane turned as Boomer was shouting, heard Bigrig cursing him back, and saw another Iraqi BMP—a kind of Infantry Fighting Vehicle equipped with a .73 smoothbore and a Sagger antitank missile launcher, the BMP was scooting into their flanks and was about five hundred yards out.

In the turret, Bigrig was getting his sight picture and punching the round selector button—HEAT—and getting the laser range finder onto the target. Godzilla's ballistic computer was calculating the distance, the barrel cant, the barrel wear and the heat factor, even the wind speed, from a sensor behind Crane. Boomer told Bigrig to traverse and the turret came about again—it was like riding a bull and made Crane a little dizzy. Godzilla had made all her calculations in a fleeting second.

Lymons, snakelike and very fluid, his moves practiced and precise, snatched up the huge HEAT round as it came up from the magazine, cleared the polished steel breech, set and capped and homed the round, slammed the breech iron, and slapped Bigrig on the right shoulder.

Bigrig got the green light from Godzilla's computer and fired. The sound shook Crane and the muzzle flash lit up all the ground in front of them as Godzilla lurched with the recoil. The BMP took a round low in the forward glacis.

The shot went right through the BMP lengthwise and came out the stern. The BMP staggered, lurched, came to a stop, and the hatch popped open. Little figures appeared in the hatch, silhouetted by flames. Crane and Boomer put out machine-gun fire and the figures disappeared back into the BMP. A second later, the BMP burst into full fire and white phosphor sparks, then it settled into the ground, blackening, its paint blistering and peeling backward away from the hole in its armor.

Down to his left, Crane saw three Iraqis running, one of them carrying an RPG-7, a weapon Crane hated down on a cellular level, a nightmare from his time in the Triangle, that tube with the cone-shaped missile in the muzzle. He was bringing his weapon to bear when a burst of automatic fire from a Bradley cut them down. The RPG clattered away over the rocks. Crane sent a ribbon of fire into the area and saw two other small gray-black shapes stumble and go down.

More shouts and curses, now from the right. He looked over at Blue Three and saw men climbing on the hull and he thought for a moment that Blue Three had been hit and the men were getting out.

Then he realized the men on that hull were Iraqis, and one of the Iraqis was trying to attach some sort of shaped charge to the turret hatch, which was buttoned up tight.

Boomer saw it as well and he was in Crane's way, and he didn't want to use the .50. Crane leaned forward to clear his line of fire— Boomer's eyes were getting huge as he saw Crane moving—and Crane had his Beretta out. He pulled the slide back, thumbed off the safety as Boomer was shouting into his headset, saying something to Blue Three, and Blue Three was answering.

Crane steadied himself on the hatch plate and aimed at the Iraqi with the satchel. It was about a fifty-yard shot. He squeezed the trigger and the man jerked, fell back. Crane fired nine more times and there were no more Iraqis on top of Blue Three.

"Jesus," said Boomer.

"Fanatics," said Crane, digging into his jacket for another magazine. "You can always get them to do something stupid."

At that moment, they heard a scrabbling noise behind them and Crane turned around to see an Iraqi, dirty and bearded, his eyes wide and white in a twisted face full of rage and fear. He had a satchel charge and was bringing it up in a sideways throw. Crane stuck the muzzle in the man's chest—the man's eyes were full of red light from the turret glow—and Crane felt the weight of the man's body as he connected with the barrel. The man screamed something at him and Crane could smell his breath. Crane squeezed the Beretta twice, the slide hammering, and two dull thuds sounded deep in the man's chest as something blew out the back of his filthy jacket. He fell away tumbling and was crushed down by a Bradley about ten feet off their stern.

And it was over.

CHAPTER SEVENTEEN

73 EASTING

Slightly stunned, the infantry scrambled out of their IFVs and did a foot recon all around the area. They found signs of a long-term camp, and dead bodies, and a couple of empty APCs, but no living soldiers in the wadi. The uphill slope was littered with burning machinery. Dead Iraqis were scattered around, looking like piles of rags in the dusty starlight. If there were others, they had broken and were gone. They buttoned up again and hit the slow road, on and on into the big gray wasteland, and all the way they hit not one damn thing. If this was AirLand War, as far as Crane was concerned, they could mail it in and wake him when it was over.

Later that day, as a bleak desert rain drifted across the horizon and the light turned from pale gray to deep dun yellow and black, Wolochek got on the 'net from his Company IFV to get an update.

He told Huckaby to take 1st Squad of 3rd Platoon in the IFV and do a sweep, see if there were Iraqis around, but not to get sucked into anything ugly. Advance to Contact, then pull back and call it in.

They settled back into a slow advance in skirmish and went forward, grinding up the slope. In their rear they could see other units mopping up the remainders, blue lights flashing like cop cars at an accident, and the radio cross talk died away after a few sit-rep checks. The silence came back in around them, just the steady growling and clanking of the tanks and the TOWs and the IFVs, spreading out in Traveling Overwatch and Combat Column now that the terrain was opening up. Everyone was getting jumpy now. Where the hell was Bob and all his goddam gear?

Boomer popped up again like a prairie dog, looking a little worried. He leaned over toward Crane.

"That contact back there? *That* wasn't operational. That was FUBAR! How'd they get inside us?"

"It's a big country. I'd say they were there a long while, up the wadi, had everything shut down so there'd be no thermal, had all the bodies *inside* their Erks and Bumpers, so we'd get no heat signature. Scouts would have passed them by in the dark. A regular VC ambush—let the point man go by, take out the patrol in enfilade."

"Shit, Dee . . . where the hell is Bob?"

At that point, three Kiowas and an Apache gunship went through their airspace at speed, a thousand feet up.

"Something's up," said Boomer.

At that point, they got the commander's call sign on the MSE Internet. About fifty miles up the line, Eagle Troop of the 2nd Armored Cavalry had encountered elements of what looked like the Tawakalna Republican Guards at phase line 73 Easting. They had fought hard, sustained losses, but they had marked out and defined the target. Now they were waiting for backup and Franks had changed his plans for the Big Red. They were now going to power forward forty miles and pass through the 2nd Armored to engage the Tawakalna. Pass through their own units engaged in a firefight. And engage a massive Iraqi armored division. Listening to LC Pat Ritter's laconic voice on the radio as he described what had to be one of the most dangerous military maneuvers in the book, neither Crane nor Boomer could think of one damned thing to say.

So they just did it.

It was a minute before midnight, the twenty-seventh of February. The rain was ceaseless and chilling, and everybody was soaked through to their boots. The inside of the M1s were hot and wet as the rain dripped through the leaky turret seals. They had cleared the last of the nearly invisible units of the 2nd Cavalry, marked off with glowing chemical wandlights, talked through the rear-echelons by the Ops Officer of the 3rd Squadron. Now there was nothing ahead of them but the Iraqis. The radio 'net talk was terse, staccato, full of tension.

"Blue One, roger. Say again, Kilo Team?"

"Kilo Team Leader, this is it. This is it. It's the Guards. Tanks. Arty. BMPs and Erks and APCs. Multiple infantry on foot. Multiple infrared contacts through ninety degrees. T Seventy-Twos, Sixty-Twos, lots and lots of APCs and BMPs. Estimate OpFor at division-strength. Bearing zero six five range five thousand six hundred repeat multiple contacts. Can you support?"

Support? Crane had to laugh. If Franks didn't support, he'd be back in Frankfurt cleaning latrines with his mustache. Jack would see to it personally.

"Kilo Leader, this is Blue One, we will support. Kilo Leader, patch yourself through to ComCon One, tell the man! We will engage immediate upon ComCon One okay. Do *not* engage yourself. Pull back and wait for support. Do not paint them again. Do not switch on ranging radar. Go to Tac Two on your MSE. Blue Team, you copy that?" Crane could hear the other tank platoons acknowledging the orders.

As they were reacting, the MSE Internet web was blistering all the way up to Rhame's mobile HQ. Rhame had been expecting this and now the time had come to take the Republican Guard to pieces. The assault tactics were doctrine, practiced time and time again in the hills and fields around Fort Riley, and in any number of sand-table run-throughs in the KTO. Everyone knew what to do.

Soon both battalions of the 34th Armor were deploying for an armored assault, almost ninety M1 tanks, along with the cavalry platoon M3 Bradleys, twelve self-propelled mortars, and elements of tanker support units. And in support of the armor, the two battalions of the 16th Infantry, each with four companies of infantry in Bradleys, a headquarters company with M2 IFVs, and anti-armor companies with M901 TOW vehicles and M113 Command-tracked vehicles. And in the air, deployed for support, two battalions of the 1st Aviation, close to eighty choppers, a mix of Kiowas and Cobras and Apache gunships. To a lizard sitting under a rock and watching, they must have looked like the worst shamal of the season.

Boomer was already dropping down the hatch. Crane heard his answer on the crew 'net, Boomer's voice low and steady. "Roger, Blue One, we copy."

The other tankers in the platoon responded and Crane felt Godzilla lurch to the left and accelerate, a blast of smoke and heat coming out of her exhaust vents. The engine noise was deafening up in the hatch and Crane dropped into the turret compartment, bracing himself in a fold-away seat behind Lymons. Lymons grinned at Crane.

"Sergeant Crane. I hear you did good up there."

Bigrig twisted to give him the thumbs-up sign, smiling, flushed with the afterburn of a firefight. Crane smiled briefly and buckled in.

The entire column was now spreading out in an assault formation as the forward elements, the cavalry scouts and the Kiowas, were sending back GPS and fire data directly to Blue One's ballistic computers. Forward fire control numbers started to appear on Boomer's Internet screen.

Crane watched Boomer listening to information on a combat tactical channel, punching numbers into his GPS as Jimmy brought Godzilla up to speed. Forty . . . forty-three . . . forty-nine . . .

Fifty miles an hour.

Inside the tank it was an altogether different experience for Crane. He had nothing to do but brace himself against the bounce and plunge of their headlong advance and watch the numbers change on Bigrig's plasma screen. The muted roar of the fifteen-hundred-horsepower turbine was changing into a deep whistling howl. Christ, thought Crane, what would it be like to sit in a stone-bermed emplacement downrange and watch something like this iron mountain come at you? Godzilla. Boomer had named the tank very well.

Intelligence reports on the combat readiness of the Tawakalna and 12th Tank divisions indicated that they were virtually untouched by coalition air power. Hussein had committed his Guard units in the original assault into Kuwait, and then withdrawn them, replacing them with inferior line units. He wanted to use the Guards as a threat force against his own forward units. If his forward units knew that a retreat would only bring them under the guns—and the fundamentalist fury—of the Guards, they might fight harder against the infidel hordes. Well, that was the plan, anyway.

Crane had a handbook listing the probable size and firepower of the Tawakalna. He tugged it out of his flak jacket and held it up to the red glow of a maplight behind the Lymons position.

Jesus. This was going to be interesting as hell.

The Guards were Hussein's SS, supposed to be the very best, the most fanatical, the least "attritted" by the air war. There was no reason to believe that this collision would be anything like the breakthrough back at the jump-off point, hammering into a broken brigade of half-starved and thoroughly cowed Iraqi conscripts.

Everybody in the Republican Guards division was a made man, part of Hussein's Takriti Mafia, and every one of them knew that if Hussein went down, they'd go with him. They had every reason to fight hard and, according to Crane's handbook, a hell of a lot to fight *with*.

The Tawakalna had two maneuver brigades left, and each brigade had two battalions of armor, sixty tanks to a battalion, for a probable total of one hundred and twenty tanks, plus mechanized infantry and mobile artillery. The 12th Tank Division had perhaps another sixty tanks operational, with support from their own mortars, and infantry fighting from APCs with machine guns. The ground forces in front of them were supposed to have air support from a battalion of Hind gunship choppers—Crane would believe that when he saw it, since most of the Iraqi choppers had either been vaporized by Apaches or had simply "bugged out" at top speed. The guys in 1st Aviation had taken to calling the Hind battalions Bob's Bug-out Brigade.

Well, no matter how you cut it, the 1st Infantry Division was about to collide with at least one hundred and eighty T-72 tanks backed up by mobile arty and mechanized infantry—probably over three thousand enemy soldiers. Crane looked around the turret chamber, at the flickering yellow numbers on the plasma screens and the red glow of the interior lights, at Lymons's glossy black skin, and at Bigrig's skinny shoulders hunched over the thermal imager, and then at Boomer Riebold. Boomer was looking into his own imager and as Crane watched him, he began to smile, a slow revealing of blood-red teeth in the cabin glow. He looked up and saw Crane watching him.

"Dee, this you gotta see. Come here—Bigrig, you getting this?"

"Roger that, Boomer."

Crane leaned over Boomer's shoulder. On the IR screen they could see a field of targets, green and pulsing slightly. Crane could see the outline of tanks and smaller indistinct shapes that looked like personnel carriers. And around the carriers, even smaller man-shaped blobs formed into larger clusters, broke apart, rejoined like green Jell-O. Boomer was humming like a small electrical engine.

"Why haven't they fired?"

Boomer looked at the laser range indicator.

"Bob's out there about three thousand yards. I don't think he can see us. All he's got are optical sights. There's hardly any light and the oil fumes are making it even worse. Bigrig, can you get that tank ranged?"

"Roger that."

The turret swiveled and the hydraulics whined as Bigrig got the main gun sights onto the distant tank. The laser range finder flickered through some numbers. So far, it looked like Blue Four was the first tank in the platoon to make contact.

"Blue Four to Blue One. I have a tank at three thousand two hundred yards bearing zero-six-five. Can I engage?"

"Blue Four, this is Blue One. Wait one. We're gonna hit them all at once. Boomer, *everybody* has targets. Break."

"Roger, Blue One."

Boomer took his mike away from his mouth.

"That I don't get. Bob knows we're here. He just got lit up by First Aviation. Why give him a chance to get set?"

"He's *already* set, Boomer. There's nothing he can do to change the game now. That's positional warfare—OpFor did it all the time. I'd say he's still betting on his ambush dispositions. Anyway, he can't actually *see* anything. He may be dumb enough to figure he was dinged by scouts, figure the rest of the ground forces are a long way away. Whatever, he's got no choice but to sit still and hope he has a strong enough position to carve us up forward and break us into a running fight, expose our flanks to Saggers and RPGs. There'll be infantry all over, in every rathole. Let me talk to Wolochek, will ya?"

Boomer handed him a link mike from the wall set.

"Baker Six Actual, this is Crane in Blue One."

"Blue One, this is Six."

"Six, we go in, there'll be antitank all around, infantry in the woodwork to the flanks. Do you want me to come back, link up with the platoon leaders?"

"Six to Blue One, negative on that. Stay up with Blue Leader, we'll deploy left and do an Overwatch. Keep us up to date if you see anything we need to watch for. Out."

"Roger, Six Actual, Blue One out."

Boomer smiled. "Glad to have you staying. What'll happen, we'll get into position, move up inside three thousand yards. What we do, we usually assign targets to everybody in the platoon, see that—"

"Boomer, I was at the NTC. Gimme a break."

Boomer grinned at him. "Sorry. With you sitting there doing squat, I forgot you were eleven bravo. I figured you were Just Another—"

"Fucking Observer, yeah. Want me to go up, get on the seven-six-two?"

"It's gonna be hot up there. If you want, okay. But don't blame me, you get your head taken off. There's gonna be a shit storm of steel flying around out there in about thirty seconds."

"I stay here, all I'm gonna do is puke down Lymons's back. Gimme your NVGs."

"So go. Watch your head."

Boomer handed Crane a set of night-vision goggles and Crane pulled the strap over his helmet. Boomer leaned back over the screen and pulled the helmet mike around. Crane slapped him on the shoulder and crawled over to the loader's hatch, pushing it up and out.

It was a relief to get his head out into the night air. There were tanks and IFVs everywhere around him, right and left and in the rear, perhaps a hundred different vehicles within a five-hundred-yard front line. He fiddled with the setting on the NVGs until he got a fairly clear image of the machinery around him, a vast green plain filled with softly luminous shapes and plumes wavering in the chilly wind.

In the next few seconds, the advance elements would have established target assignments and agreed on fields of fire. Everybody had a priority target and a series of secondaries. The idea was to open up all at once, destroy as much of the enemy's Command and Control units as possible, and then blow the shit out of everything else. Up ahead the Iraqi forces were deployed in an ambush formation, in positions that should have concealed them from ordinary night eyes, hull-down behind hasty berms of sand, camouflaged with brush and canvas rigging, backed up into wadis and riverbanks and rocky defiles. They also had their ears on, but so far no Iraqi units had been able to intercept, let alone decipher, the fast-burst encrypted information that was flying around them on tactical 'nets.

The terrain was rough and broken ground, a tilted irregular plain almost ten miles wide by twenty miles deep, pocked with sinkholes and little ravines, low sand hills and rocky crests. Bob had dug himself in all over the place, in every location that provided the least bit of fire protection.

The trouble was, it was a cold night, there was fog and mist and oil smoke everywhere, and Bob was stone blind. Worse than that, Bob was warm.

Warm enough to show up on hundreds of thermal imagers, and those thermal imagers were attached to tanks or TOWs or Apache gunships that could kill from a very long way away, much farther than anything Bob could throw. If the first volley was telling enough, they might be so rattled that the whole division would break and scatter, and once they lost unit cohesion, they were dead.

Godzilla had been purring up a little grade and was now hull-down, the main gun clearing the rise but the bulk of her body hidden by the slope. On the helmet 'net, Crane listened to Boomer's low and slightly lazy voice, and the Internet cross talk, short, sharp bursts of information, laconic and flat, as the company commanders worked out their dispositions and made their final target assignments. Now they were just waiting for the word to come down from Rhame. They got it about a minute later.

A half second later, they blew the night to pieces.

CHAPTER EIGHTEEN

NORFOLK

Along a mile-wide front, passing through the forward units of the 2nd Armored Cavalry, the 34th Armor, along with elements of Lieutenant Colonel Baker's 16th Infantry—all in all, a universe of iron—opened up in a shattering rippling volley of tank and TOW fire, an outburst of fire and thunder that could be seen from twenty miles away, could be seen through the cloud cover like flashes of sheet lightning.

Later, some of the Air Force guys who had been manning a radar screen on one of the J-STARS told one of the brigade officers that they all saw the whole AO light up, watched the clouds flickering and glowing from the cockpit of the J-STAR, an eruption of light that rippled and rolled and flickered across miles of thin ragged clouds, as if the land underneath it had broken open and begun to burn.

Down in the middle of it, Crane was literally stunned by the *size* of that first bombardment, and he believed at that moment that he knew what it must have been like at Verdun or the Somme or Dresden. The cracking and booming of main guns underlay the hissing shriek of TOWs and Hellfires and the ribbons of fire from the chain guns. The darkness was literally made day, the cold wet air began to burn, the world became one solid rolling explosion of fire and thunder, an insanity of molten iron and white-hot incoming rounds.

Underneath the first volley, the forward units of the Iraqi tank lines dissolved into a landscape of burning machinery. Hundreds of men died in the time between one breath and another, never knowing what had killed them, seeing the steel around them glow white hot, feeling their eyes boil away, or blown into vapor and smeared across the walls of their APCs and BMPs, or pounded into ruined meat by concussion.

On the Internet, the Military Intelligence monitors heard brief cries and half-issued commands, curses, and shouted warnings—all cut off as the barrage came down on them and the shot lanced in, the TOWs and the missiles. Units of the Guard that were hull-down and forward were literally erased from the terrain. What had been an army minutes before was now a disintegrating melee of burning iron and cooking men.

Firing at will now, the armor accelerated, main guns traversing and settling—*blam*—and the area around the tank would light up white and red, the earth would rock and dust swirl upward from the shock, and the tanks would roll forward out of their own shock wave, looking for new kills, firing as they came.

Pounded, deafened, Crane hunched into the turret as his face and shoulders caught the backblast from Godzilla's main gun along with the guns of Blue Three and Blue Two beside them, and all the guns down the line.

The green landscape in his NVGs blossomed into a solid sheet of fire. Crane ducked his head to save the circuits and stowed them under his hatch plate. Ears ringing, nose running blood, he held on to the hatch-rim grips as Godzilla roared across a little wash and bounced up a gravel slope. His world was strangely muted, as if there was a wall of thick glass around him, a bell jar of soft sounds and rapid muffled drumming as thousands—millions—of red streaks and blue-white tracers and high-arching howitzer rounds slammed out of the line and flew into the Iraqi positions.

It was like nothing he had ever seen before. Nothing in his whole lifer career had ever come close, not in Vietnam, not in his dreams or visions or nightmares. It was something biblical, like the cracking open of the world, and as he watched it, the lights flickering across his face in a liquid dance of red and green and blue and white and orange, he experienced a wild soaring upsurge, a burst of nameless joy and wonder, for he was alive and here and not yet killed, alive inside the red thundering heart of war.

Dimly, as if through water, he heard Boomer shout, and then Godzilla—over the slope—was plunging downward, traversing, looking for her secondary targets, the long barrel settled, a momentary stillness, and then another shattering explosion and a flat streak of fire as the red-hot round lanced into a target.

Now the entire front was a latticework of crossed tracer fire, eruptions of fire and earth, and in the distance he could see huge Iraqi T-72s laying down smoke grenades and throwing up wakes of dust and gravel as they cut left and right, treads churning, main guns firing wildly, trying to get out from under the rounds and dodge the Apaches and Cobras arcing and swooping over them.

Bright green fountains of tracer fire wavered and shimmered through the darkness as Iraqi turret machine-gunners tried to catch a chopper in the fire. The entire night skyline was a trembling, scintillating web of interlacing tracer fire, green and red and blue-white, with here and there the heavier cables of TOW rockets as they sliced into the Iraqi units. Iraqi APCs were rushing back out of the killing zone, soldiers clinging to the hulls and running alongside them—and in a few seconds, they were *inside* the Iraqi positions and there were targets *everywhere.*

Godzilla had forty rounds—make that thirty now—a combination of HEAT and sabot, and in five minutes Boomer and Bigrig had fired off ten rounds and made nine confirmed kills. Lymons was keeping a count and he made it six T-72s, all in the first three minutes, a T-62, and two BMPs.

The one unconfirmed was being shared with Blue Two, whose round had come in at the same second, totally obliterating what had looked to Bigrig's infrared to be a BTR-60 armored personnel carrier covered with a mound of fleeing soldiers. It had gone up in a yellow gout of fire, little black mannequin figures twisting and breaking up in silhouette in the flames, and secondary lancets of green tracer as the ammunition and small-arms magazines popped off.

It was at that point that Crane began to feel a kind of sickness, and his fleeting exhilaration dissipated. So far, the Iraqis hadn't managed *one* aimed shot.

All they were doing was spraying out fire and shot in a panicked attempt to back up out of the battle and get away alive. He could see their cohesion coming apart, see their fields of fire dissolve into a disorganized output of erratic tracers and random grenades. Even the T-72s were missing every shot, *if* they even made the attempt.

They had seen what happened to the braver tankers right at the start. Because the T-72 had to slow down almost to a crawl to acquire a good target and make the shot, they were obliterated by the faster and more accurate fire coming from M1s, agile gun platforms that could fire on the fly at thirty miles an hour going sideways down a ditch. It was simply no contest and although Crane felt no sympathy at all for the men dying in all that molten armor, it was still an ugly thing to see.

Once they had closed in with the Iraqi forces, Boomer had come up top to man the .50-caliber, because now one of the main threats to Godzilla would come, theoretically at least, from flanking foot soldiers or light antitank vehicles.

As Godzilla ground forward through a dense thicket of pine bush and bramble, Bigrig fired again, blowing most of the brush away and setting the rest on fire. Flames swirled up around the hull and blistered the paintwork around the steel plates covering the treads. Boomer looked disgusted but said nothing, staying with the .50 as the turret swayed and jolted and they headed back downgrade and out onto another broad stretch of open desert. In the distance, they could see Iraqi tanks in a full-out retreat. They were also dispersing, fanning out into the terrain, the entire armored division breaking up into random panicked units. And any tank in range, any armored vehicle, was immediately fired on by at least two or three M1s. The competition for kills was becoming intense, and underneath that was the slowly developing rage that comes over soldiers who see their enemy in full flight.

It was a kind of sadism, perhaps a response to the prebattle fear, but Crane could feel it growing even in these relatively innocent troopers. Now the Iraqis were deeply into the shit. Unless they managed to lose the pursuit, they'd be hunted down one by one and crushed without quarter.

Hardcore.

War is a nasty thing. People who start them are hardly ever the people who end them, and the people who end them are never what they were at the beginning. No one gets out without being touched by fire, and that fire changes everything, changes it forever.

Later they called it the Battle of Norfolk, although Crane remembered it chiefly for the long straggling lines of beaten Iraqis that they raced by in their pursuit of the fleeing Republican Guard tanks. They had no time to take prisoners, and no place to take them, and no intention at all of letting a string of sorry-assed ragheads foul up what was beginning to look like an all-out barnburning massacre. Leave them to the MPs coming up behind.

They just waved at the Iraqis—many of whom were waving those surrender passes—and barreled on through into the eastern reaches of Kuwait, through to Highway 1 out of Kuwait City, across the Tigris and the Euphrates, gaining speed and bloodlust with every mile and every blown-up and butchered Iraqi vehicle.

The breakthrough became a rout in about one hour, and in a little while the entire advance was strung out in a high-speed charge, tanks and IFVs and APCs and every vehicle that could keep up, a thundering herd, racing east over the desert, deep into Iraqi-held territory, with the bitter wind in their faces, and the clouds of smoke rolling like black ink in bad water . . . T-72s went up in white showers of steel, their crews shot to bits as they scrambled out. T-62s pounded the same way, and BMPs and Erks and APCs loaded with frightened soldiers. Godzilla blew her last round on a BTR-60 and had to fall back to refuel and reload, but Boomer rode her hard and within an hour they were back up with the pack, part of a wave of American iron that rolled across southeastern Iraq that night, killing and burning as they went, an all-out armored runaway charge that went on through the night and into the early dawn. It was a seamless war-dream of hunting and killing and destruction, of tanks rocking from blowback and loaders sweating with the shells, of little orange numbers flickering across amber screens, the crackle and hiss of cross talk and sudden shouts and bursts of static, of green ghosts wavering under blossoms of white flame in a shimmering green landscape.

It was a fine madness, all thunder and speed and searing exhilaration, a night that none of them would ever forget, and they smelled a total victory, a complete and crushing ruin hand delivered to the goddam Iraqis by the goddam United States Army—with a little help from the Marines—but any way you cut it, a definite and undeniable all-out ball buster of a war.

Simply put, it was victory, sweet and neat and totally complete, shoved up Saddam's personal and deeply deluded butt, and when they pulled up at dawn with their M1s sitting on top of the only highway out of Kuwait and watched the distant flaring lights and heard the groundswell of concussion and the bass-drum booming of the war gods as they incinerated a milling press of fleeing Iraqi thieves down on the Baghdad road, all they felt was the blood singing in their ears and pounding in their chests.

Every combat soldier hears about this feeling, and some of them even get to enjoy it, and what the men of the 1st Infantry were feeling then was an almost sexual lust to turn northeast, go to Baghdad, drive into Saddam's bedroom, tear up the four-poster and drag the sorry little fuck out from under it and put three rounds into the back of his head.

At eight on the morning of February 28, they regrouped on a butte overlooking the AO, with the Baker Company IFVs all around, and Mosby and Polanyi, and the LTs and all the junior sergeants. Everyone was cleaning weapons, servicing the tanks and vehicles, refueling and refitting. Wolochek was somewhere down-range, probably in a huddle with the adjutant and the HQ Company officers. Mosby was watching Crane stitch up a deep cut on Lymons's head with a set of needles and thread he had taken from a Holiday Inn in Junction City. After a silence, he set aside his SAW and squatted down beside Crane.

"Sergeant . . . so waddaya think?"

Crane looked up from Lymons's wound. Mosby's face was streaked with lime dust and he had a three-day beard. He'd taken the batteries out of his razor and used them to replace the dead ones in Polanyi's night-vision goggles. Crane could see changes in Mosby's face, some of them good.

"What'd I think of what?"

"The Hoo-Yah. Is it what you thought it would be?"

"No, Darryl."

"The casualties, right?"

"Yeah. Aside from the blue-on-blue, we lost a guy in the breach, defusing a mine, and another guy wounded by DivArty."

"Polanyi and the rest of the guys, we all got confirmed."

Crane looked at him in silence. "Yeah?"

"So, now we know."

"Yeah. You do."

Mosby looked back over his shoulder to the platoon AO, where Polanyi and Orso and Mitchell were scrubbing away at their weapons and talking happily. There were about fifty troopers in the general area, and another hundred or so spread out around their IFVs and M1s all down the side of the butte. A flight of Kiowas droned high up in the northern skyline, and the murmur of voices sounded on the wind. Crane figured Mosby had something to say, and he gave him time to say it.

But Mosby only shook his head after a long silence and then he patted Lymons on the shoulder and grinned at Crane. Grunting, he straightened and slapped some dust off his knees. He smiled again, looking about forty-two years old for that brief moment, and then he went back to his squad. Crane watched him go and knew he was looking at another lifer in the making.

The wind had been building all morning and now it started to whistle through the rocks so they didn't hear Boomer swearing until he slammed the hatch cover back.

He popped up out of Godzilla, jumped down, and walked over to where Crane was sitting, looked down at Crane with his face blank and shocked. They all looked at him, their talk fading away into an uneasy silence. Boomer looked down at Crane for a full minute.

Crane waited.

"It's over."

"What's over?"

Boomer looked northward, along the great salt valley that rose up into Iraq, along the road to Baghdad.

"The war. The fucking war. It's over."

"Waddya mean, it's over? Like hell it is!"

"Bush ended it. That's it."

Some of the men began to groan, others laughed.

"Bullshit, Sergeant," said Bigrig. "We're going to Baghdad. We got these motherfuckers on the run. No way they'd stop us. No way!"

Crane looked past the tankers and the APCs. The Baghdad road was a thin black thread lying on the yellow skin of the land. It snaked and twisted up through the long shallow valley and rose into the brown hills and red rock cliffs to the north.

He looked back up at Boomer, and then past him to DerHorst, who was bandaged and burned above his left eye. DerHorst was staring back at him, saying nothing.

"Goddamnit," said Crane, after a silence. "God *damn* it."

"Yeah," said DerHorst. "Exactly."

CHAPTER NINETEEN

PERIMETER WIRE

SEPTEMBER 1993

Crane leaned back in his green swivel chair, groaned, and stretched, looking out the slatted blinds of his office at the troops going by on Normandy Drive. His air conditioner was wheezing away in the frame like an emphysemic banshee, but the single-story red brick building was still an oven, and the grass on the little lawn would have been a brown stubble if one of the grunts hadn't been watering it every day. The light was changing a bit, as it does in September, maybe not quite so hot white, more amber in it, and the shadows were longer. A dusty wind carried the sound of a platoon doing a mile run a block over, the hoarse voices singing, "I don't want no teenage queen—I just want my M Fourteen—if I die in a combat zone—box me up and ship me home. . . ."

The sound of the cadence faded away and disappeared behind the roaring of a convoy of trucks from the Engineers, going somewhere out into the ranges to screw up something, and when that faded there was the thump of boots in the hall and the rumble of voices from the other noncom offices. He looked around his office, at the pale green walls and the posters for the New Modern Army—"Be all you can be"—at the bulletin board jammed up like a collage with Polaroids of the guys, time sheets, service docs, ordnance reports, motor pool beefs, shots of a boot party at Lucy's in JC, Mosby and Orso putting a black guy—Mitchell—through the Bouncing Betty initiation, a news photo of one of those plywood signs they'd put up in Saudi—"Welcome to Iraq Courtesy of the Big Red One"—behind his desk, framed certificates from various noncom courses, a yellowed and faded map of Vietnam with three darts sticking into it, marking off the Iron Triangle, an old black-and-white shot of DuPuy pinning a CIB on Crane's bony in-country chest, and two flags on mahogany-and-brass poles, the Stars and Stripes and the blue and gold of the Army.

Christ.

Thirty years.

Crane looked back down at the papers on his desk.

Training reports. Readiness reports. Medical calls. Requests for loans. Complaints about Montgomery Bill accounting requirements. One of the Baker Company grunts wanted bereavement leave to go back to Wichita, some great-aunt or other had had her ticket punched and was taking the midnight train to Valhalla. A storekeep from JC had written complaining that four grunts from Baker Company had been rude to him the week before and he wanted them court-martialed. Here was Polanyi—he'd made his stripes and was a squad leader—asking for permission to move his leave up a month. He wanted to take his wife and kid to Yellowstone and the gates closed in late September, and he couldn't wait any longer because he was being transferred to Fort Belvoir to do a second hitch with the Engineers.

Mitchell was tagged for Range Data. Most of the LTs were off to play the Great Game, taking courses at Kansas State or politicking for a posting to Leavenworth or Fort Monroe or *anywhere* in a Battle Group. Shabazz was gone to Fort Sill to study artillery. Ackisson had taken an Early Out and a big payout from the Drawdown fund and was studying to be a chiropractor in Oklahoma. Fanand and Seafferman were out of the Army, and DerHorst was on his way to Intel. The halls were crowded with brand-new LTs and cherry boots fresh in from Benning and Bragg. A new kid named Karpis needed dental work and wanted it done before his parents arrived to see him in October, but there was a line-up for dental work and Karpis was way back there. Other grunts were on the sheet, looking for outpostings to a trade service or hammering him for a training rotation somewhere, Signals at Fort Monmouth being the current top pick among ambitious grunts. Get those marketable skills, hit civvy street running, get a trick haircut, lease a Bimmer, buy a Hugo Boss suit . . .

It seemed that almost everybody in Baker was on his way to something else, that an entire nation of young men and women were on the prod for success and fame and four weeks paid vacation. Christ, the Custer Hill golf course used to be strictly officers. Now every green boot in Riley was out there every afternoon, tricked out in pastels and dragging a set of Ping Eyes around the terrain.

Everybody was headed somewhere, bug-eyed with plans and ambitions, and the only fixed point in the whole three-ring circus was First Sergeant Dee Crane and this puke green office in a red brick building up on Custer Hill. Even the OC, Rhame, had rotated, and now they had a new MG down at 1st Division HQ on Heubner.

No, somebody was staying eleven bravo. Mosby was coming back from the noncom school at Leavenworth later today, and Crane had a note here to go get him at Marshall Field, take him to Harry's for the sergeant's party later.

Mosby had made corporal in May of 1991 and sergeant in the spring of 1992. Now he was coming back—covered in glory—from Leavenworth and was probably going to make staff sergeant by the end of the year. Crane was proud of him.

And off to the left there, under a copy of the *Manual of Arms* and the *Uniform Code of Military Justice*, radiating threat and change, was Crane's resignation form, filled out but not signed. Yet.

He looked back out through the venetian blinds, seeing the soldiers in the street, everyone back in their forest camos. The chocolate chips were stored away, pressed and crated. The ground war had been so short, a lot of the troops had been able to turn in their chips and get a uniform credit as payback. Well, they'd had a lot of payback of one kind or another, hadn't they? It was as if the country had been trying to make up for something.

The 1st Infantry had stayed in Saudi for another three months, policing the battlefield, destroying any remaining Iraqi armor and ordnance—the mines were out there in the millions and the Army had decided that the mines were a Kuwaiti problem. They could afford to hire civilian specialists to clear them off—which they had—and many of them had died trying to do that job in the year that followed. And civilians had put out the oil fires—over six hundred of them—losing a few men in that as well.

Crane and DerHorst had been busy getting their men back out of the war zone and seeing to it that nobody stepped on something lethal while they did it. They established rear-area AOs and set up resupply strips and generally handled about two hundred problems a day from the end of February to the middle of April, when they were finally relieved and DEROSed back to Riley, supposedly covered in glory. Supposedly.

But Crane still remembered Lieutenant Colonel Fontenot's announcement after his 2nd Battalion of the 34th Armor had gotten up to Safwan Air Base and secured it so Schwarzkopf and Franks and the rest of the Third Army brass could take the Iraqi surrender there.

Fontenot had implied that the Iraqis had bugged out in panic as soon as they saw the first M1s clear the horizon line. His words were "... they didn't want to tangle with the First Infantry Division ... and we took the last objective of the war."

Well, yes.

Sort of.

It turned out that somebody at VII Corps had gotten some wires crossed—or not—and somebody else, precisely *who* being an object of very hot debate, had told the CINC, meaning Schwarzkopf, that Safwan was already taken—it had been a 1st Division objective— when in fact not one 1st Division trooper had gotten anywhere near the place. The only humans anywhere near Safwan at that time had been an entire regiment of Republican Guards, and since there had already been one shoot-out after the cease-fire—the 24th Mech had smoked a Republican Guard brigade in the Euphrates valley, taking three thousand POWs, after the Guard commander had fired at some of their Bradleys—it was reasonable to infer that the Iraqis who were at that point squatting on Safwan could be seen as a threat to the formal surrender ceremony. There they were, contrary to the after-action faxes littering Schwarzkopf's desk.

When Schwarzkopf found out about the misfire, he apparently went straight up fifty feet and landed right on top of Fred Franks. Franks got chewed out like a lance corporal, chewed out for not being at Safwan and for not using his VII Corps aggressively enough during the Hail Mary sweep across the KTO. He still got a promotion, but the inference was pretty insulting to Franks, and Crane found the image hard to shake.

They had made a classic breakthrough at the first berms, blown the lines apart, lost not a man, and then they had accomplished, basically, dick until they hit the Tawakalna on Tuesday evening.

Crane did not believe that either Franks or Rhame—who was a hard-nosed and aggressive commander and nobody's idea of a man who would dodge a fight—had tried to avoid Iraqi units.

But the non-negotiable reality of the thing was that VII Corps had in no way equaled the rapid advances of other line units in the same sector, including the 24th Mechanized and the 2nd Armored Cavalry. It was a matter of record that even the highly publicized Battle of Norfolk had been triggered by contacts developed by the 2nd Armored Cavalry, that they fired the first shots in that engagement, and that the 1st Division had not been allowed to pursue their war as aggressively as other units because Franks was so cautious.

Franks had not believed that the first after-action reports of a massive Iraqi collapse were accurate. He saw their Area of Operations as a "killing sack" highly vulnerable to chemical and biological attacks, which could kill thousands of men under his care and control. That was a valid fear, since no one in the KTO had any way of knowing that Saddam's delivery systems for these weapons, his missiles, were so degraded by bad maintenance and so inaccurate that they presented as much of a threat to his own forces as they would have to an enemy concentration.

And it was also true that Americans had been gassed in the First World War and the memory of that gassing was alive and terrible in the senior ranks of the Army. Still, there was no getting around it; the 1st had done well, but not as well as it could have, although no one at Riley was saying this out loud.

As for Franks, it was Crane's personal belief that Schwarzkopf was abusing Franks because, like Everest, Franks was there. The dirty little secret of the war was that after-action reports carried out by the 1st Division Intelligence teams showed that the Iraqis were not nearly as strong or as numerous as the Pentagon had been telling the American people. This tallied with Crane's suspicions in the field, and it sure as hell conformed to common knowledge about the combat readiness of the Warsaw Pact forces. Even back at the NTC, the observers had admitted that they credited their own OpFor units with a far higher degree of mechanical fitness and durability than you would see in a real Soviet motorized rifle regiment.

But the Great Game had to be played, and the official record claimed that the 1st Division had fought its way through two hundred and sixty klicks of enemy-held territory—well, there was enemy somewhere inside it, anyway—they had destroyed close to eleven divisions of Iraqi forces, wiped out six hundred enemy tanks and five hundred personnel carriers and in the process taken more than twelve thousand enemy prisoners, a performance that earned the division two more battle streamers, the Defense of Saudi Arabia and the Liberation of Kuwait.

But Crane was eleven bravo and had a long memory. When the 1st came back to America, it was like six months of the Fourth of July. The entire nation threw a party for the returning heroes—the ticker-tape parade down Fifth Avenue, the marches in Washington, the television coverage and the songs and the speeches, all played out against a background of grinning troops in chocolate-chip camo marching column after column down Main Street America, flags fluttering in the great American wind, the bands huffing away at their brass, the drums booming and rattling, the stamp and shuffle of men and women marching by on their way back from history.

For Crane—and for any man or woman in the armed forces who had ever been to Vietnam—it was a bittersweet experience. Bittersweet first of all because the 1st Infantry lost eighteen men during Operations Desert Shield and Desert Storm, and not all of them in combat.

Five troopers had died in aviation accidents during the build-up and deployment in November. Another three had died in traffic accidents or turnovers when their IFVs had flipped over and tumbled down a sand dune or thumped into a hidden wadi. Two were killed by mines.

And two were killed by blue-on-blue fire, shot up by an Apache pilot during a preliminary advance before the ground war started. They were in the right place, but wrapped in darkness and rain and poor IR capabilities. The Apache pilot put two Hellfires into their Bradleys, thinking they were Iraqi scouts. That happened in war a lot more than any of these cheering flag wavers could guess. One of the reasons a seasoned patrol in Vietnam hated to take on an FNG was that, in a firefight, he was as likely to kill *you* as he was a VC. There were more names on the Wall who had died from blue-on-blue than anyone would ever know. Civilians who liked to whine about that kind of thing usually had no idea of just how wild and chaotic combat really is; soldiers get killed by their friends in every war, and the twitchier the technology, the greater the risk.

And there were other ways to get it. One died from a heart attack when he thought he was being gassed. Five died in combat, taking rounds from Iraqi soldiers. Of course eighteen dead out of a deployment of seven thousand soldiers sounded pretty good, unless you were the one who had to write their families. But it was bittersweet for another and older reason as well.

When Crane finally got diagnosed as fugazy at Ben Cat in '69 and was ordered home, he had spent a lot of time in downtown Saigon, hanging around Annie's Bar with a lot of other DEROSing grunts, belting back the Bammy-Bows and watching the girls in their *ao dais* go by on Tu Do. But sooner or later they'd all get

around to that moment when the guy would climb down off the
Pan Am jet in San Francisco and walk out into the lights and the
music of the real world.

Crane was telling another soldier, a Spec 5 from the 9th in from
Dong Tam, what he was going to do in San Francisco and who he
was going to do it with and how often when a leathery-looking
captain with a missing left cheekbone and a left eye that looked
like a shattered glass ball and a Thundering Herd shoulder flash
leaned over to their table and said, "Well, boys, whatever you do
when you get back to the World, the first thing is you go into the
washroom at the airport and change into civilian gear, because
they're waiting for you in the concourse."

"Who are?" said the Spec 5, but Crane had an idea.

"Jody. Jody and your sister. And when you come down the
ramp, they'll throw a sack of baby shit at your breast bars and ask
you how many babies you bayoneted."

"Bullshit—no disrespect, Captain," said the Spec 5.

"Don't mean nothing to me," said the captain. "Don't say I
didn't tell you." He smiled in a slow and considering way, revealing a set of brand-new teeth and stitches in his lower left gumline.

He turned away and after a while he got up and walked out of Annie's with one of the girls. When they got to the door the girl in the *ao
dai* was suddenly illuminated by the bright white sun out in the street
and her body under the tunic looked slender and graceful and her
hair seemed to glow with auburn and black firelights.

Crane watched her go and remembered what the captain had
said. When he got to San Francisco he changed into Levi's and a
white tee shirt but they spotted him anyway. Later he figured it
was his Army haircut.

Well, everybody knew that story, and "So what?" was all you
could say. But when they'd had all the parades and the speeches for
the Gulf War vets, it was hard not to remember that captain and his
shattered eye and the brand-new nylon stitches in his gumline.

During the Topeka parade, the avenues had been lined with people, old vets in their VFW and Legion caps, housewives and office
workers and teenagers in baggy clothes and trick haircuts, city offi-
cials and cops who looked too young to drive let alone ride those

big escort Harleys, and everybody was cheering and waving, their voices hoarse and their faces bright red with pride and patriotism.

Or at least, that's how it looked. But going down the road with Baker, Crane had seen a few faces in the crowd that weren't smiling, guys with sad eyes, guys with Vietnam-era ribbons and colors, and every time Crane saw one, he felt just a little shamed.

At the time, none of the kids in the division had any trouble taking the bows and getting the parades, but as the weeks and months had gone by, some of them began to wonder if there wasn't something false about the whole thing.

For one thing, here they were, late summer about three years after their first deployment to Saudi, and Hussein was still in power, still poking his finger in America's eye every chance he got. Schwarzkopf had a book out—so did everyone who was ever there, it seemed—in which he was saying that those people who wanted the U.S. forces to go on into Baghdad were just rear-echelon chicken hawks who would never dream of putting themselves in the line of fire. That wasn't true, since a lot of the ordinary soldiers who had been there were at least *thinking* that the war should have been pushed to a more clear-cut ending. That feeling had started around the time the Iraqis had used their treaty permission to fly choppers in southern Iraq to blow the daylights out of rebel forces, not to mention what they had done to the Kurds in the north.

Schwarzkopf's answer to that was, Well, yeah, but suppose we *did* take Baghdad, suppose we could even *find* Hussein, let alone kill him, then guess who would have to *pay* for all of Iraq's requirements. America would be an occupying force. American troops would *still* be there. It was a damn good point. But the survival of so many of Saddam's personal troops, and the power he had to do harm in the region, much of that could have been eroded by a few more days of hardcore search and destroy—if you're going to *fight* a war, then by God you *finish* it—and Schwarzkopf knew that damn well, because he was Infantry and eleven bravo himself.

But the men and women who were thinking that around Riley weren't saying it very loud. There seemed to be a general agreement to pretend that the Gulf War was a complete success, a resounding victory in which the great combat record of the 1st Infantry had been renewed. For Crane, that was the truth, but not the whole truth, since he was in a position to understand what true combat was really like.

He wouldn't say it to the kids, but if they spent the rest of their lives believing that what they had gone through in the Gulf was anything like combat, then they were very lucky kids. If the drums sounded a little hollow, well, they had in every war, and they always would. If you had hard combat, like they'd had in the Triangle, then no one wanted to know about it. And if your combat was relatively painless, as it had been in the Gulf, then it was just the other side of the same grim fact, and the troops were being celebrated because there was no pain in it for the citizens, and no questions that might generate answers they couldn't handle.

War was always going to be outside the civilian world anyway, because that was where they wanted it. As far as Crane was concerned, there wasn't a contradiction between the celebrations around the Gulf War victory and the silence around the Vietnam War Memorial; if the Gulf War had killed a lot of young men and women, America wouldn't be giving anyone a parade. They'd be lynching the politicians who got them into it. Crane figured the parades were more of a tribute to the low rate of casualties than they were a party for returning victors.

A few days before, Crane had been sitting at the long bar in Harry's when a news report came on Tory's television. It showed the aftermath of a Special Forces fiasco that had taken place in Mogadishu that week. Somali gunmen had shot a Ranger chopper out of the air. The poor bloody pilot was a hostage, shown on video, shaken and bruised and clearly working hard to control his fear, which came off the screen so strong it made Crane burn in his belly.

And a large contingent of Rangers had been ambushed at the same time. It looked like there were maybe twenty killed, more than the 1st had lost in the Gulf War. So far, more servicemen had been killed in Somalia than in all of Desert Storm. And this night at Harry's, they all sat in silence, watching a crowd of Somali kids drag a naked U.S. soldier around by the ankle. He was dead, and showed signs of being mutilated. His right leg was broken, and the whole body was starting to come apart. Even more disturbing was that the man's wrists were bound up in nylon restraints. Crane recognized them as Army gear. They had used thousands of them on Iraqi prisoners in Saudi. No one at the bar seemed to realize that the cuffs meant that this trooper was killed *after* he was captured. You don't cuff a dead man. This American soldier was probably tortured and murdered by those skinny little Somali shits who were dragging him around, the same skinny little Somali shits they had supposedly gone in to save from starvation. It was a vile obscenity and Crane said nothing about it to anyone, not at Harry's and not back at Custer Hill. But watching it put him right back in the jungle, and he stayed awake for two days and two nights just so he didn't have to watch the scene over and over again in his skull.

At the time, the whole room at Harry's Bar was stunned and silent. And someone from the back of the room said something about how America should just go in there, kick their asses. Crane didn't turn around, but he was pretty sure the voice belonged to a civilian.

So where was this guy when Clinton was talking about sending American troops off on a feel-good mission to Somalia? Even after the Gulf War, the civilians hadn't learned a damn thing. You don't send troops to do things that troops can't do. The Army is for killing, not for feeding the hungry and doing Peace Corps work. Any mission that has no clearly defined goal, and any mission that includes an order *not* to fight, was guaranteed to present you with a picture like this one sooner or later.

Clinton and his whole cadre of boomer yuppies wanted to feel *good* about the Army. They had the same delusions about the Army that they had about police forces, the same obsessions with doing good and being liked. So Clinton had turned an Expeditionary Force over to UN control, to accomplish an impossible mission, and every civilian in the United States had happily gone along with it, because what could be wrong with feeding the starving?

You want an answer?

Look again at that dead soldier, being dragged naked through a street in Mogadishu. He might be alive right now if the mission had been to go into Somalia to crush the warlords, disarm them, and turn the pacified country over to a competent local government. But that would have required a full-out war, fought to a bloody conclusion, instead of a warm-fuzzy free lunch program that everybody could get behind.

It was the kind of thing that Crane expected of Clinton and his crowd. Clinton had been a draft dodger, no matter how you phrased it. He and his wife came out of that sixties antiwar hippy culture, and they had grown up believing that it is better to feel good than to do good. Any use Clinton would make of the military would have to make him feel good about it inside.

If Crane had needed any confirmation of that, he got it in the summer of 1993, when Clinton ordered an air strike in retaliation for an attempt on George Bush's life when he was visiting Kuwait. Clinton ordered a cruise missile attack on Iraqi Intelligence headquarters in Baghdad.

So far so good.

Then he went on television to make sure everybody understood that this counterstrike was "proportional" and "commensurate with the provocation." What he seemed to be saying was that an attempt on the life of an ex-President by a hostile power was worth a certain number of "hit points," the way a war-game observer would assess a tactical move. This drove the older noncoms and the officers at Riley crazy.

Where was it written that one dead President equalled one Iraqi building? Where was the rule book that you used to calculate the comparisons? What if they'd missed Bush but killed Barbara? Would that mean they'd only take out half the building? What if only a dog died? Would Clinton call in an air strike on a petting zoo in Basra?

As far as the Army was concerned, Hussein and his forces were terrorists, and it made no sense at all to talk about dealing with them "proportionally," especially in a situation that Clinton himself described as "an attack against our country and against all Americans." That was the same kind of "proportionalism" that made such a hell pit out of the Indochina War.

At that point, a lot of the noncoms and rankers in the 1st began to see a similarity between the Clinton approach to the Iraqis and the sudden pull-back at the end of the Gulf War; was that "proportional" too?

So many days of ground war and so many bombing sorties in exchange for one invasion of Kuwait? Eighteen dead soldiers from the Big Red One equals so many acres of burning oil? Was that why they pulled up before the kill? So Bush and Babs could feel good about their part in it? For more of the same old cold warrior "signaling"?

If so, was this poor dead grunt being desecrated in Mogadishu a sacrifice to Clinton's need to feel good about himself? God help them all if Clinton decided he needed to feel good about Bosnia too.

It was all too depressing to think about. So after a while Crane said the hell with his reports and the hell with Karpis and his dental problems and the hell with Polanyi's trip to Yellowstone park. He locked his office and said "later" to the Spec 5 clerk in the front office, and went to get Mosby down at Marshall Field.

The field was out in the open, across the Kansas and down a long stretch of road that ran from the shaded lawns and buildings of the main post down toward a flat delta that lay in the lee of a broad yellowstone bluff to the south. The interstate ran along the base of that bluff and Crane could see the tractor rigs and the four-wheelers racing by the gates. A huge water tower rose above the hangars and outbuildings of Marshall Field. On the side of the tower there was a huge red *1* and the words "Fort Riley, home of the Big Red One."

Mosby's chopper was already inbound when Crane pulled up by the landing pad. He watched the old transport Huey thunder in and flare up just as the rails touched, a real in-country touch-and-go that took him back thirty years, as it always did. Mosby clambered out in his Class As, carrying his kit bag and grinning like a demented coyote. Holding on to his hat, he bent down and frog-jogged over to Crane's tan Chevy.

"How'd it go?"

"*Out*standing, Sergeant Crane! Where's Top?"

"With Polanyi and the guys. You remember what I told you?"

Mosby smiled again and dropped into a singsong recital tone: "The caliber seven-six-two M Sixty machine gun is a belt-fed gas-operated automatic weapon issued with an attached bipod and a tripod mount optional excellent weapon to suppress ATGM gunners vehicles and troops the night-vision device is the AN/PVS-Two and should be boresighted and zeroed on the IAW TM eleven five-eight-five-five dash two-oh-three dash thirteen prior to night patrols tracer burnout is approximately nine hundred meters—"

Crane was pulling out onto the interstate. He looked sideways at Mosby and said, "They asked you about the Sixty? Why?"

"Why not? I was ready for anything. I think they asked me about the Sixty just to see if I had history on the weapon. Which I do. I think I'll get the ticket. I screwed up on Internet protocol with coalition forces but I was okay on all the MOPP drills and the nerve agent stuff was golden."

"Good. Good work."

"Thanks, Dee. It was all you."

"Bullshit. I'm happy for you. You'll get staff for sure."

"Jesus. My dad will freak out."

Mosby's dad. Right. Mosby was someone else's kid. The thought made Crane feel strange, saddened him for a while. Now and then, when he felt like this, he could feel an old man's impatience coming over him, and a feeling that his time was narrowing down to one last military act, and after that . . . well, whatever, it was not yet.

But he was proud of Mosby and proud of all the eleven-bravo troopers he had taken to war. He had never shared any of his doubts about the war with the kids. Oh, they had them all right, at least the more intelligent ones did. But let them enjoy their victory and enjoy being combat vets.

Too many Vietnam-era soldiers were running around the landscape saying Yeah, but, and generally raining on everybody else's parade. One more raggedy-assed Nam vet wearing too-tight boonie-rat gear and whining about his miserable existence and Crane would personally go over and throw up on him.

The Wall said it all. There were no more POWs and MIAs. All

that stuff was a marketing scam run by redneck combat freaks and backed up by politicians who wanted to jerk the Vietnamese around to get votes back home. Everybody knew that you *always* reported a guy MIA instead of KIA, because that way, his widow got a kind of extended payout while the Army blundered through the paperwork. Otherwise, she was chopped, given a flag and his insurance money and a ride to the front gates.

The MIA thing was just a way for old grunts to hang on to the limelight for a while longer, even if they didn't know it. The time had come for old grunts to fade away. Including Crane.

They pulled up in front of Harry's Bar on Poyntz Street. Through the glass Crane could see a press of uniforms. Carla was behind the bar, serving and smiling, and they could hear the music out in the street, George Thorogood playing "Bad to the Bone," which had become a kind of Baker Company anthem since they'd come back from Saudi.

Mosby popped the door and half stepped out. Heat flowed in around him and his flushed young face was shiny. He looked hard and polished and his sergeant's stripes were bright yellow in the sunlight. His breast bars shone like colored silk. He was pure eleven bravo and Crane looked at him from the shade of the car.

"What's the matter, Dee? You not going in?"

"I'll be there. I got a few things to do."

Somebody called Mosby's name. They looked across the street. DerHorst, Polanyi, Orso, about twenty other soldiers, were standing in the window, holding up tankards of beer, waving and calling.

"You gotta come in, Dee!"

"I will. Gimme an hour."

"Promise! You been dodging the crowd lately."

"I'll be there."

"Okay." Mosby shut the door and waved over his shoulder as he jogged across the street toward Harry's Uptown. Carla was watching Crane as he pulled away.

He waved to her and accelerated up the street. He turned left at the town center and left again on Leavenworth. College kids were walking along the shaded street, heading back to their rooms or getting ready for the evening.

In a little while, he was westbound on Riley Boulevard. He drove through Ogden and on into the east gate, past the stone cairn by the railway track, past Camp Funston and on along Heubner until he reached the Main Post grounds. He turned right off Heubner and rolled quietly to a stop on Barry Avenue.

The post chapel was just across a little field, under a stand of oaks and cottonwoods. Beside it was a smaller building, made out of roughcut yellow limestone, the old St. Mary's Chapel. Crane climbed out of the Chevy and walked across the dry grass of the lawn, feeling the late afternoon heat on his shoulders and back.

Inside the chapel it was cooler but very still. The two little rows of hardwood pews glistened with lemon oil and the air smelled of lemon and sandalwood and floor wax. A kind of amber sideways light was flowing in through the stained-glass windows. All along the sides of the chapel were tablets of wood with the names of old soldiers set down in brass and bronze, sergeants killed in the Indian Wars or before that, at places like Shiloh and Antietam.

In the chapel, it was possible to feel very close to them, to feel that you were a part of something very old and very fine, and that even if you had no family of your own, there were people who would remember you, remember what you had done and the places you had seen.

Up on Custer Hill there was a great hall and plaques with the names of men who had died at places like Berzy-le-Sec and Normandy and the Kasserine, Katum Airfield, the Plantation, Song Be, or Thunder Road. There were eighteen new names up there now, eighteen troopers of the 1st Infantry Division who had been killed in a war that everyone was saying was a great victory, although Bush was gone now, and Saddam Hussein was still in power.

Fighting halfhearted wars was getting to be a pattern now, and Crane hoped with all his heart that Clinton would keep them out of Bosnia. But he had come to accept that halfhearted missions were probably eternal, leaders being what they were, and the ambiguous nature of victory in the Gulf was no different than the victory of any other war; they only looked good from a distance.

Well, whatever Clinton was going to do, Crane was out of it.

Mosby was halfway to his staff stripes. DerHorst would make LT or better. Wolochek was a major and they had given Baker Company to Petrie—he was a captain now. Everybody was moving up or shipping out and even Custer Hill was changing. Crane had gotten into the habit of coming down here to the old chapel because it was one of the few places left at Fort Riley where he didn't feel like a mile marker in someone else's rearview mirror.

It was his intention to sit down quietly here for a little while, think about things, let his mind clear. Mosby was right. Lately he had been avoiding the guys, even his own ranks. He guessed he was getting ready to let go, and he thought about that Army discharge paper on his desk up at Custer Hill.

The time was coming. He was too old for another deployment. It had taken him months to get back to health after the Gulf deployment, and he still had aches and creaks from the long winter wait out in the Saudi desert. It was like he was chilled to the bone and only a long rest in the sunlight could warm him. There was a shaft of sunlight coming in through the stained-glass window and resting on his shoulder. He could feel the heat on the side of his face. It calmed and warmed him. He closed his eyes and tried to remember a prayer.

Sergeant?

Crane was dreaming about a river, lying by the river on a broad green bank, under the shade of old trees. The day was very warm and in the morning there had been a storm—a summer storm, like the ones they had in Kansas, where the sky would turn green and bruised looking and great anvil-shaped clouds would sail like galleons across the horizon line, rippling with fire along their edges and glowing deep inside. The sound of them was like a low pleasing voice in another room, maybe your father's voice, the way you heard it through the walls when you were young. Then the rain would come, lancing, sheets of it, and the dry grasses in the fields would bend as the pattering drops came down, bend and then rise again, and the rain would gentle and roll onward, down into a long valley and up the far side, like a manta ray gliding over the floor of an ocean. . . .

Sergeant?

And as he lay beside this river, looking out into the late afternoon light on the broad brown waterway, he saw that a chain of
lily pads was floating down on the current, a long chain of interlocking green vines and tendrils, like a floating island, with white
flowers and red flowers and yellow flowers, and there was a scent
in the air—it was jasmine, or perhaps lotus, but heavy and hyp-
notic, the breath of the East. . . .

Sergeant Crane . . .

Moths and a kind of cobalt blue butterfly he used to know from
somewhere in his youth and dragonflies and tiny flying things
were drifting and gliding over the moving island and there was
haze in the air that softened the light on the water. Crane lay
under the trees and looked out at the broad river and the slow
sweep of the lilies floating past and after a while he raised his eyes
and looked at the far shore, where a cool deep green darkness lay
under all the trees, although the sunlight was strong and bright
on the upper branches, and the sky was very blue and high like a
bowl of glass. Crane thought if he could reach up and strike the
glass it would ring high and very clear and the ringing would go
on for a long time and not really end but just seem to float away
out of hearing.

Sergeant . . . Sergeant . . .

Crane looked back down toward the far shore again and there
was a man there, standing under the heavy trees and looking back
at Crane. It was that captain from the Thundering Herd, the guy
with the damaged eye who had warned him about the hippy chicks
waiting for him Stateside, and when the light changed Crane
could see there were other men behind him, Half Moon and Airborne, Weeks and Midget Suarez, and many others, standing under the heavy branches with tall grasses all around them. . . .

Sergeant Crane.

Crane came awake suddenly. He was very hot, and his face was
wet and pale. He looked up into the face of a young black soldier
who was leaning over him and had a hand on his shoulder. Behind
the man there was a soft amber glow and Crane knew the glow
was from stained-glass windows.

"I'm sorry to wake you, Sergeant. We have to close up. Are you okay?"

Crane wiped his face. His palm came away damp and he held it off his thigh, not wanting to stain his uniform. He looked down at the hand, seeing the light around it, as if his hand were glowing.

"Sorry . . . sorry. I guess the heat . . ."

"Yes, sir. It's a warm day. But it's September. It'll cool off soon. Can I get you a glass of water?"

Crane shook his head and stood up. He looked around at the little chapel, at the hardwood arches and the plain white plaster vaulting, at the little stone altar in the nave. Two brass candlesticks, buffed and glittering, caught the slanting afternoon light and sent it rippling around the white walls. Beyond the stained glass a cottonwood swayed as the wind shifted, making the sun shimmer on the far wall, a liquid scintillation of green and gold.

Crane thanked the trooper and walked away down the aisle toward the old wooden doors.

He stepped outside onto the broad green lawn. Oaks and cottonwoods shaded the little chapel and the larger post chapel beside it. On the far side of the park a row of large old stone houses lay beneath a line of shade trees. Each house had a little white fence around it, and flowers in the garden. On the screened porches there were bikes and tricycles, skateboards in splashes of hard color against the ocher and deep green of the houses. Crane walked through them and along a quiet street, looking at the homes and thinking about the men and women who lived there, and the lives they had together.

Crane reached the top of the little lane and turned right, walking along past the low wooden veranda of Custer House. On his left beyond the bronze horseman the Cavalry Parade Field rolled away toward the museum and the buildings of the post annex.

The Main Post of Fort Riley was quiet at this time of day, the troops at work up on Custer Hill, in the motor pools and the training halls, and out in the ranges. Down here by the Kansas the old fort seemed to float on a river of time, a citadel for dead men.

Crane walked across the cavalry field toward Battery Rogers, his boots hissing in the dry grass, the sun burning down on his uniform shirt.

Duty. Honor. Country.

But don't lose. Above all, don't lose.

His car—the same tan cruiser—was parked down by the post HQ annex, a big stone temple-looking construction with "Patton" carved into the stone above the pillars. He climbed into it—Christ, it was hot.

He turned on the air conditioner and drove slowly through the Main Post grounds, past the old yellow buildings and the hundred-year-old oaks and cottonwoods, until he reached the road that led down across the Kansas River and the interstate beyond it. When he cleared the old forest and came down the long twisting lane he was suddenly into the hard yellow light of the afternoon sun. It lay on the Kansas River like liquid fire, shimmering and wavering on the water and shining through the dusty cottonwood leaves.

He pulled the car over and sat there by the side of the road, watching the light on the water. He rolled the windows down and felt a cool breeze roll in from the river. It smelled of earth and sweet grass.

Soon he would have to retire. Next year, probably. They were hammering at him to take a big payout. He didn't have a lot of choice. He thought he would go back to Lake Placid for a while, because he missed the Adirondacks, missed the clear cold and the way the deep snow lay on the land all winter, and the colors of the leaves in the fall.

It would be hard. He had been nothing but a soldier all his life, but he was still young, only fifty-one, and could have another life. A second life, up in New York, in Lake Placid or Utica—see the Schultz and Dooley Museum again, and the House of a Thousand Animals. Carla had married one of her doctors last year. She seemed happy. Crane still lived alone.

Now that the afternoon was fading, the prairie wind was stirring and it made the surface of the Kansas shimmer with yellow and gold and red light. The hazy windshield was a web of flickering fire and he thought about the war, about everything he had seen, the dead and the living, and the places he had known, and he knew that he would leave the Army, make a new life for himself, see his own people again.

But he also knew as he watched the way the yellow fire rippled along the broad brown back of the Kansas River that he would never again feel his life so strongly and never again see the light in quite this way, and he sat there for a very long time as the wind rose and the light changed, caught in the narrowing iris of time.

Through the open window, he could hear someone calling a drill from a mile away. It was very still. It was as if time had stopped. At times like these, Crane felt that he was out of time, that he had stepped out of it when he joined the United States Army so many years ago. He had a lot of memories, some of them very fine, few of them connected to war. There had been good friends—all of them civilians now, or dead. He had some rank, although not as much as he could have had. He had never married, so there were no children, and no in-laws to avoid at Christmas. All around him at Riley, young men were racing past him on their way up the career ladder, playing the Great Game. The guys who weren't going to stay in the Army were transferring out of Combat Arms into an MOS that would give them marketable job skills in civilian life.

And what about him?

What did it all add up to for him?

Well, he had combat ribbons, and a good record. Maybe there'd be work for him with the state patrol, maybe as a training officer. If he wasn't too old? And there was security. There were big corporations in Kansas City and Wichita. Maybe one of them could use an experienced soldier to run their . . . their what?

What the hell did Crane know about security? They'd give him a job checking the underground parking lot and sitting in the lobby giving directions.

Middle management? Yeah, the only thing that set him apart from every other office manager was that he knew how to do it with a side arm on. And middle-management types were losing their jobs all over the country.

Damn, this was a depressing line of thought.

He had savings, and he'd get a big buyout to retire. Enough to go up to Montana, buy a place on the Yellowstone. Or set up in Livingstone, buy a bar.

MacArthur hadn't been telling the whole story. Old soldiers may never die, but they don't fade away either. What happens is, everything *else* fades away, and one afternoon late in your career you find yourself sitting in a tan Caprice by the side of the river, watching the light change and thinking about how much of your life was just an illusion, that while you were telling yourself all the stories about eleven bravo and the Army and the holy code of the warrior, everybody else was out there in civilian life, making a future for themselves. He could feel the Laphroaig at home, feel it calling him. Or he could get over to Harry's, catch the tail end of Mosby's party, make small talk with Carla.

Soon.

But right now, it was good to listen to the distant cadence and hear the rush of the Kansas River under the cottonwoods, and kid himself a while longer that even a soldier whose whole world was slipping away could close his eyes for a moment, smell the sweet grass, feel the cool mist off the water, hear the creak of his old leather garrison belt, remember the places he had seen and the things that had happened, and feel that in a small and fleeting way he had been a part of some great thing.

A FEW FINAL WORDS

In *Vom Kriege* (*On War*), Carl von Clausewitz cut a niche for himself in the mind of modern military men with the phrase, "War is nothing but a continuation of political intercourse with the admixture of different means," a line commonly shortened to "War is just politics by other means." Seeing war as just another way of settling economic and political competition, of furthering the interests of a state, has assigned to the experience of combat a rationality that it does not in any way deserve, which may be the chief reason for our continuing delusions about war itself.

This is not to suggest that there are no wars that needed to be fought if something good, some particle of grace and freedom and justice, was to have any hope of survival. Few people who have any clear recollection of the words and the actions of the Nazis in Europe and the Japanese atrocities in China and Korea and Singapore will tolerate much in the way of clever undergraduate revisionism about World War Two. Unfortunately, other conflicts in this century cannot deliver the same sort of moral comfort. And getting back to von Clausewitz, even the long-term consequences

of what Studs Terkel called the Good War don't support the Clausewitz thesis at all.

In 1939, Britain and the Commonwealth nations were (relatively) strong economically, and the remnants of the British
Empire were still visible, if not viable. In the meantime, the United
States was struggling with unemployment and the aftereffects of a
shattering Depression. Germany was undergoing a remarkable economic transformation, and Japan was seeing China and the
South Pacific as a fallow field, fertile with imperial possibilities.

At the end of the war, everything had changed. The British
Empire was in ruins, England herself a client state, and the Commonwealth on the point of disintegration. She lost India the next
year, and has been in retreat ever since. Germany was in ruins,
and Japan had a boot on the back of her neck, although richly
deserved.

And the boot belonged to the United States, one of the few
nations to emerge from that war with all its power not only intact,
but magnificently enhanced. None of these is an outcome that
could have been in any way anticipated by any of the politicians
who started the war or who saw it as their duty to attempt to end
it. And fifty years later, the two aggressor nations have become
economic superpowers, and the future of the United States is in
play.

So if von Clausewitz was right, he was right in a way he had not
intended. The trouble seems to be that his errors have become
the bedrock assumptions of global military strategists and the gov-
ernments they serve. Seeing war, seeing combat actions, as a sensible and predictable way of implementing geopolitical goals is
one of the great unexamined assumptions of our age.

No one can effectively argue that the West's great struggle
against communist aggression (a worthy end) was in any accept-
able way advanced by the deaths of fifty-eight thousand young
American men in Vietnam. Even if there were some tangible ben-
efits from the Vietnam War—it may have "signaled" to other communist or totalitarian nations such as North Korea, China, and
Russia, that the U.S. was prepared to fight for its beliefs—it also

shattered the myth of U.S. invincibility and created a terrible domestic rift that persists to this day. Our adventures in Grenada and Panama had ambiguous consequences, and recent events in Somalia have made it blindingly clear that "feel-good" missions without clear and definable goals can, and usually will, have obscene and tragic outcomes.

Desert Storm seems to have been a success, in that Hussein, although still in power, has had his power largely erased, for a military price that was miraculously low. But the region is still a volcanic terrain boiling with tribal and religious hatreds, as it has been for a thousand years. Bosnia has re-emerged at the end of the century in a welter of ethnic hatred and atrocities, which is roughly where it was when this century began. What happened last year in Rwanda and Burundi is, sadly, business as usual in that blood-dark continent. In the past one hundred years, in spite of all the ringing rhetoric and gallant assaults, all the wars we have endured have been like sudden and savage hurricanes, rolling in from dark seas and tearing the fabric of our nations to shreds, leaving ruin and lasting change in their wakes. There's not much of von Clausewitz in any of it; there's a great deal of Dante, or Wagner, or Kafka.

I'm not the only one to sense this absurdity, and in this book I have been guided by the thought and the work of better men and better writers than I could ever be. John Keegan's brilliant and relentless analysis of the great battle of the Somme clarified and strengthened my own observations of the futility of artillery bombardments, but it was his lucid and compassionate insights into the very essence of the combat dynamic that helped me make some kind of sense out of the letters my father's cousin sent before his death in the Kasserine, and, in a much more modest way, out of my own experiences in Southeast Asia—every Valentine's Day I think of the Perfume River—my observations of mercenary soldiers in Costa Rica and southern Nicaragua, and, for that matter, my rather harrowing years with homicide cops in the South Bronx and narcotics investigators in places like Los Angeles, Vancouver, Detroit, and Central America.

Beyond Keegan, there is only Paul Fussel, whose writings on war and the lives of soldiers are without parallel—wryly funny, bitter, pointed, and yet full of mature affection, telling detail, and, finally, transcendence. Anyone wishing to begin a true understanding of combat and the soldier's life can find no better guide; his voice resonates throughout this book. John Toland's massive work, *1918*, is the definitive work on that terrible year, and the inspiration for my own aria on the inner life of Private Rose.

For the very best thinking about modern military strategy and the future shape of the American Army, you can't find a better source than the work of Colonel Harry G. Summers, Jr. (Ret.), whose *On Strategy* books, *A Critical Analysis of the Vietnam War* and *A Critical Analysis of the Gulf War,* have shaped, and continue to inform, the best thinking about armies and what they ought sensibly to attempt.

If you really want to understand the way things work at the National Training Center in Fort Irwin, but you don't want to try it for yourself, you need to read *Dragons at War* by Daniel P. Bolger, a young officer in the 24th Infantry Division (Mechanized) at Fort Stewart. Bolger's stern and rigorous assessment of his time at the NTC is a stellar illustration of what is meant by the term "professional soldier." Bolger, who was much criticized for his honesty by senior officers playing the Great Game, is precisely the kind of soldier the U.S. Army, and America, needs. I don't know where he is right now, but I hope he's still in a U.S. Army uniform.

Other professionals have furthered my understanding of the military world, including many men and women serving with the 1st Infantry Division at Fort Riley. The stories they told me, the insights they gave me, were given at a certain risk, the same risk faced and accepted by Daniel Bolger. The military mind is mistrustful of civilians, and hates ambiguity. My interpretations of the stories I was told form the record of this book. If elements of these stories strike you as hard or cruel, I ask you to consider the time and the places in which these events took place; if you were there, you will not judge.

I spent a total of nearly a year at Riley and in the surrounding towns—including far too much time at Harry's Uptown Bar in downtown Manhattan—and it was too short a time to spend in such company. All of the reported conversations detailed in this book are the result of hours and days of talk—some of it tearful, some manic, all of it heartfelt and honest—with soldiers of the Big Red. I've tried to get the talk right, but all of it is necessarily re-created. What is true rings truly; anything that may ring false is my own fault, due to my own errors, nuances I missed or fumbled, facts I have surely bungled, in spite of Beverly Lewis, my editor, whose work on this book has been, as usual, at once graceful, fine, and supple, and yet hard as iron.

And what was it all about? Why have I been tugging on your sleeve all this time? I called the book *Iron Bravo*, from the combat arms MOS designation, eleven bravo. What I wanted to achieve was an insight into a question that has troubled me for most of my life.

I come from a long line of soldiers, almost two hundred years. Strouds have been professional soldiers for centuries; there were Strouds—usually cavalry—at Waterloo, in the Crimea, at the Retreat from Kabul, at Cawnpore and Lucknow, and in all of this century's major wars. I've seen the thing for myself, and watched as thousands of other young men and women have looked at what John Keegan called the "Face of Battle." It is a terrible face, a Gorgon's face, and no one who looks at it walks away unchanged. Yet still the wars come, generation after generation.

Why? What sustains the soldier? It's not anything von Clausewitz wrote about. He was writing for princes, not soldiers. Soldiers don't fight wars, they fight battles. They don't see the Higher Purpose. They fight for each other, and for a sense of themselves as soldiers. This is a great mystery, and something more easily stated than understood.

I suppose I hoped to find an answer to this question by concentrating on one career noncommissioned officer. My father, who was a captain in the Dragoons, always said it was the noncoms who were the living memory of an army, and the conduit for ten thousand years of battle experience. Certainly that was my own belief. That's why I looked to Crane for reasons, for an answer to my own questions about combat, war, and futility.

And what was my answer?

I believe that this century has seen the brutality of war intensified beyond the limits of human endurance; modern warfare achieves nothing but slaughter. It is the celebration of murder. Modern war delights in refinements of technique, in the perfection of machinery. It couples the soul of an actuary with the appetites of a demon. It has exceeded the ability of the species to control it. The modern soldier commutes between this world and the pit. The fact that many soldiers are transformed by the alchemy of battle, that they are made into finer stuff by the crucible of combat, does not change the fact that they are burning. War is the madness of states.

Carsten Stroud
Thunder Beach, 1994

GLOSSARY

Abrams	M1A1 65-ton 60-mph 120-mm very advanced U.S. main battle tank
AEF	Allied Expeditionary Force; World War I U.S. troop commitment
Air Cav	The 1st Air Cavalry Division
AIT	Advanced Individual Training; postboot MOS training
AK47	Kalashnikov assault rifle (Russian design); usual OpFor weapon
ANGLICO	Air/Naval Gunfire Liaison Control Officer; your link to Navy guns
ANZACs	Australia and New Zealand Army Corps
AO	Area of Operation; infantry unit tactical assignment, local terrain
ao dai	Vietnamese woman's dress; long skirt slit to hip, worn over pants
Apache	AH-64 gunship with miniguns, Hellfire and TOW rockets

arc light	B-52 bombing missions; usually along Cambodian border
ARVN	Army of the Republic of Vietnam; also *Arvins*
AWACS	Airborne Warning and Control System; Boeing E3 Sentry 707
ba	Vietnamese; a married woman, used as a title of address
Bammy-Bow	Ba Mu'oi Ba; brand of Vietnamese beer
basee-day	*ba si de;* homemade rice alcohol
BDUs	Battle Dress Uniform
beaten zone	The sector where most incoming rounds will strike (kill zone)
berms	Military defensive fortification; specifically the forward glacis
blivet	Collapsible water or fuel container
bloop gun	M79 40-mm grenade launcher; Vietnam era
BLU-82	3,000-pound gravity bomb; also known as Daisy Cutter
BMO	Black Moving Object; U.S. Army slang for a Moslem woman
BMP	Bronevaya Maschina Piekhota, Russian Infantry Fighting Vehicle
BMP-2 IFV	Kuwaiti tracked troop carrier with AT-4 launcher/30-mm
boonies	From boondocks; out in the bush, far from home, in enemy country
Bradleys	M2 Bradley Infantry Fighting Vehicle
BTR-60	Iraqi Armored Personnel Carrier
Buffs	B-52 Stratofortress bombers
bunky	Old U.S. Cavalry term for a bunkmate or buddy
CALFEX	Combined Arms Live Fire Exercise; NTC weapons-training drill
camo	Camouflage clothing
chain gun	General Electric–made electronic machine gun; very fast rate of fire

Charlie	Viet Cong, from Victor Charlie, the radio call letters
cherry	Green; see FNG
chickenshit	Army discipline and standards enforced solely to crush individualism
Chieu Hoi	Literally, "Open Arms"; surrender program for VC and NVA troops
Chobham armor	Armor composed of ceramic blocks in a resin matrix inside steel
CIB	Combat Infantry Badge; award for courage in a real firefight
CINC	Commander in Chief
Class As	AG 44, 344, 444 Standard U.S. Army "walking out" uniform; green
Claymore	Convex tripod hand-detonated C4 mine with 700 steel balls
CNXed	Canked; canceled at the highest level of command
CO	Commanding officer
co	Vietnamese for unmarried woman or "miss"; used as a title of address
Cobra	Hellfire- and TOW-missile-equipped airmobile gunship chopper
COHORT	Unit COHesion and Operational Readiness Training
defilade	In a position out of the line of direct enemy fire
DEROSed	From DEROS, Date of Estimated Return from Overseas
di di mau	Vietnamese for "hurry, move it"
dishdasha	Saudi robe
Div Arty	Division Artillery; guns assigned to support your mission
djebel	Hill or round-top; Arabic
downrange	Closer to the kill zone
Drawdown	Clinton's plan for reduction in the U.S. military establishment

duma	Vietnamese patois; roughly, "go fuck your momma"
Early Out	Unscheduled ETS or End Tour of Service; usually a wound
enfilade	Fire directed along the long axis of an enemy formation
EPWs	Gulf War terminology for enemy prisoners of war or POWs
Erks	ERC-90 Armored Car; Iraqi wheeled minitank
fire base	Compound in the AO containing TOC, Div Arty, combat troops
FIST	Fire-Support Team; troops assigned to call in artillery fire
FLIR	Forward-Looking Infrared; nighttime target ID system
FNG	Fucking New Guy; a green troop in your AO, about to die
fougasse	Jellied petroleum or gasoline-and-soap combination; antitank
FRAGORD	A fragmentary or incomplete military order
free-fire zone	Anyone found in this area is an enemy and can be fired upon at will
Fritz helmet	Recent-issue Kevlar-and-ceramic U.S. Army helmet, from the shape
FUBAR	Fucked Up Beyond All Recognition
fugazy	Totally nuts, brave, but completely insane (from sniffing fougasse?)
G1	Company-level adjutant/Personnel officer
G2	Company-level Intelligence officer
G3	Company-level Operations officer
G4	Company-level Logistics and Supply officer
get-go	Lock-and-load line; jump-point, the very beginning
golden BBs	Antiaircraft rounds as they look when you're the target
GPS	Global Positioning System; satellite-based navigational system

hardcore	Vietnam-era term; professional and without mercy, life takers
HEAT	High-Explosive Antitank; a tank round fired at an enemy tank
Hercs	C-130 Hercules, main troop and equipment air transport
HESH	High-Explosive Squash Head; a tank round (see HEAT)
Hoo-Yah	Desert Storm and related operations in KTO
Huey	UH 1 Vietnam-era multipurpose airmobile chopper, still in use
humvee	HUMV—recent multiconfiguration replacement for the Jeep
IFVs	Infantry Fighting Vehicles; various tracked configurations and arms
intox	Intoxication; as in "I and I" (intoxication and intercourse)
J-STARS	Joint Services Tactical Airborne Radar System on a 707 airframe
JAFO	Military slang for Just Another Fucking Observer
jarheads	U.S. Army slang for United States Marines, from the haircuts
Jedi Knights	Graduates, School for Advanced Military Studies, Fort Leavenworth
Jody	Draft dodgers, slackers back in the World, pogues; Vietnam era
ka-bar	U.S. Marine Corps fighting knife
kaffiyeh	Arab headgear
kakeshya	Lakota (Sioux) term for extreme torture of an enemy prisoner
Kevlar	Brand name of interwoven fiberglass antiballistic cloth
khong-zau	Vietnamese for "nice, very nice"
KIAs	Killed in action
kill zone	Area upon which presighted fire will land; small-unit tactics term

Kiowa	OH-58 Kiowa Scout chopper
klick	A kilometer
KTO	Kuwaiti Theater of Operations
LAWS	M-72 Light Antitank Weapon System; throw-away bazooka
LRRP	Long Range Reconnaissance Patrol; infantry unit on extended patrol
LT JG	Lieutenant, Junior Grade; lowest-ranking officer, also "butter-bar"
Lurp	Unit member of a Long Range Reconnaissance Patrol (Vietnam)
LZ	Landing Zone; Vietnam-era Airmobile term
M9	Combat earthmover; armored-assault support bulldozer
M113 APC	Saudi tracked IFV with one 12.7-mm machine gun
M203	Combined M16A2 assault rifle and underbarrel grenade launcher
MAC	Military Airlift Command
MACV	Military Assistance Command—Vietnam
MAST	Mobile Army Surgical Team
MILES gear	Multiple Independent Laser Engagement System
monster	Twelve Claymore mines rigged to detonate simultaneously
MOPP	Mission-Oriented Protective Posture NBC suit; also a condom
MOS	Military Operational Specialty; what you're trained to do
MP	Military Police
MREs	Meals Ready to Eat; individual food packets, universally loathed
MRR	Motorized Rifle Regiment; main Iraqi or Russian assault division
NBCs	Nuclear and Biological Contaminants
NTC	U.S. Army National Training Center at Fort Irwin, California

nuoc mam	Sauce made by percolating water through a vat of salted fish
NVA	North Vietnamese Army; Regular Army troops (enemy)
NVGs	Night-Vision Goggles; available-light electrical image intensifiers
OCS	Officer Candidate Schools
ODs	Olive Drabs
OER	Officer's Efficiency Report; U.S. Army career report card
OpFor	Military abbreviation for Opposing Forces
OSUT	One-Station Unit Training; for infantry, Fort Benning, Georgia
PAOs	Press-liaison officers from the Public Affairs Office (see PUNTS)
payback	Violent retributive military action
PFC	Private First Class; postboot rank
pogues	Anyone not "operational"; rear-echelon time-servers, of no use at all
point man	Forward scout for an infantry patrol in high-risk areas
Prick-25	PRC-25 Motorola field radio carried by RTO; Vietnam era
PsyOps	Psychological pressure applied in a combat environment
pungi stake	Pointed bamboo stake covered with feces or venom
PUNTS	People of Utterly No Tactical Significance; REMFs downrange
Puzzle Palace	MACV headquarters building at Tan Son Nhut near Saigon
PX	Post Exchange; on-base general store
raghead	Contemptuous slang for any Saudi, Kuwaiti, or Iraqi
rat-fuck	Doomed from the get-go; a fugazy mission, brave but nuts

RC-292	Ground plane antenna used to extend range of PRC-25
REFORGER	REinFORcement of GERmany; European war games
REMFs	Rear-Echelon Mother Fuckers (see PUNTS)
Riley	Fort Riley, Kansas and related cantonments in the AO
ROK	Republic of Korea
round	Slug or bullet, as distinct from cartridge that includes case
RPG	Rocket-propelled grenade launcher; Charlie's Choice
sapper	A military tunneler; in Vietnam, a VC infiltrator and assassin
SatNav	Radio-wave satellite-linked triangulation hardware (see GPS)
SAW	M249 5.56-mm Squad Automatic Weapon; replaces M60 7.62-mm
Scud	Iraqi missile, or KTO cocktail "drink all you want, still can't hit shit"
shin loi	Vietnamese patois; roughly, "tough shit"
Sikes-Fairbairn	British Army commando stiletto
slick	Airmobile Huey; slick because it had no exterior projections
Spec 4	Specialist Fourth Class; one rank above PFC, most common rank
Spookies	AC-47 (later AC-130) planes equipped with minigun pods
Starlifter	C-141B Starlifter; workhorse of the Military Airlift Command
Stoner	M63 multipurpose 5.56-mm machine gun with 200-round mag
strack	Slang for Strictly According to Regulations; high standards, perfect
Stukas	Luftwaffe dive-bomber
suq	Town market center, bazaar; from the Arabic

sutler	A civilian storekeeper licensed to sell goods on a military base
T-10C	Issue parachute for Airborne troopers
T-72	Main Soviet/Iraqi battle tank
TACMs	Corruption of ATACAMS; "steel rain," long-range missiles (U.S.)
Tet	Vietnamese New Year celebration; January '68 Viet Cong offensive
the World	Anywhere but inside the war zone
Thirty-Three	Brand of Vietnamese beer (dreadful, and so rare)
TOC	Tactical Operations Center; ground-force operations base
TOW	M901 Antitank guided-missile-tracked fighting vehicle
TRADOC	TRAining and DOCtrine Command; U.S. Army training department
TREs	Target-Rich Environments; lots to shoot at
uprange	Closer to the source of the fire
ville	Any concentration of huts or hootches in the AO
wadi	A dry wash or riverbed; from the Arabic
Warthogs	Slang term for the A-10 Thunderbolt close-support aircraft
Willie Pete	White phosphorus; marking or incendiary explosive round
XO	Executive officer; officer in charge of administration for the CO